Effective Communication for the Helping Professions

Jennifer MacLennan
D.K. Seaman Chair
Technical and Professional Communication
College of Engineering
University of Saskatchewan

Prentice Hall Allyn and Bacon Canada
Scarborough, Ontario

Canadian Cataloguing in Publication Data

MacLennan, Jennifer
  Effective communication for the helping professions

Includes index.
ISBN 0-13-013234-9

1. Business writing. 2. Business communication. I. Title.

HF5718.3.M25 2000   808'.06665   C99-930845-9

© 2000 Prentice-Hall Canada Inc., Scarborough, Ontario
Pearson Education

ALL RIGHTS RESERVED

No part of this book may be reproduced in any form without permission in writing from the publisher.

Prentice-Hall, Inc., Upper Saddle River, New Jersey
Prentice-Hall International (UK) Limited, London
Prentice-Hall of Australia, Pty. Limited, Sydney
Prentice-Hall Hispanoamericana, S.A., Mexico City
Prentice-Hall of India Private Limited, New Delhi
Prentice-Hall of Japan, Inc., Tokyo
Simon & Schuster Southeast Asia Private Limited, Singapore
Editora Prentice-Hall do Brasil, Ltda., Rio de Janeiro

ISBN 0-13-013234-9

Vice President, Editorial Director: Laura Pearson
Acquisitions Editor: David Stover
Marketing Manager: Sophia Fortier
Developmental Editor: Susan Ratkaj
Production Editor: Cathy Zerbst
Copy Editor: Lisa Berland
Production Coordinator: Peggy Brown
Art Director: Mary Opper
Cover Design: MaryBeth MacLean
Cover Image: DigitalVision
Interior Design: Lisa LaPointe
Page Layout: Janette Thompson (Jansom)

1 2 3 4 5   04 03 02 01 00

Printed and bound in Canada.

Visit the Prentice Hall Canada Web site! Send us your comments, browse our catalogues, and more at **www.phcanada.com**. Or reach us through e-mail at **phabinfo_pubcanada@prenhall.com**.

Table of Contents

Preface	vi
Acknowledgements	viii

chapter 1 — Style in Professional Writing – an Overview — 1

Focus on Your Purpose	3
Remember Your Reader	5
The Six C's of Professional Writing	6
Points to Remember	12
Sharpening Your Skills	12
Online Exercises	12

chapter 2 — Sharpening Your Professional Writing Style — 16

Preparing to Write	17
Common Faults of Professional Writing	17
Points to Remember	22
Sharpening Your Skills	22
Online Exercises	24

chapter 3 — Letters, Memos, and E-Mail Messages — 30

Types of Professional Letters, Memos, and E-mail Messages	32
The Parts of a Letter	45
The Parts of a Memo or E-mail Message	51
Letter and Memo Format	54
Points to Remember	57
Sharpening Your Skills	57
Online Exercises	67

chapter 4 — Informal and Semiformal Reports — 70

Why Write Reports? — 71
The Parts of a Report — 72
Report Situations — 74
Standardized Report Forms — 81
Formal, Informal, and Semiformal Reports — 82
- *Points to Remember* — *91*
- *Sharpening Your Skills* — *95*
- *Online Exercises* — *98*

chapter 5 — Formal Reports and Proposals — 99

The Parts of a Formal Report — 100
Using Visuals in a Formal Report — 103
Proposals — 107
Sample Formal Report — 111
- *Points to Remember* — *111*
- *Sharpening Your Skills* — *111*
- *Online Exercises* — *128*

chapter 6 — Oral Reports and Presentations — 129

Types of Oral Presentations — 131
Preparing Your Presentation — 132
Choosing a Topic — 133
Preparing a Briefing — 139
Delivery — 140
Visual Aids in Oral Presentations — 144
The Importance of Practice — 146
- *Points to Remember* — *147*
- *Sharpening Your Skills* — *147*
- *Online Exercises* — *148*

chapter 7   The Job Package   150

The Résumé   151
    Points to Remember   *160*
Sample Résumés   164
The Letter of Application   189
The Application Form   190
The Letter of Recommendation   193
    Points to Remember   *198*
Taking Your Job Search Online   199
The Job Interview   202
    Points to Remember   *212*
    Sharpening Your Skills   *213*
    Online Exercises   *215*

appendix a   Grammar Review   227

Word Groups   228
Joining Clauses   230
Six Common Sentence Errors   230
    Sharpening Your Skills   *234*
    Answer Key   *236*

appendix b   Punctuation   238

Reviewing Common Punctuation Marks   238
Title Treatments   243

Index   245

Preface

I am delighted to write this note to accompany the brand-new edition of *Effective Communication for the Helping Professions*. My goal in this book has been to provide a brief introduction to the study of professional communication as it is carried out within human-services occupations. Although I have avoided burdening this introductory text with technical terms, my approach to communication study remains fundamentally grounded in the ancient art of rhetoric. Throughout the book, I have emphasized that effective communication involves more than an exchange of information; it also contributes significantly to building and maintaining positive professional relationships. As a result, the book treats communication, both in writing and in formal oral presentation, as a thoroughly human process, and focuses on the importance to any act of communication of clarity of purpose, a strong sense of audience, and an effective, competent projection of the writer or speaker.

In the past few years, I have been involved in a number of projects that have influenced the approach and assumptions that drive this book. One of the most important of these has been piloting a large number of special communication projects, in which senior rhetoric students have had to use their theoretical knowledge of communication to develop practical strategies for training, teaching, public speaking, and writing. These experimental projects have given us real insights into how an understanding of communication principles can inform and enhance the practice of communication, both professionally and personally, and have resulted in the opportunity for several of my students to present their findings to the annual conference of the Northwest Communication Association.

A second important development has been my recent move from a Department of English to an endowed Chair in Professional Communication. This new position provides an exciting opportunity to explore the relationship between theory and application, and to develop more effective strategies for enhancing practice through an understanding of process. In my new role as communication specialist in a professional college, I have been challenged to put rhetorical theory to work in much the same way that my students were able to do in our special projects. I have also used the same approach in the writing of this book: its rhetorical foundations are not only implicit in the principles of effective communication that I have advocated in the text, but are also evident in the approach I have taken in communicating with my audience of student readers.

Teaching the strategies of professional writing and speaking to students in the helping professions has traditionally been something of a dilemma, since most of the available texts approach the subject from the point of view of business. Unfortunately, a business model isn't always the best one for human-services occupations, in which communicative requirements often differ significantly from those imposed by business. This book responds to the needs of helping professionals with advice and examples geared specifically to their unique context. Some of its specific features are as follows:

1. It includes coverage of both content and relation in professional communication, and emphasizes the human interaction at the heart of all communication.
2. It discusses not only letters and memos, but also addresses the use of electronic communication in professional situations, including both e-mail and Internet job searches.
3. It examines the role of reports to human-services occupations, and discusses the types of reports most commonly used in the field, including incident and occurrence reports, accident and injury reports, misconduct reports, assessment or evaluation reports, progress reports, proposals, and research reports.
4. It fully discusses oral presentation skills.
5. It deals comprehensively with the job search process.
6. It employs examples and illustrations exclusively from the helping professions.
7. It avoids business metaphors and examples that might alienate those in the helping professions.
8. It provides appendices on both grammar and punctuation.

My goal has been to produce a book that will serve both professors and students in communications classes; I have also tried to make it practical enough that its readers will continue to refer to it even after the course in which they first used it is over.

Acknowledgements

I would like first to thank those who have used my *Effective Business Communication* and who have recognized the need for a specialized text for students in the helping professions. I am also grateful for the suggestions of my reviewers, whose contributions have helped ensure that this book is well-suited for its intended audience. They are David McCarthy of Centennial College, Genevieve Later of University College of the Cariboo, Shelly Lyck of the Loyalist College of Applied Arts and Technology, and R.A. Bonham of Malaspina University College. I have very much appreciated their comments and suggestions.

I have also greatly valued the contributions of my editors at Prentice Hall; David Stover has been, as always, a pleasure to work with. I am indebted also to the hard work of many other people who saw the book through production, in particular Susan Ratkaj, Cathy Zerbst, and Peggy Brown. I am especially indebted to my copyeditor, Lisa Berland, for her careful attention to detail and nuance.

I have been fortunate over the past year in having the warm support and friendship of my colleagues at University of Saskatchewan: Dean Franco Berruti; the Advisory Committee to the D.K. Seaman Chair: Gary Wacker, David Male, Gordon Putz, Lee Barbour, and Richard Burton; the staff of the Dean's Office: Roxanne Vandeven, Brenda Bergen, Brenda Rowe, Dot Brown, Colleen Sopatyk, Colleen Teague, and Cathy MacKenna; and everyone with whom I have been privileged to work in the College of Engineering. I also remain grateful to the people whose continued collegiality has been very important to me: John Moffatt, Sue Poulson, William Lambert, Ken Tokuno, Lori Leister, Barbara Warnick, Ray McHugh, Marg McKeen, Frank Vandenheuval, David Kaminski, and Richard Fiordo.

Finally, of course, I can't begin to appropriately acknowledge the support of David Cowan, whose belief in me has made all things possible. Thank you, from Meestie and Feral and me.

In memory of Calvin W. MacLennan, 1920–1998.

chapter 1

Style in Professional Writing
–an Overview

> **LEARNING OBJECTIVES**
>
> ▸ To understand the two principles upon which all effective professional writing is based.
> ▸ To learn the Six C's of professional writing and incorporate them into all your writing.

No skill is so vital to the work of a community-services professional, or indeed to everyday life, as effective communication. Through our work we interact with dozens, or even hundreds, of people daily; we communicate by letter, memorandum, telephone, and electronic mail. Everyone in the organization is busy — often too busy to finish all that needs to be done. As a result, messages that are clear and easy to understand will be dealt with first, while those that are unclear, incomplete, or impolite will be set aside for later or possibly forgotten entirely.

Since much of the contact we have with clients and other agencies is through the things we write, whether they are distributed in "hard copy" or by electronic mail, much of our success in community-service professions depends on writing clearly so that our messages are dealt with efficiently. It is important to state our meaning directly and edit our messages carefully, so that we can prevent misunderstandings or delays that can cost time and money, or cause embarrassment to the organization and ourselves.

Achieving clarity in writing is not easy, but the good news is that with a bit of effort almost anyone can learn to write effective professional communications. Professionals who communicate effectively are able to do so because they have mastered both style and form in their letters, memos, and reports; they are also careful to be clear and coherent in their electronic messages. Their messages get dealt with more efficiently, and they seem to get more done. They know the secret of effective writing: they think of their written works not as products but as tools, not as works of art but as communication between people. They know that all good professional writing is based on two main principles: focus on your purpose, and remember your audience. These two principles underlie all good communication, in the professions and elsewhere; the forms of professional writing are designed to help us use these principles.

To communicate effectively, you must first know exactly what you want to say. You can't make any message clear to a reader unless you know, before you begin to write, exactly what your purpose or objective is. What do you want to accomplish through this e-mail message, letter, or memo? Second, you must have a clear idea of the audience for whom you are writing. Why does this reader care about your message? What is the reader's interest in the information? What background does this person have? What will the reader need to know to make a decision?

All good writing, whether in a professional setting or in other spheres of your experience, means recognizing that you are participating in an act of communication involving three components: a message you wish to communicate, an audience or reader for whom the message is prepared, and a speaker or writer who creates the message. Part of the function of every professional message, no matter how routine, is to create and maintain a smooth professional relationship between the writer and the reader. Thus, you need to think as you write not only about the content of your message but about how you are building and shaping your professional relationships through your communication with your clients, colleagues, and managers. This element is called the *relation,* and is present in every act of communication. It is frequently as important as — and sometimes more so than — the content of any message.

Once you have recognized that your job as a writer includes building effective professional relationships by thinking of the purpose and the audience for your message, you can begin to think about how professional communication is typically organized. Most professional writing contains essentially the same parts:

1. The main message statement ("the main thing I want to tell you is that..."). In a report, this is referred to as the summary. In an electronic-mail message, a written memorandum, or even a letter, this information usually appears in the subject or "re" line.
2. Any background information the reader may require. This information is placed in your introductory paragraph or sentence.
3. The full development of the e-mail, memo, letter, or report. This part — sometimes referred to as the discussion or body of the work — provides any necessary details.
4. The closing sentence or paragraph (the conclusion). It should remind your reader once again of your main point and should indicate any results you ex-

pect or intend. It may also suggest to the reader any appropriate action he or she should take in response to your communication.

Remember these parts and always use them as a guide when you are writing any professional correspondence. After all, you want your message to be communicated, and as a writer, it is your responsibility to help your reader understand that message. Following these guidelines and jotting down your main ideas first can make your written communication more effective and the writing process easier because you will have organized your ideas about the message before actually composing the final version.

A professional communication of any kind should also be arranged attractively. In the case of e-mail, effective presentation is more of a challenge, since computer screens and electronic-mail systems differ, and it's more difficult to control how an e-mail message will appear to the recipient. However, print messages can and should be carefully laid out on the page. This means the writer should create an effective balance between the printed or written material (print) and the blank areas of the page where no print appears (known as white space). A page that is crowded from one edge to the other without visual breaks may intimidate the reader; on the other hand, generous margins, paragraphing, and standardized formats can help a reader understand your message more easily and quickly, and can also help make a positive impression.

Before we move on to consider the standardized formats of professional writing, let's look more closely at the two important principles of communication that will help you to forge effective professional relationships:

1. Focus on your purpose; and
2. Remember your reader's needs, expectations, and background knowledge.

Focus on Your Purpose

Before you begin writing, ask yourself why you are writing this e-mail, letter, memo, or report. What do you want it to do? Is your primary aim to pass on information? Or is your goal to persuade your reader to act or believe something? If you are primarily interested in informing your readers, you can state your facts clearly and simply. If, however, you want to move your readers to action, convince them of a point of view, or encourage them to accept a change in plans, you will need to use more persuasive techniques in your writing. These are covered in Chapter 3.

This awareness is equally important no matter what you are writing, from an ordinary letter of request to an application for a job. In today's office, electronic mail (e-mail) has replaced some of the functions that used to be served by internal memos and even letters; nevertheless, for formal situations, the letter and the memo are still the most frequently used forms of professional communication. As well, although the e-mail memo is often considered a less formal method of communication than a paper memo or letter, style and content are still a consideration.

We will begin our discussion of purpose and audience by considering the memo (including e-mail) and the letter. Reports, of course, are more complex, and these are dealt with in Chapters 4 and 5. The parts of a job application are discussed in Chapter 7.

Memos (both paper and e-mail varieties) and letters may address only one issue or involve a number of related issues. They may be as short as one page or as long as two or three pages. Whatever their length or contents, however, one principle remains constant: if you are not clear about exactly what you want to say, you cannot say it well. It is also important to organize your writing with your most important purpose foremost. You cannot hope to make your professional writing effective unless you know in advance exactly what you want it to do. You should keep the following guidelines in mind when writing a letter or memo, or when drafting an e-mail message.

Put Your Main Point First

Writing on the job differs from the other kinds of writing that you may be used to reading or that you have learned to do. In your work-related writing, you should begin with the main point of your message. Putting your main point first will seem awkward at the beginning, because it will seem a little like giving away the punch line before you've told the joke. We have all been conditioned to write in a more or less chronological order, which usually results in the main point coming last. This arrangement is ideal for a novel or a movie script, but disastrous in a professional situation. Think about your reader's situation: he or she may have many time demands, and may receive several dozen or more reports and memos daily, in addition to numerous e-mail messages. All of these messages require attention and action. You can't afford to waste the reader's time with a message that doesn't get to the point. Put the main message at the beginning of your communication, preferably in a subject (or "re") line. You can teach yourself to put your main idea first by beginning your rough drafts with, "The main thing I want to tell you is that...." Doing so will help you to focus on your main message. Be sure to delete this clause in your final draft.

Be Specific

Make sure you can identify exactly what you wish your reader to know and what response you expect. Be as concrete and specific as possible. For instance, if you wish to request a file or document, book a room, or refer a client, state this purpose clearly, identifying the document required or the specific room you wish to book. Don't waste your reader's time; get to the point quickly, and provide as much concrete detail as is necessary to get the job done.

Simplify Your Message

Try to keep your letters, memos, and e-mail messages as simple as possible: don't clutter them with irrelevant information. If you can, stick to one main topic and include only what is necessary to the reader's understanding of your message. If you must deal with several topics in one letter or memo, be sure that each is dealt with fully before moving to the next issue. Cluster related information and get to the point as quickly as possible.

Remember Your Reader

Most professional writing, like all effective communication, whether primarily designed to inform or to persuade, must catch and maintain a reader's attention and interest. You cannot do this if you don't understand the person for whom you are writing. Since any professional communication is really an attempt to convince your intended reader that your position is valid and your recommendations necessary, you must present the information in a manner most likely to convince that specific reader. Effective communication is audience-centred; that is, it focuses not so much on what the *writer* feels like saying, but on the things the reader needs to hear in order to make an informed decision. Good communication puts the reader's needs first. In order to do this, you need to identify your reader as to needs, level of knowledge, and expectations.

Needs

Consider first the information that your reader needs in order to make a decision. What is the reader's interest in this subject? What will the reader be doing with the information? How much detail is needed? Leave out any information that is not immediately relevant to the reader, no matter how interesting it may seem from your point of view. If you are to communicate your point successfully, you must address the reader's need for the information you are providing.

Background Knowledge

Keep in mind your reader's level of expertise. If you are writing to someone who has no prior knowledge of your caseload or specialization, you will need to explain substantially more than you will if you are writing to someone who is well acquainted with them. On the other hand, it is just as inconsiderate to provide unnecessary detail to someone who knows a great deal about your work as it is to provide inadequate detail to someone who does not know very much about it. Also, the kind of prior knowledge your audience brings can influence the way you choose to present your information as well as the amount or kind of information to present.

Expectations

What you say, and how you say it, will be very much affected by what the reader is expecting from your work. A reader who has been expecting a negative response will be relieved and delighted by good news. However, a reader who has been anticipating positive results is likely to be disappointed, frustrated, or angry if those expectations are not met. Ignoring or overlooking your reader's frustrated expectations when you write will only aggravate the situation and may damage your relationship with your correspondent. On the other hand, acknowledging a reader's legitimate disappointment can help to cushion the impact of bad news and emphasize your professional concern and interest in the reader's viewpoint. Such positive reinforcement can go a long way in cementing effective professional relationships.

In order to make the communication a success, it is the writer's responsibility to pay attention to the relational level of the message as well as to its content. To create and maintain effective relationships within your professional circle, you will need to think carefully about the needs and expectations of the reader who will receive your communication. If you do this each time you create an e-mail, a memo, or a letter, you will not only communicate your content more effectively, but you will also maintain more successful interactions with clients and colleagues.

The Six C's of Professional Writing

Beyond clearly identifying both your main message and your reader, you will also want to attend to the actual style of your writing. Good professional writing — like any other effective writing — exhibits a number of identifiable characteristics.

1. Completeness The first thing you must do is to make sure no important details have been overlooked. Have you included all of the information your reader will need in order to understand and act on your message? After you've written the first draft of your e-mail, memo, letter, or report, always ask yourself, "Have I said everything I needed to say?" Use the following questions as a guideline to ensure that you have included all the information your reader needs. Be sure you have answered any that are relevant:

Who?   What?   How many?   When?
Where?   How?   Why?

2. Conciseness To be concise means saying as much as you need to say in as little space as possible without being curt. This process is more difficult than it sounds, because it involves more than simply brevity. You need to eliminate unnecessary information while preserving the details necessary to full understanding. Once you have completed your first draft, and have made certain that all essential information is included, you need to be sure to take out any *irrelevant* information that has crept into your message. Ask yourself whether the reader really needs to know a fact you have included. If the answer is no, then cut it and avoid repeating yourself unnecessarily. It's also a good idea to avoid wordy expressions and clichés, such as:

at this point in time	if this proves to be the case
it is probable that	it has come to my attention that
until such time as	please do not hesitate to

There are many more clichés common to career writing; many of them can be found in the discussion of good writing style in the next chapter. You should learn to recognize these deadeners of style and clarity and eliminate them from your messages.

3. Clarity In addition to making sure you've included all the details you need and eliminated those that are irrelevant to your reader's needs, you need to pay close attention to detail and organization. Be as concrete and specific as you can, identifying exactly what the problem is and what you would like done. Try to avoid ambiguous phrasing: the message should be clear on the first brief reading. Your reader should never have to puzzle out your meaning and should have no unanswered questions after reading your correspondence. Organize your message in a logical way, moving from problem to solution, from request to thanks, from general to specific.

4. Coherence Any professional correspondence should "hold together"; the parts should be logically connected one to the other. Coherence is achieved partly by a sensible organization, but in addition to a movement from problem to solution or request to thanks, you should also use connective words or phrases to guide your reader from one point to the next. If you have organized your ideas well, coherence should be easy to attain by adding connectives. Some that you may wish to use include:

since	as well as	in addition to
therefore	however	on the other hand
naturally	of course	as a matter of fact
also	nevertheless	for instance
for example	once again	furthermore
moreover	thus	

5. Correctness Check the accuracy of all information — names, dates, places, receipt numbers, prices — that you include in any correspondence. Correctness, of course, also includes correct spelling, grammar, and sentence structure as well as attractive formatting. Never send a letter without proofreading it first — to do so is unprofessional and reflects badly on the writer. As well, a mistake could be costly.

Proofreading is not simply rereading or running the spell-check program on your word processor. When you proofread, you read with the clear intention of improving your written message. You look not only for errors in spelling and grammar, but also for any places where your message is unclear. If possible, take a break — even a short one — between the writing and the proofreading, and try reading your work out loud. Both of these strategies will help you to uncover mistakes you might otherwise miss. The next chapter offers some more detailed advice on this important process.

6. Courtesy In professional life, as in all human interactions, things usually go more smoothly if people are pleasant and courteous to one another. Your relationships with clients and colleagues are very important, and every communication you send can build or undermine those relationships. Since your attitude is displayed clearly in your writing and will affect the relational level of your message, it's important to pay close attention to *tone* in what you write. To check this important aspect of your own professional communication, read over your work carefully, putting yourself in the place of the reader. Make it a habit to be pleasant and be sure to say please and thank you for any services or favours requested or received. Even if you are writing to someone whom you believe has done you wrong, give this person the benefit of the doubt, at least initially: allow the recipient to save face by taking the attitude that the error was the unintentional result of a misunderstanding. This approach will be much more effective in resolving difficulties than will a confrontational or accusatory tone.

These Six C's are among the most important qualities of good professional writing. If you can incorporate them into your own work, your writing will be vastly improved.

Of course, there's more to any communication than simply *what you say*; how you present your message is as important in professional writing as in any other human interaction. Part of the way we can demonstrate our good judgement as writers and as community-service professionals is through our recognition of effective layout and correct format. Letters and memos are fairly standardized in their appearance, and violation of these standards may suggest a sloppy or unprofessional writer.

E-mail messages, of course, are far less consistent in their format: some writers, perceiving e-mail to be a casual medium of communication, ignore all conventions of punctuation, spelling, and capitalization. However, you should know that not all readers appreciate *receiving* such unconventional messages, since they can be much more difficult to decipher. It is much better, from the point of view of reader consideration, to observe the conventions of spelling, punctuation, and grammar than to take the chance of annoying a correspondent.

Letters and memos, of course, are always more formal than electronic messages. An effective letter or memo is always word-processed or typed, with a clear, dark printer cartridge or ribbon on clean, good-quality paper. It makes use of generous margins (never looks too crowded or too spaced out) and appears balanced on the page. It may make use of other visual techniques to make it both more attractive and easier to read. For example, if it includes several important facts, these may be indented in list form to set them apart from the rest of the information.

Figure 1.1 shows the first draft of a letter that does not observe the Six C's or the rules of effective layout. Compare it carefully with the corrected version

figure 1.1 The first draft of Trish Trcka's letter contains many flaws. Try to identify the errors yourself before reading the analysis.

Trish Trcka[1]
PO Box 123
Drayton Valley, Alberta
T5Y 7H8

9/28/01 [2]

Ministry of Tourism
Province of British Columbia
Parliament Buildings
Victoria, British Columbia
V1R 7H9

Dear Sir: [3]

I am writting[4] you this letter because[5] I am interested in taking a trip to British Columbia.

It has come to my attention that[6] your ministry can offer some valueable[7] information to potential tourists who are concidering[8] visiting your beautiful province.[9]

It would be greatly appreciated[10] if you could provide me with some documents[11] outlining your attractions, accommodations, and special events.

Thank you in advance for your assistance in this matter[12]. Your immediate response will be appreciated.[13]

Sincerly[14] yours,

Trish Trcka
Trish Trcka.[15]

(Figure 1.2), noting where the improvements have been made and why. Errors in the first draft have been numbered for easy reference in the analysis.

Analysis

[1] Since Trish's name appears under her signature, she should not include it here. This is a common error.
[2] Trish should write out the date in full for ease of understanding.
[3] A subject or "re" line would help to clarify what Trish seeks and could replace the entire first paragraph.
[4] "Writing" is misspelled.
[5] "I am writing you this letter…" is clearly unnecessary: the reader, who has Trish's signed letter in hand, does not need to be told again that she has written it.
[6] "It has come to my attention that…" is a cliché and should be avoided. It is also unnecessarily wordy and pompous.
[7] "Valuable" is misspelled.
[8] "Considering" is misspelled.
[9] This kind of effusiveness borders on being sickly sweet and serves no useful purpose; Trish should try to sound more sincere.
[10] "It would be appreciated…" is a cliché, and so probably does not sound sincere. Since Trish is making a personal request she should also increase the sense of human contact in her letter by avoiding the passive construction.
[11] The phrase "some documents" is vague; Trish has not identified clearly what she wants. She should be specific about her needs.
[12] "Thank you in advance for your attention to this matter" is another cliché; as such, it is wordy and sounds insincere and stuffy. A simple "thank you" would be better.
[13] "Your immediate response will be appreciated" is not only another unnecessarily wordy and tired phrase, but it borders on rudeness by implying that the people in the Ministry of Tourism won't respond quickly enough unless she orders them to do so.
[14] "Sincerely" is misspelled.
[15] No period should follow her name.

In addition to the above mistakes, Trish has made another major error in this letter: she has not provided some of the specifics that would enable the people in the tourism office to help her most effectively. If she can, she should indicate where in the province she plans to visit and when she will be there. Activities and events vary around the province and are often seasonal. As well, Trish should take care to centre her letter vertically on the page. This kind of detail makes a letter more attractive and even more pleasant to read. Take a look at Trish's improved letter (Figure 1.2).

figure 1.2 The improved version of Trish's letter observes all of the Six C's of effective professional writing.

PO Box 123
Drayton Valley, Alberta
T5Y 7H8

September 28, 2001

Ministry of Tourism
Province of British Columbia
Parliament Buildings
Victoria, British Columbia
V1R 7H9

Re: Tourism information for Vancouver and area

I am planning a visit to British Columbia during Christmas week and would appreciate any brochures or other information you could provide regarding attractions, accommodations, and special events in the Vancouver area from approximately December 20, 2001, through January 3, 2002.

I plan to make the trip by car and expect to stay overnight in the Kamloops area. I would also like some information about accommodations in that area, if you have it, and would appreciate a provincial road map as well.

I have heard many positive things about Vancouver and am looking forward to this trip. Thank you very much for your help.

Sincerely,

Trish Trcka

Trish Trcka

Analysis

1. Since Trish does not know the identity of her reader, nor whether the reader will be male or female, she has simply deleted the salutation, a practice that is increasingly common. A more old-fashioned approach, but one which is still courteous, is to use "Dear Sir or Madam" in place of "Dear Sir."
2. The "re" line specifies what information she wants and for which area.
3. The opening paragraph avoids clichés and gets right to the point: the request for information and the dates and destination of the planned visit.
4. Additional details about the trip help the reader to determine what information Trish will need. She specifies some of the documents, such as a map, that she believes will be useful to her. Note that she includes her method of travel only because it affects what the ministry people will send her.
5. A brief compliment and her thanks close the letter effectively.

points to remember

1. All effective professional communication is based on two primary principles:
   - Know your purpose and be able to state it clearly.
   - Understand your reader's needs, expectations, knowledge.
2. Always watch your own tone; make it a habit to be pleasant.
3. Good professional style observes the Six C's of professional writing:

   | Conciseness | Clarity | Coherence |
   | Correctness | Completeness | Courtesy |

4. Good professional communication displays effective balance between print and white space.

sharpening your skills

Read the following professional communications (Figures 1.3 and 1.4). Following the model analysis of Trish Trcka's letter, suggest ways they might be improved, keeping in mind all six principles of style in professional writing.

online exercises

1. Many of those who do a lot of writing on the job fall into habits of sloppiness or obfuscation. Will Stockdell is a professional writer whose "Writing

figure 1.3 In how many ways does Ichio Hudecek's letter violate the Six C's?

Ichio Hudecek
980 Main Street,
Saint John, New Brunswick
E1G 2M3

March 3, 2002

Ms. Sheena Truman, Director
Publications Department
Social Service Support Activists
555 California Street
Vancouver, British Street
V1R 7H9

Dear Sir:

I am writting you a letter to ask you about the booklets I ordered from you about six weeks ago. I still haven't received it even though you have already cashed my cheque.

If you don't send them to me right away I'll have to report you to the department of consumer affairs.

Yours truely,

Ichio Hudecek
Ichio Hudecek

figure 1.4 This e-mail message is unlikely to help solve the problems the class has with Mr. Wolf Child. What is wrong here?

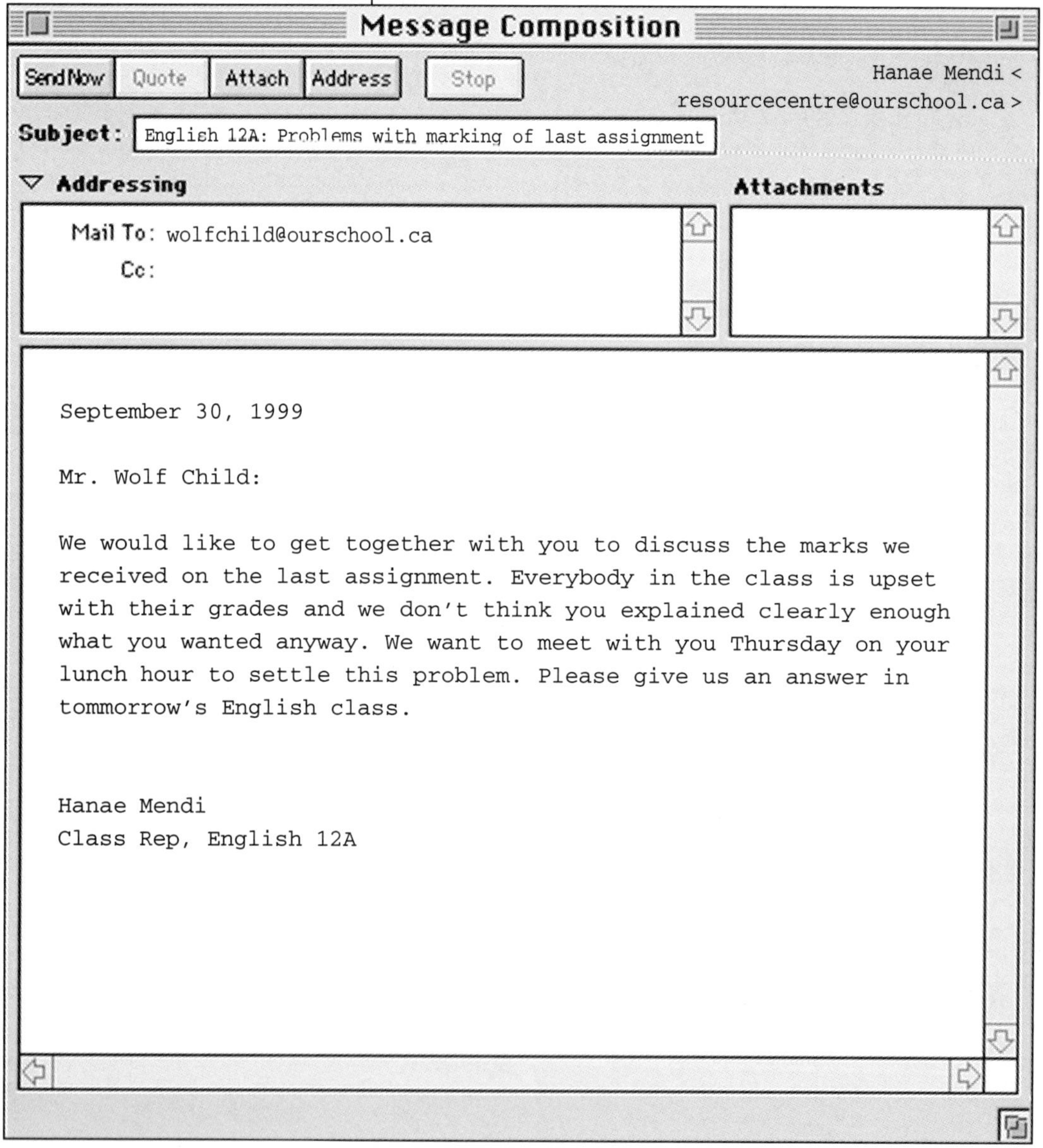

```
===================== Message Composition =====================
[SendNow] [Quote] [Attach] [Address]    [Stop]         Hanae Mendi <
                                              resourcecentre@ourschool.ca >
Subject: | English 12A: Problems with marking of last assignment |
▽ Addressing                                Attachments
    Mail To: wolfchild@ourschool.ca
        Cc:
```

September 30, 1999

Mr. Wolf Child:

We would like to get together with you to discuss the marks we received on the last assignment. Everybody in the class is upset with their grades and we don't think you explained clearly enough what you wanted anyway. We want to meet with you Thursday on your lunch hour to settle this problem. Please give us an answer in tommorrow's English class.

Hanae Mendi
Class Rep, English 12A

Improvement Page" for professionals offers some concrete advice on how to improve your writing. At Stockdell's site, **blondie.mathcs.wilkes.edu/~stockdwm/badwriting.html**, you will find a discussion of several common writing problems, along with suggestions for their solution. How does Stockdell's advice compare with the Six C's of Professional Writing listed in this chapter? Discuss with the rest of your class.

2. How does professional writing differ from the kind of writing you were taught to do in your high-school English classes? List as many differences as you can think of, then go to the Web page called "Differences between Literary and Business (Professional) English," **www.smartbiz.com/sbs/arts/pbw2.htm**. How does your list compare with Tom McKeown's list? What is the biggest difference between writing on the job and literary writing?

3. As you learned in this chapter, all communication involves an element of relation. At **www.smartbiz.com/sbs/arts/exe164.htm**, you will find a page entitled "26 Tips For Better Communication." Study the list carefully to determine how many of these principles focus upon this often neglected element of professional communication. To what extent does improving your communication skills mean paying more attention to the relational elements of your communication? How much of this advice is focused on the principle of remembering your audience? Briefly summarize the main principles represented by the items in this list and send it to your instructor in an e-mail message.

4. At **www.engr.usask.ca/dept/techcomm/whatis.htm** you will find a short essay of mine entitled "What is Rhetoric?" Compare the information in this essay with the discussion of professional communication in this chapter. To what extent does this book approach professional communication as a form of rhetoric? Why do you think I have avoided using the specialized terminology of this essay in the introductory chapter of this book?

chapter 2

Sharpening your Professional Writing Style

LEARNING OBJECTIVES

- To analyze and put into use an effective method for planning your professional correspondence.
- To examine several common causes of unclear writing and learn how to edit them out of your own writing.

It is one thing to know that, in theory, you need to put the main message first and weed out wordy and clichéd phrases; it's another entirely to accomplish these things in all your writing. Even when you clearly recognize the importance of the Six C's, it is sometimes difficult to put them into practice in your own writing. This chapter is designed to help you do just that.

Most writers experience difficulty in achieving the sharpness of style that good professional writing requires, because bad writing is surprisingly easy to produce, while good, clear, effective writing — which looks simpler on the printed page — is actually much more difficult to achieve.

Conciseness and clarity seem to be the two most challenging of the Six C's for most writers; also, because they are closely linked, improving one often means improving the other. For this reason, we will focus on these two qualities in this discussion of writing style. The only way to achieve clarity and conciseness is to increase organization and reduce wordiness. This process often requires several drafts, but it can be learned, and you can use it to make all of your writing — in your professional life as well as elsewhere — more effective.

Preparing to Write

Before you begin to write, plan your communication carefully. Using the Professional Writing Planner (Figure 2.1) as a guide, identify the important elements of your message and the probable needs and expectations of your reader. Jot down the major points you wish to cover and juggle them around to achieve the most logical order. Consider carefully the way in which these points can be presented, choosing your words with care as you work. Then write your rough draft, beginning with "The main thing I want to tell you is that…." Be sure to cross out this clause in later drafts, especially the final draft.

Common Faults of Professional Writing

Once you have planned your letter or memo, you must look at it critically to determine whether it is as effective as it could be. Concise writing is hard work, and almost every writer produces first drafts that need correction. Although you should give some thought to planning and organization when you write the first draft, don't imagine that it will be perfect. Expect — and be willing — to revise your work to make it more effective. With practice, this process will become easier and less time-consuming. One good way to learn to edit your own writing is to look for specific, common faults of professional correspondence. The following are some of the real troublemakers.

1. Failure to identify the central issue Before you begin to write, be sure that you can identify your main idea and that you understand exactly what you want your reader to know. This information must come first, and it should be expressed clearly. Before you work on the body of the letter, write down your main idea. You may even, as we discussed, begin your rough draft with the words, "The main thing I want to tell you is that…." (Remember to cross this out for your final draft.) In fact, you might even wish to put the point into a "re" line; doing so will not only force you to put it first, but will also help your reader to grasp your message more quickly.

2. Use of clichés Clichés make any writing uninteresting and deaden its human connection. Nevertheless, use of clichés is one of the most common faults in job-related writing. Below are some of the most common abstractions and clichés. A complete list of all the possible clichés of writing would take up the rest of this chapter, but I have provided enough examples below to give you a taste of what to look for and avoid. As a general rule, any phrase that sounds as though it "ought" to be in a piece of formal correspondence probably should be eliminated from yours!

figure 2.1 A Writing Planner can help you in all your written communications. You may adapt this general form to the specific demands of your writing situation by changing the questions to suit your needs.

PROFESSIONAL WRITING PLANNER

Before beginning your letter or memo, consider these points carefully.

1. What is the topic of this letter or memo?

2. What is my focus or purpose? Am I providing information or promoting an idea?

3. What is my main point? (This will appear in a subject or "re" line.) "The main thing I want to say is that...."

4. Who is my reader? What is his or her interest in this subject? What does my reader already know and what further information will be needed or wanted?

5. What background information does my reader need as preparation for what I am going to say?

6. What are my primary supporting points? Which details are important? Have I answered any *Who, What, When, Where, Why,* and *How* questions the reader might have?

7. What, if any, action do I wish my reader to take after reading my letter or memo? Have I made it possible for her or him to do so?

at this point in time	if this proves to be the case
in the amount of	it is probable that
postpone until later	under separate cover
it has come to my attention that	reach a decision
until such time as	please do not hesitate to
on or before	whether or not
send you herewith	enclosed herewith find
with reference to	give consideration to
at the present time	due to the foregoing consideration
in view of the foregoing	in the near future
due to the fact that	in accordance with your request
in the event that	it will be our earnest endeavour
in accordance with your request	at your earliest convenience

Unfortunately, many writers, not knowing what else to do, fall back on the clichés they have seen in the writing of others. Inexperienced writers often imagine that professional correspondence is supposed to sound hackneyed, because so much of it does. You will do yourself, and your readers, a favour if you avoid this trap. Because such clichés add words without adding meaning or clarity, because they say in several words what could more clearly be said in one, and because they obscure rather than clarify your meaning, they are bad writing.

Most of these cumbersome and meaningless phrases can be replaced by much simpler language, often a single word that communicates much more forcefully and directly. For example, "at this point in time" could be replaced by "now"; "if this proves to be the case" could be written simply as "if"; "postpone until later" could simply be "postpone." Some of them, such as "it has come to my attention that," could be eliminated completely without any loss of meaning. See if you can translate these awkward and stuffy phrases and clauses into plain language. Always proofread your own writing for such phrases and replace them with more direct language.

3. Use of the passive voice The passive voice expresses not action done *by* the subject, but action done *to* the subject, a crucial difference. For example, "Assistance would be greatly appreciated" is almost always better written, "I would appreciate your assistance...."

In certain types of very formal writing, the use of passive voice is considered appropriate, but it distances writer from reader, deadens style, and often causes a loss of clarity. For these reasons, it is sometimes used (along with vague and clichéd wording) as a deliberate strategy by writers who want to confuse or obfuscate: official government documents and administrative memos are often written in such opaque language. However, deliberate obscurity or unintentional muddiness is not a desirable quality in writing designed to communicate. You want your writing to stand out for its clarity, directness, and human connection. Consider how much more vivid and powerful, not to mention shorter, the following sentences are when they are written in the active voice.

Larry completed my project.
   is better than
The project that I was working on has been completed by Larry.

Shirley conducted the required tests.
   is better than
The tests that were required have been conducted by Shirley.

Doug hired John Smith to complete the literacy foundation fundraising project.
   is better than
John Smith was hired by Doug for the completion of the fundraising project for the literacy foundation campaign.

We have evaluated your application.
   is better than
Your application has been evaluated by us.

One way you can make your own writing more powerful and concise is to eliminate unnecessary use of passive voice wherever you can.

4. Overuse of phrases and dependent clauses as modifiers Very often we find ourselves using several words where we could use just one. Believe it or not, long windy sentences are actually easier to create than are clear, concise ones, because they don't demand as much care or attention to meaning, and they require no concern for the audience's needs. But they also make very dull, boring, tedious messages that remain unread or unheeded.

Excessive use of phrasal and clausal modifiers is among the most common causes of this kind of wordiness, and when it is combined with the passive voice (as in the examples above) it can be dull, or even confusing, to read. As a rule, you should not use several words when one will do the job. See how much more concise the following examples can be.

- the project I am working on (my project)
- the equipment that our department recently purchased (our recently purchased equipment)
- the store on the corner (the corner store)
- the present that I bought for my father (my father's present, *or even* my present for my father)
- the application for funding belonging to this client (this client's funding application)
- the reason for which I am writing (my reason for writing)
- the case files that I recently acquired (my recently acquired case files)
- property that belongs to the agency (agency property)
- a friend whom I have known for a long period of time (a long-time friend)

Watch, in particular, for an overuse of the words "of" (or other prepositions), "which," or "that." Rewrite such phrases or clauses into one or two words whenever you can do so without a loss of precision or thought.

5. Unnecessary repetition of ideas Repetition can be a powerful tool for persuasion when it is used effectively and deliberately. It can engage and motivate an audience into action. However, two things must be said about repetition as a strategy: first, effective repetition is primarily an oral device that usually does not achieve the same effect in writing. Second, much repetition in writing is cumbersome and unworkable; it may even seem unnatural and overdone. In professional writing, where the goal is to communicate efficiently and clearly, unnecessary repetition can actually be a hindrance to your message.

In a memo, letter, or e-mail, you need to say what you mean in as little space as possible. To make your writing really effective, you should avoid any unnecessary repetition. To avoid this problem, cluster related information and make each point only once. If you say it clearly the first time, you can eliminate the useless and often confusing repetition that weakens your writing and obscures your message.

6. Failure to cluster related points In organizing your message, you must be sure to place related points together: jumping back and forth is confusing to the reader and is one of the things that leads to the unnecessary repetition we have just discussed. If you find yourself writing the clause "as I said above..." you probably need to do more to cluster related information.

If, for example, you are writing a letter to obtain tickets and accommodations for a convention, you should cluster all information pertaining to the tickets into one paragraph and all information about the accommodations into another. For added clarity and visual appeal, you can place the main details in indented lists.

7. Failure to identify the desired action A frequent function of persuasive professional correspondence is to prompt a specific kind of action from the reader. You are writing because you want results. Although as a writer you may feel that the appropriate course of action is obvious, what you want done may not be quite so clear to the reader, whose idea of a suitable response may differ from yours. Don't expect your reader to come automatically to the same conclusion you have reached about what must be done. State directly, in clear and specific language, what you expect the reader to do. If there are several steps to be taken, list and enumerate them for the reader's convenience.

8. Incomplete information Before writing your final draft, check once more to be sure you have included all relevant information. Ask yourself Who? What? Where? When? Why? and How? to be sure that you have supplied all the necessary details.

points to remember

Learning to edit out the common faults of career writing will improve your communication and make your messages easier to understand and act upon. Keep in mind the rules discussed in this chapter whenever you write a piece of correspondence. Here they are in summary, with a few additions.

1. Always be prepared to write more than one draft.
2. Always begin with your main idea.
3. Put the main point into a subject or "re" line where possible.
4. Cluster related points together.
5. Check wordiness by eliminating unnecessary repetition, excessive use of clauses and phrases, clichés, and the passive voice.
6. Include all necessary information.
7. Identify desired action.
8. Be courteous — always consider your reader's feelings and watch your tone.

sharpening your skills

SECTION A

Revise the following sentences, taken from actual memos and letters, to make them clearer and more concise.

1. In the event that any employee should be the final individual to exit the premises of this agency on the eve of any given working period, it would be greatly appreciated by management as a gesture of fiscal responsibility if such individuals should leave the offices in a state of darkness.

2. It has come to my attention that your firm is offering a new position that has never been available before to any new applicants from outside the organization. Please be advised that I would like to express my interest in this very attractive position and feel that you should be interested in my background as well.

3. If this writer can be of any further assistance to you in this matter, please do not hesitate to contact myself at the above-mentioned office location.

4. With reference to your communication of the above-referenced date, enclosed herewith find the documents which you requested at that point in time.

5. At the present time, I am not at liberty to give consideration to such requests due to the inability of this office to evaluate whether or not this aforementioned request is in accordance with present practice of this agency.

6. It is our earnest endeavour to process applications with greatest efficiency; however, in the event that you are not in receipt of a requested response on or before the closing date, please do not hesitate to put yourself in contact with personnel at this location.

7. Due to the difficulties involved with the aforementioned request, I would like to take this opportunity to thank you in advance for your assistance in this difficult matter.

8. Due to the fact that this writer was unavailable over the period of the previous month because of absence due to vacation, your correspondence of the above-referenced date did not receive the immediate attention of myself, for which I send you herewith my most sincere apology.

9. A cheque for the amount specified to cover the loss experienced due to the above incident of April 30 has been prepared by this office. Your appearance is requested at your earliest convenience to complete the necessary paperwork and to receive such payment. We trust this is in order.

10. In the event of circumstances beyond our control which affect delivery of this service, some alterations to the planned schedule may be required.

Section B

1. In his famous essay "Politics and the English Language," the writer George Orwell rewrites a familiar passage from *Ecclesiastes* into modern language. Here is the original, followed by Orwell's rewritten version:

   I returned and saw under the sun, that the race is not to the swift, nor the battle to the strong, neither yet bread to the wise, nor yet riches to men of understanding, nor yet favour to men of skill; but time and chance happeneth to them all.

Compare Orwell's version, rewritten in modern English:

   Objective considerations of contemporary phenomena compels the conclusion that success or failure in competitive activities exhibits no tendency to be commensurate with innate capacity, but that a considerable element of the unpredictable must invariably be taken into account.[1]

Of course, Orwell's point is to demonstrate how much less clear the modern language is than the original. As a class, compare Orwell's passage with the passage from *Ecclesiastes* and explain why the original is more effective.

2. Just for fun, try your hand at this reverse process by rewriting some clear passages into "modern" language, using the clichés and abstract phrases we

---

George Orwell, "Politics and the English Language," *The Orwell Reader*, ed. Richard H. Rovere (New York: Harcourt, Brace, and World, 1956), 360.

have been discussing. Try rewriting some of the examples of good writing in Chapter 3 in such a manner, or apply the process to a familiar fairy tale — "The Three Little Pigs" or "Red Riding Hood." Compare and discuss your choices with those of the other members of the class.

S E C T I O N   C

The following pieces of correspondence (Figures 2.2–2.6) are real examples that I have collected over several years. Read them through to spot weaknesses similar to those we've discussed above, and edit for conciseness and clarity.

online exercises

1. At Purdue University's On-Line Writing Lab site, **owl.english.purdue.edu/Files/90.html**, you will find a list of guidelines for revising your professional writing. Although it specifically targets business writers, the advice on this site is useful for writers in all professions. Scroll down the page to reach a set of questions similar to the Writing Planner on page 18 of this chapter. Plan two separate communications — letters, memos, or e-mail messages — using the online form for one and the Writing Planner for the other. What differences did you find? Discuss your observations with the class.

2. Compare the advice offered on the page "Ten Tips for Better Letters," **www.smartbiz.com/sbs/arts/exe195.htm**, with that given in "Ten Easy Ways to Write More Effective Letters," **www.smartbiz.com/sbs/arts/dir5.htm**. Although both of these pages are on the same site, the two are very different in focus. What reasons can you find for this difference? Is there any way in which the two pages seem to share a point of view or approach? To what extent do they confirm, or extend, the advice provided in this chapter? After considering both these sites, and the material presented in this chapter, write a memo to your instructor outlining what you have inferred to be the most important advice for a professional writer.

3. As we have discussed in this chapter, one of the biggest difficulties for writers of letters and other correspondence on the job is the tendency to reach for abstractions and clichés rather than simple words and phrases that are clearer and more concrete. In "Simpler Words and Phrases," **www.smartbiz.com/sbs/arts/tpl5.htm**, you will find a list of commonly used abstractions and suggestions for alternatives that are clearer and more direct. Exchange with a classmate a letter or memo you've recently written as an assignment for your communication class. How many of these overly complex phrases or words did you find in your colleague's writing? How many did she or he find in yours? Can you simplify your work any further? Can you think of an instance in which such simplification might not be appropriate? Discuss your findings with the class.

figure 2.2 Despite her good intentions, Roxanne Vandeven's message is obscured by wordy, vague writing. See if you can improve her letter.

The Second Time Halfway House
25 Headframe Street
Forestville, Ontario
K8Y 4R2

April 25, 1999

Mr. Iqbal Zafar, Director
Legal Aid Services
34 Centre Street
Cedarton, Ontario
K7Y 2F6

Dear Mr. Zafar:

With reference to your correspondence dated April 22, 1999, in accordance with your request for information about Luchia Gaschler, it will be my most earnest endeavour to provide you with a most glowing reference of her character.

First of all, Lucy Gaschler was in our employ for a period of four years; she is at the present time seeking for a position in a more advanced capacity elsewhere. During that period of time Lucy performed a wide variety of duties which were expected of her in her position of counsellor aide which she performed to the utmost of her ability. We never had at any time a reason to doubt Lucy's ability to be able to do her job and we perceived at all times that she was a good worker who was conscientious in her work, honest, and utilized courtesy in dealings with clients.

In giving consideration to Lucy's personal characteristics of her personality, in line with your suggestion, we have found Lucy to be easy to get along with for everybody who had to work with her and at all times could be depended upon to do what was needed at that point.

Due to the foregoing considerations, it would make me happy to be able to provide you herewith with a positive recommendation of Lucy and in the event that you are in need of further information, please do not hesitate to contact myself in the near future.

Yours very sincerely,

Roxanne Vandeven

Roxanne Vandeven
Manager

figure 2.3 This career statement fails to deliver a clear, coherent message. How would you improve it?

WHY I CHOSE EARLY CHILDHOOD DEVELOPMENT

When interacting with people, I find it most intriguing working with preschool children in this particular field. Early Childhood Development gives you a better in-depth look at what certain behaviours and ideas affect the different stages of development in young children.

Communication is the most important part of Early Childhood Development. Communicating with the children, their parents, as well as their teachers gives you an opportunity to observe human nature. Observing human nature with children is a very good example of getting to know the child.

When observing human nature, you find the different aspects of children, such as What are the child's likes and dislikes? How artistic/creative are they? What are the child's reactions to ideas?

These are just some of the examples and questions you will be asking when you begin to observe children.

By getting to know children as you work with them you will feel good and better about yourself when you look back on those special moments that you will always treasure.

As I look back at all the experience which I received when taking care of children. I found the observations which I did, to be very challenging, interesting, and very useful for comparisons.

During the beginning of last year's school year, I tutored students between grades 2-3 level with arithmetic and phonics. For each evening with them, I tried to think of new ways to explain a problem which they found difficult. After each tutoring session I would record each observation about each child.

By the end of the school year, their was a tremendous change of each child which I tutored. The children, their parents, as well as the teachers were quite amazed. I received a great many thanks and appreciation notes for the time that I spent with them. I felt good about myself and for the time I spent with them. It was challenging and very rewarding to be with them.

figure 2.4 Why might this candidate not get the job he wants? What flaws can you find in this statement, which was required as part of the candidate's application?

STATEMENT OF CAREER INTEREST: CORRECTIONAL SERVICES

In response to your requirements which you stated to me in your advertising for the position of Correctional Worker in your institution, I would like to write to you to tell you about why I think a Correctional Worker is important to their society. I have always wanted to have a career as a Correctional Worker and I would be happy to outline for you why in this essay.

As a correctional worker, a lot would be offered to society by me. Because society is organized according to rules it will always be the case that there will be people who will for whatever reasons they might have will break them. Sometimes very serious infractions like murder or assault. In the best interests of all concerned who are members of our society and who have input into our social situation, these offenders are separated from the rest of their society and they need to be supervised for the protection of those in society.

As well as being able to be in a supervisory position over the inmates I will also be able to offer another service to my society in addition to keeping it safe. I believe I can give some aid not only to those who are in society but also to those who are incarcerated behind the walls of our prisons and jails where we keep criminals and that is that they should be able to be encouraged to be rehabilitated. As a Correctional worker it will fall to me to be able to help to offer some counselling and support to the offenders who may want to correct their behaviour or ways of life which led him to be in this place in the first place. I am most interested in this role of the Correctional Worker who will be the one to be working most closely with offenders within the walls of the prison system. These are the two roles I believe are the most important for a Correctional Worker.

figure 2.5 Though Lucy has included most of the necessary details, her letter is ineffective. Why?

Lucy Wollersheim, Director
Heartbeat Haven Women's Shelter
27 Wormsley Road
Airdrie, Alberta
T4X 1U7

November 25, 2001

Qwik-Print Productions
Manager, Lino Panucci
1702 Dutch Street
Vancouver, British Columbia
V8K 8H9

Dear Mr. Panucci:

I am writing to tell you about my new program brochures which I bought from your company last summer. I have always liked your service in your company and enjoy dealing with you. I am returning the brochures to you.

Your order forms are always nice and clear and the illustrations are beautiful, which is what led me to order this one from you in your Spring and Summer mailing list, on page 26.

I am really writing because the ones I got were printed in blue and green, and I ordered them in pink and mauve, in August I think. I need the right ones sent back right away because I am planning to hold the conference at the beginning of January. The 150 brochures cost $69.95.

Thank you very much for your help in fixing this mistake. If you can't send it to me would you please refund my money I paid you?

Yours sincerely,

Lucesca Wollersheim

PS The order number is 307 - 62WP

figure 2.6 In what ways does this letter violate the Six C's of effective writing? How can it be improved?

HOTEL BonAmi
where good friends meet

19 Sherwood Avenue
Mississauga, ON M2R 7G5

phone: (905) 987-6543
fax: (905) 987-5432
email: hba@inet.ca

Friday, November 10, 2000

Mr. Ray Pronyshyn
Waskasoo College
20015 Laketree Place
Forestville, Ontario
P1A 5X7

Dear Ray:

Further to our conversation of the above-referenced date, please be advised that the following positions are presently available at our BonAmi Airport International Hotel: Security Officers; Child Services/Day Care Specialists; Recreation ProgramsAssistant (November and December); Life guard.

If it should prove to be the case that any one or more of your current students presently in your Community Services Program should be interested in the above-mentioned positions of employment, it is my hope that your staff or faculty will inform them to contact myself at their earliest convenience.

I appreciate your co-operation in this matter and please do not hesitate to contact me if you should be in need of any further information or assistance.

Thanking you in advance for your assistance,

Best regards,

Judy Cheung

Judy Cheung
Assistant Customer Services Manager, Recreation and Security

chapter 3

Letters, Memos, and E-mail Messages

| LEARNING
| OBJECTIVES

- To master standard letter and memo format.
- To understand the common types of professional correspondence and know when to use them.
- To learn the parts of a letter and memo.

Whether they are sent by surface mail, by facsimile machine, or through electronic mail, the letter and the memo are the most common forms of professional communication. Although information can be exchanged by telephone, this method isn't satisfactory for all situations. For many practical reasons, written communication may be preferred: it allows a precision not possible in oral exchanges and creates a permanent record for your own files. Whenever someone in an agency exchanges written information with someone in another organization, the letter has traditionally provided the appropriate vehicle. Within an organization, written communication is usually conducted via the memorandum, while informal messages may be sent by electronic mail (e-mail). If a message must be sent across Canada or to another country, e-mail, or even regular postal service, is still much cheaper than long-distance telephone calls.

Electronic mail provides a quick and inexpensive means of communicating with people within an organization or with other people and agencies in locations around the world; generally, communication by e-mail is less formal than letter or memorandum. Although its use is widespread, e-mail is still considered largely an informal medium. It is also, as many of you know, not a secure form for discussing personal or sensitive issues. As a result, it has not yet replaced the letter or the memo as the dominant form of correspondence, particularly for the formal and legal demands of professional communication. Still, the principles of effective writing that follow are also applicable to written communication sent by electronic means.

Part of communicating your message effectively is choosing an appropriate method or medium of communication. Here are some general guidelines for choosing between oral and written communication, or between a letter or memo and e-mail. You should use a letter or a memo rather than a telephone call for any information that might be considered "official" or formal, and for any information that is to be retained on file. A call or even a personal note will suffice if the information is for one person only, if no copies will be distributed elsewhere, and if it is not for the record.

E-mail, on the other hand, may be used for a whole variety of communication situations, is handy if you have to send the same message to a number of people, and can be quite casual in its set-up. However, because it cannot as yet carry your signature, it is not usually considered suitable for formal needs, and busy people who are inundated with dozens of e-mail messages a day may not give an important piece of communication the attention it deserves.

As well, despite its casual air, you should remember that anything you send via e-mail may be retained indefinitely by the recipient or forwarded without your knowledge or permission to someone else virtually anywhere else in the world. Your personal e-mail files may also be viewed with impunity by your employer. You should not use e-mail communication for confidential messages unless you can ensure that they will be securely encrypted and decoded only by the intended recipient.

Generally, you should use a letter or memo when:

- a copy of the information you are sending must be retained on file;
- the information concerns organization policy;
- the information is important; and
- copies of the document will be formally distributed to someone other than the individual to whom it is addressed.

Because letters and memos are used so frequently in professional situations, consistent standards of content, format, and style have evolved to help make the task of writing easier. Eventually, as electronic mail replaces "snail mail" as the standard for professional communication, style requirements are evolving for its use as well. Observing conventional standards in your writing will not only help to make your message more easily understood, but will also create a positive impression and help to establish you as a professional. Both memos and letters — as well as e-mail communication — observe the same rule: get to the point and don't waste the reader's time. To be effective, they must be accurate, clear, and written in an acceptable format.

Types of Professional Letters, Memos, and E-Mail Messages

Letters, memos, and e-mail messages can carry both good and bad news and may serve a multitude of purposes, from providing information to soliciting financial support. As a general rule, you should use letter or memo format for formal messages and reserve e-mail for more informal purposes. Whether they carry good news or bad news, letters, memos, and e-mail messages can be divided into two main categories: request and response. Whichever form your message takes — letter, memo, or e-mail — it will follow the same general guidelines.

Making a Request

A *request* may be written for any number of purposes: to order merchandise; to request information (printed materials, catalogues, travel flyers) or an appointment; to reserve a conference or hotel room; to apply for a job; to ask for favours (a reference, for instance); or to invite donations.

Basically, a request is any message that initiates contact with another person; the writer should aim to establish an effective working relationship between correspondents. These days, professional contacts may be initiated via e-mail as well as by letter; the following guidelines also apply to these exchanges.

Request messages should observe the Six C's listed in Chapter 1, keeping in mind that a major part of courtesy is making reasonable requests — don't ask the person to whom you are writing to do your work for you. Here are three questions to ask yourself before you write.

1. Am I being specific about what I want to know or what I'd like done?
2. Am I asking someone else to find information or perform a task that I could easily accomplish myself?
3. Is this request going to inconvenience the person in any unreasonable way?

If you can easily find out the information you need from a library or other source, or if you are vague about exactly what you want, you should reconsider your request carefully. Do not ask others to do for you what you could easily do for yourself. Of course, you should also be sure to say please and thank-you.

Writing a Response

A *response* is any message written in response to a request, an advertisement, or a situation. These might include letters of recommendation, information, congratulations or condolence, adjustment, refusal, or complaint.

Once again, the Six C's apply, with a few additional considerations. An effective response is both prompt and helpful. Always give the reader a positive impression and make your letter complete.

Good-News and Bad-News Messages

Within the two general categories of request and response are many situations that require a letter, a memo, or an e-mail message, and these may be broadly categorized as "good news" or "bad news" messages. Some of these present special problems for a beginning writer. Letters, memos, and e-mail messages carrying good news, such as congratulations or recommendations, make it easy to establish a positive writer-reader relationship; those that carry bad news — letters of complaint or refusal, for example — demand more careful handling.

It is especially important to watch your tone when delivering bad news. Try to cushion your bad-news message with suitable positive language and a positive tone. Be especially careful to avoid suggesting or implying that the other person is somehow responsible for the situation, even if you believe this to be the case. Always assume that you could be mistaken, and give your correspondent the benefit of the doubt if you can. What you really want is to have the problem solved, and creating unnecessary bad feelings will only lessen the chances of this happening. Be pleasant and take care to avoid a sarcastic tone.

Both good-news and bad-news messages require the same qualities of completeness, conciseness, coherence, correctness, and clarity as other professional correspondence. Bad-news messages also require an especial emphasis on courtesy. In a difficult or challenging situation, especially one in which bad news is being presented, it is particularly important to be courteous to your correspondents in order to make certain that your wishes are complied with.

Following are several common writing situations; messages of congratulations, fundraising appeals, and public service announcements could be considered good-news messages, while messages of complaint and messages of refusal are considered bad news. Keep in mind that any of these types of messages may be sent in memo or e-mail formats, as well as in letter format.

Congratulations or Acknowledgement

Of the four special types of good-news messages, the letter of congratulations or acknowledgement is the most pleasant to write. A letter (or memo) of congratulations may be written to an employee, a colleague, or a client on the occasion of achievement or accomplishment. Perhaps someone you know has received an award, published a book or article, earned a promotion, made a significant contribution to an agency project, or simply provided long or effective service that deserves to be recognized. Whatever the occasion, the letter of acknowledgement or congratulations should be positive in tone and to the point. Such letters should be:

- specific (identify the achievement or occasion);
- positive (make sure your tone is warm and your comments flattering);
- sincere (nothing is more insulting than congratulations that sound insincere; avoid being too effusive or ironic); and
- brief (as in any professional communication, say what you have to say, then stop — many people ruin effective acknowledgement or congratulations messages by not knowing when to quit).

Figure 3.1 contains a memo of acknowledgement from a supervisor to a staff member who has contributed an extraordinary year's work to the organization. Figure 3.2 is an e-mail message expressing congratulations to a colleague who has received the organization's Employee of the Year award. Compare the two. Based on your knowledge of professional writing, which is the more effective? Why is this so?

Letters of Complaint

Although not so pleasant to write, bad-news messages are unfortunately much more common than messages of congratulations. Most human-service agencies do their best to handle correspondence and requests for their services in a professional and efficient manner; however, occasionally mix-ups do occur. Applications may be misplaced, cheques lost, wrong information sent, or mailings waylaid.

Most agencies will do all in their power to keep such mistakes from happening, since any organization functions more smoothly when good will is maintained through effective client or staff relations. If you always make it a rule to assume, at least initially, that the mix-up is an honest error and to treat such incidents as unintentional, your complaints will be dealt with more promptly and positively.

The first rule for letters or memos of complaint is to be especially courteous. No one wants to receive abusive, sarcastic, or threatening letters; phrase your bad news in as positive terms as possible. Problems will be more easily solved if you allow your correspondents room to correct the situation without making them look foolish. They will be more interested in helping you and they will be more anxious to maintain your good will if you approach them in a friendly, non-threatening manner.

It is also important that in a complaint you specifically identify the nature of the problem and the action you wish taken. For example, if you have ordered program materials and after waiting a reasonable length of time have not received your order, you will want to identify the missing items by name, catalogue or item number, catalogue issue, and page number. You should state the date of your order, the cheque number, if there is one, and the amount of the order. If you have a standing account with the firm, cite your account number. Be sure that all of this information is correct. Be sure also that you tell the reader exactly what you want done about the problem. The reader's idea of a satisfactory solution may differ from yours.

Below are the points to remember for letters of complaint.

- Phrase your comments positively.
- Be sure to identify the exact nature of the problem immediately.
- Provide all relevant details.
- Request specific action.
- Be courteous. Thank correspondents for their help.

figure 3.1 Note how Michael Cea's warm tone and use of specific details make his letter of congratulations effective.

Friendly Face Youth Services
internal correspondence

DATE: April 14, 2001

TO: Gwynne Nishikawa

FROM: Michael Cea

RE: Appreciation of your contributions during the 1999/2000 fiscal year

Just a note to say thank you for all the work you have done for the Second Chance Secondary School project during this past year. I have especially appreciated your willingness to take on extra projects for the students, and your help with the mid-year assessment report for the Municipal Budget Committee.

Considering that you also managed to develop a new computer training program for the Job Readiness and Placement group, your contribution has been truly commendable and beyond any requirements of your job description.

Thank you for all that you have done and for your valuable assistance. Few, if any, members of the organization have done more to make this a successful year.

Please accept my heartfelt thanks for a job well done.

Mike Cea

cc. Personnel File
MC:jm

figure 3.2 In what ways is this message of congratulations flawed? (Consider both content and relation.) What does it suggest about its author?

Message Composition

From: Randy Alexander < Randy_Alexander@commserv.ca >

Subject: Employee of the Year Award

Mail To: Peter_Holowaczok@commserv.ca
Cc:

January 25, 2002

Congratulations on winning the Employee of the Year Award. It doesn't usually go to somebody who has been in the organization only two years — you must really be something special. I have been here for four years and though my work is really deserving, nobody seems to notice. I haven't even been nominated. I suppose I haven't made friends with the right people; I never was much good at lobbying.

I have heard it said that the work you've been doing in Public Relations is really outstanding, especially that slick brochure you produced for the new Drug Awareness Week campaign. Most everybody believes that it's really well designed. I saw it — it is pretty good, but could I give you a little advice? I didn't think that the photo of the Minister and Deputy Minister was appropriate for the cover. I have a talent for graphic design, and it's not what I would have chosen.

Please let me know if you'd like to get together sometime to talk about layout; I took a course in graphic art in college and could probably pass on a few useful hints. Also, I'd like to have a chance to talk with the new golden boy from PR.

Congratulations again on winning the award.

Sincerely,

Randy

In the letter on page 37 (Figure 3.3), Lam Huan is making a complaint regarding some student loan payment cheques that have been mistakenly processed too early and have been rejected by his own bank. Note that though the loans officer is at fault, Huan wisely does not cause more difficulty by being sarcastic or abusive.

figure 3.3 What features make Lam Huan's letter of complaint effective? Compare Huan's letter with the letter in Figure 3.4; in what ways does Ing Jang violate the principles of effective professional writing?

---

90 Victoria Crescent
Scarborough, Ontario
M2E 2R4

November 20, 2001

Accounting and Process Control
National Exchange Bank
Student Loan Business
PO Box 12345
Rochester, New York 10098

Re   Returned cheques dated November 1, 2001, and December 1, 2001
        Loan Payment Account #555693737 - 9

I received the above cheques from you, with a letter indicating that they were rejected by my bank due to insufficient funds. However, the cheques were processed by your department on October 20, 2001, and received by my bank on October 25. The reason for their rejection was thus not insufficient funds but postdating. Although American banks may operate differently, Canadian banks do not accept postdated cheques.

I dated the cheques according to their payment dates, and mailed them in advance to make certain that they would reach you on time. Since I would like to prevent such a mix-up happening again, is there some way to ensure that in future my cheques are not processed until the appropriate dates have arrived?

I am enclosing a third cheque to cover both payments. Since the original cheques reached you before the November 1 and December 1 due dates, I would appreciate an adjustment to any additional interest charges. Thank you.

Sincerely,

Lam Huan

Lam Huan

figure 3.4 How effective is this letter of complaint? Can you think of any ways it could be improved?

22 Ulethe Crescent
Scarborough, Ontario
M3R 5Q8

March 14, 2002

Manager
Moms and Tots CoOp Day Care
Midtown Youth Services
222 Bank Street
Toronto, Ontario
M4T 2H6

Dear Manager:

My son goes to your day school for Children of Teen Age Mothers. He has been in the program for two months and I have already had problems with your staff. I don't really know the name of the woman I spoke to but I want to complain about her immature behaviour to my son and I.

When I went to drop off my son for day school yesterday, the girl in charge told me I couldn't leave him there anymore. Just because of that other kid's broken tooth and the language she said my son uses, is no reason to keep him out of day school. Anyway, I don't know what language she is talking about. He must of picked it up from day school. Why don't they punish those other kids? Anyway, this isn't the first time either that your staff threatened me about my son. He is only four, and it's not his fault the other kids are sissies. She said I have received a letter of warning twice before but I never saw any letters.

This woman should be fired for her rudeness to me. Now I have no place to leave my son so I can have a few hours to myself. Also, the ministry of Social services is on my back to go to school. How can I when you people are always picking on my little boy? He needs a place to go where he won't be picked on by your staff.

I think you should fire the woman I spoke to and anybody else who is rude to clients. After all, this is a public centre, so as a citizen you people work for me. I hope I don't see her anymore.

Sincerely,

Ing Jang

Ing Jang

Persuasive Messages

Throughout this book, I emphasize the necessity in any professional writing of identifying the reader's needs, expectations, and interests. Such an understanding of your reader is always necessary if you are to write effective professional communications, but is especially important when you move from merely informative to persuasive writing. All persuasive communication must engage the attention and interest of its intended audience and motivate that audience to act as requested. As well, an effective persuasive message will help to guide the reader to the appropriate action through an enabling strategy, a device that makes it easy and convenient for the reader to do what is requested.

Fundraising letters are among the most common form of persuasive writing in the human services, although they are not the only ones you may have observed. Though these can be considered good-news letters and should, like the previous types, be positive in tone, they are more challenging to write because you are not only asking the reader to accept your message, but inviting the person to respond with a donation. A persuasive message must appeal to the readers, influencing them to donate to a cause, volunteer their time, or provide some authorization or sanction. You need to establish a human connection with the reader through the relational aspect of your message; to do this, you should sound upbeat and personal, and above all, honest and sincere. Outline to the reader the benefits of the program for which you are raising funds. Keep your letter personal; don't bully, patronize, or pander to the reader, and avoid obvious gimmicks.

Fundraising letters may be sent to potential donors or to established supporters of your organization; your approach will differ slightly depending on which is the case for you. The following are some of the things your fundraising letter to a new donor should do.

- Catch the reader's attention immediately. You may do this with a question, an unusual statement, a story, or a quotation. If you can, make a personal connection with the reader.
- Motivate the reader to respond by showing what a donation can accomplish. Appeal to the reader's good will and community spirit; show her how she will benefit. Emphasize the advantages of your program; if you can offer tax receipts for donations, be sure to point this out clearly.
- Make it easy for the reader to respond to your request. If you can, provide a donation form, a postage-paid envelope, or instructions as to how to donate by phone, fax, or e-mail. Offer instalment payments or direct debit as options, if possible
- Keep an enthusiastic tone. If you can, use the reader's name to make the message more personal.
- Communicate your sincerity. If you don't sound as though you mean what you say, your reader will reject your message, no matter how earnest you feel. Be sure that your sincerity is reflected in what you write. Especially avoid the standard clichés of professional writing, which will make you sound insincere or even phony.

The fundraising letter to an established donor is nearly identical, with the following additions.

- As an established donor, your reader will be more predisposed to read your mailer through, so you do not have to work quite so hard to catch attention.
- The established donor already has shown a commitment to your cause; briefly emphasize the advantages of your program and outline the achievements of your cause to date. Remind your donors of the importance to your community of their continued financial support; outline the potential losses that will occur without their support. Indicate that tax receipts are available.
- Be enthusiastic. You should definitely use the reader's name to personalize your letter.
- Be sincere and emphasize the effective relationship you've had in the past.

All fundraising letters must appeal to the reader strongly enough to make that person respond actively. They should be positive, warm, and persuasive, appealing to the needs, interests, and expectations of the reader.

A Note on "Hard Sell"

Fundraising, as a form of persuasion, requires careful identification of reader interests and concerns. This is a perfectly legitimate, basic principle that underlies all effective persuasive communication. However, there are other bases of appeal that are less respectable: instead of identifying and responding to an existing need, some promotional material seeks to create a false sense of urgency or fear. This kind of advertising appears to be designed to manipulate readers by appealing to their fears and doubts instead of to their good will or generosity. Some flyers use a hysterically enthusiastic style and tone and as a result, their voices are not as convincing. Modern readers, who are overwhelmed with requests for donations from television, radio, the World Wide Web, and print media, are quite sophisticated about gimmicky "hard sell" approaches. They may be wary and suspicious of such methods, and will reject your message as insincere if they detect such an attitude. Remember to keep your tone positive and warm, not crass or offensive, and to keep your audience's concerns genuinely in focus.

The following example of an effective fundraising letter (Figure 3.5) encourages donations for a medical cause. Contrast it with Figure 3.6, a letter circulated in a downtown neighbourhood to advertise a new child care facility that has just opened.

Public-Service Announcements

As a human-services professional working in the public sector, you may be responsible for writing public-service announcements to be broadcast over the radio or television or printed in the newspaper. Public-service announcements are primarily informative and communicate a simple message as clearly as possible. Like all effective messages, PSAs should observe the Six C's — completeness, conciseness, clarity, coherence, correctness, and courtesy.

Since the air time for a public-service announcement is donated by the radio or television station, the writer of such an announcement must structure it in such

figure 3.5 What are the qualities that make this fundraising letter effective? What methods does Huston use to engage her readers' interest and gain their support?

Waskasoo College

PO BOX 1977, FORESTVILLE, ON P6R 2T7

April 29, 2001

Dear Friend:

Like many of us who live in the city of Forestville, you may have fond memories of playing at the old City Recreation Park. Unfortunately, in the last ten years the park has fallen into disrepair and is no longer a place where children and families can go for recreation and fun. With your help, that can change. This spring, students from the Recreation and Leisure Studies Program at Waskasoo College have been at work on a special project: with permission of the mayor and city councillors, they have begun to refurbish the old recreation park. They have already embarked on a clean-up of the site, where they plan to establish a playground, picnic park, and games field.

As you may know, what is left of the old playground equipment is in dire need of repair. The students have donated their time to the clean-up and have organized teams to help with the building of new facilities and the repair of any of the old equipment that can be salvaged. Once the park is rebuilt, the mayor has promised to fund supervised recreational activities for children throughout the summer.

Unfortunately, all this hard work leads nowhere without financial support. That's where you come in: the Recreation and Leisure Studies Student Society of Waskasoo College invites you to participate in this worthwhile project with a donation of equipment, materials, or money to assist the students in rebuilding the park into a site we can all enjoy and be proud of. Our goal is to raise $5000 in corporate and private donations to support the work the students are doing. Donations of any amount will be welcomed.

We hope you will come out to the site to see the progress we have already made, and that you will be able to assist us in our efforts to complete this worthwhile project. Cash donations may be sent directly to the WCRLSS or dropped off at any Benjamin's Drug Store location. To donate materials or equipment, please contact Dajat Singh, Chair of the Recreation and Leisure Studies Department.

Sincerely,

Megan Huston
Megan Huston, President

Dajat Singh
Dajat Singh, Faculty Advisor

figure 3.6 A promotional letter like this one is a good idea for a new service, but these writers could use a little help. What improvements to their letter would you suggest?

Short Stuff
Your Children are First in Our Hearts
22619 Cowan Blvd, Lethbridge, AB T5N 5Y5
(403) 345 2473

Dear Working Parent:

We are recent graduates of the Early Childhood Development program at Waskasoo College, and we have just opened our very first day care service to offer you the best in up-to-date child care. We learned just about every technique imaginable in school, and we are anxious to try them out on your child.

As the new kids on the block, we are anxious to make a go of this centre, and we think it will be good for you to try somebody new for a change. We need to establish a clientele or we won't be able to stay in business for long, so we hope you will try us out.

To make our new centre more attractive to you, bring this letter with you when you come in to register your child. We will give you 5% off your first month's rates. Also, we guarantee to satisfy your child care needs, so if we do make a mistake in caring for your child, we promise we will correct it to your satisfaction. So instead of going to your usual day care facility, come in and try us. We're anxious to please you and to have a chance to practice our various techniques.

Sincerely,

Missey

Missey Ivanics

Sutri

Sutrisna Kanagaratnam
Co-Owners

42 EFFECTIVE COMMUNICATION FOR THE HELPING PROFESSIONS

a way that the complete message can be broadcast in 15 seconds, the average length of time for a short commercial. The announcement is typically contained in a letter addressed to the manager of the radio or television station, or the editor of your local newspaper, requesting that your announcement be included in their public-service spots for the appropriate dates. Be sure to make your request courteously and to express your thanks for the service.

An effective public-service announcement typically is under 100 words long (or conforms to length guidelines provided by your local media). It is usually contained in an indented paragraph within the letter, although it may be placed on a separate page and accompanied by a cover letter. It should be sent to local radio and television stations and to the local newspaper. A public-service announcement provides the essential information as briefly as possible, including:

- the name of the event, which should be mentioned both at the beginning of the announcement and again at the end;
- the sponsors of the event, if this is important to the message;
- when and where the event will be held;
- admission price, if any, or an indication that admission is free;
- a phone number to call for further information.

The public-service announcement should be phrased exactly as you would like it to be read on air or printed in the newspaper. Figure 3.7 shows an effective public-service announcement within an appropriate covering letter.

Refusals

These bad-news messages are often the most difficult to write. Great delicacy is required whenever you must turn down someone's request, whether that request has come from a candidate for employment or from a client who wants an adjustment of a fee or a resolution to a conflict. While you do not want to trivialize or underplay a difficult situation, you also don't want to exaggerate it through unnecessarily negative language.

As in all bad-news messages, tone is important to a refusal. You must be tactful in refusing to provide the service, and you must preserve the client's good will if possible. Be sure to observe the rule of putting the main message first. You should use as positive terms as possible under the circumstances to cushion the refusal, and you should especially avoid sarcasm or accusation. State the message briefly and then politely explain your reasons for the refusal.

At least initially, it is best to avoid placing responsibility for the refusal on the reader, even in cases where that person shares part of the responsibility. It rarely helps to point fingers at anyone; it is preferable instead to stress your own inability to comply with the request. Keep in mind that your most important goal is maintaining good will. For example, if you are writing a letter of refusal to someone who has been turned down for a job, stress that the position was offered to another candidate because that individual more closely suited your needs, not because the person you are writing to is inadequate. Likewise, if you are refusing a reference, it is better to stress your inability to supply it, rather than

figure 3.7 — A good public-service announcement is brief and concise, while including all the information listeners or readers will need. It is framed within a polite letter of request to the managers and editors who will be airing or publishing the message.

Community Awareness on Literacy

2550 Colombo Road
Port Hastings, Nova Scotia
B1R 1M2

September 30, 2001

Mr. Norman Stormon, Manager
CKMA Radio
PO Box 980
Port Hood, Nova Scotia

Dear Mr. Storman:

Would you please include the following announcement in your public-service spots for October 14 and 15?

> Community Awareness on Literacy will hold an **OPEN HOUSE** for new volunteers on Thursday evening, October 16, at the Downtown Library on Colombo Road. Anyone interested in volunteering for our *Each One Teach One* program or any other of our activities is invited to attend. Admission is free. Refreshments will be provided. For more information on the Community Awareness on Literacy **OPEN HOUSE**, please phone 543-9459.

Thank you very much for including this important event in your community calendar spots. As always, we are grateful for your support in advancing literacy in our community.

Sincerely,

Ruth MacLeod

Ruth MacLeod

Director, CAL

suggest that the person is flawed. The following are some points to keep in mind when writing a letter of refusal.

- Identify the subject in a subject or "re" line.
- Indicate briefly your inability to comply with the reader's request, using as positive terms as possible.
- State your reasons simply, taking responsibility for your refusal.
- Avoid sarcasm or accusation.
- Be polite and sincere.
- Suggest someone else your correspondent might approach for assistance, if possible.
- Offer the person your best wishes for better success elsewhere, if it's appropriate to do so.

In the letter of refusal in Figure 3.8, the bad news has been cushioned with positive comments, and the reader has been invited to reapply for a future training session. As well, the writer has recommended another volunteer organization that might enlarge the candidate's skill base in preparation for future service with his organization. Contrast it with Figure 3.9; both letters have a similar message to relate. Which of the two would you rather receive?

Remember, no matter what kind of message you are writing, be sure to identify your main point first and communicate your message as clearly and concisely as possible, maintaining a polite tone throughout.

The Parts of a Letter

All letters contain the same parts and may be written in any of three standard formats. All are also single spaced. Also, whether the letter is sent by ordinary post or via fax, all letters consist of the same standard parts:

1. Return Address This is the normal address of the writer of the letter; it does not include the writer's name. In a personal letter, the return address is your home address; if you are writing on behalf of your organization, it is the organization's name and address. If you are using agency letterhead, you do not need to include a separate return address.

2. Date Though there is a move toward dating letters numerically, it is still better to write out the date; styles of numerical dating vary, and this inconsistency can cause confusion, especially as we move into the new century. There are currently three forms in use:

Canadian	12/06/02	Day/Month/Year
American	06/12/02	Month/Day/Year
"Metric"	02/06/12	Year/Month/Day

figure 3.8 What strategies did John Moffatt use to soften the news of rejection for Molly Crump? Contrast this example with the e-mail message in Figure 3.9. Which would you prefer to receive?

Community Distress Centre

PO Box 3550
Calgary AB T3N 5H6
1-800-568-9547

February 15, 2001

Ms. Molly Crump
55 Elwood Close
Calgary, Alberta
T5W 3F6

Dear Ms. Crump

Thank you for participating in our recent training session for our Telephone Crisis Line. Although the trainers felt your practice sessions showed solid potential in counselling, I am afraid we will not be able to offer you a spot as a Crisis Counsellor for this year.

This decision is not meant to reflect on your potential to be an effective telephone counsellor; rather, it is an indication of the large number of very fine volunteers who participated in this year's training session. We simply could not accommodate all who applied.

We would like to encourage you to reapply for next year's training session. In the meantime, we suggest that you obtain additional volunteer experience in one of the many programs offered through the Leisure and Human Services department of the City of Calgary. We believe such an experience would help you to better prepare for the demands of serving on our Suicide Crisis Line.

We extend our best wishes and look forward to seeing you again next year.

Sincerely

John Moffatt

John G. Moffatt
Managing Director

figure 3.9 How might Martin Oordt respond to this letter? Suggest some ways David Kaminski's message might be improved.

THE COLLEGIAN

The Voice of Waskasoo College • Student Union Building, C-870

April 1, 2002

Martin Oordt
125 Coulee Court
Forestville, Ontario
P2W 0W3

Dear Marty:

Thanks for submitting your latest poetry for consideration by the *Collegian's* editorial staff. As you know, we usually welcome submissions from students and members of the community at large.

We would prefer, however, not to receive any more poems from you. Although I admit that we published one of your poems last year, you should know that poetry is not really our "thing" and we used the other poem only because we had a little bit of space to fill and your work just fit.

We are more interested in other kinds of submissions — photos, drawings, and fiction written by the college community; I am pretty sure that our readers don't know much about poetry and don't really want to see it in the *Collegian*. If they did want to read such stuff, they could take an English course! After all, we are interested in things that are relevant to real life and most people agree that poetry is boring. Besides, I'm not even sure how to judge the quality of your poetry.

I hope you won't be too upset by my letter, but I thought you would want to hear the truth. If you decide to take up a more interesting kind of writing, please let us know. We might like to have something else from you.

Sincerely,

David Kaminski

David Kaminski

Without some further cues for interpretation, it's very difficult to ascertain whether this date is December 6, 2002, June 12, 2002, or February 6, 2012. If your employer prefers numerical dating, you should use your format, but otherwise, avoid this unnecessary confusion by writing the date out in full — in this case, June 12, 2002.

3. Inside Address This is an important part of the letter; it provides information for the files of the organization to which it is sent. It should include the following, in this order.

Name and title	Mr. Dajat Singh, Chair
Name of organization	Recreation and Leisure Studies Program
	Waskasoo College
Address of organization	PO Box 1977
	Forestville, ON
	P6R 2T7

If the person's title is very long, it might be placed on a separate line, but the order of the parts remains the same.

Name	Ms. Soo Liang Chan
Title	Assistant Manager, Human Resources
Name of organization	Waskasoo College
Address of organization	PO Box 1977
	Forestville, ON
	P6R 2T7

4. Salutation This is the opening of your letter; traditionally, it's "Dear...." Use the name of the person to whom you are writing, if you know it. If you don't know it, and it is important that you have it (for instance, in a job application letter), telephone the organization and ask the person's name. If you can't bring yourself to do this, you may be able to locate the correct name on the agency's Web site, if there is one. If you can't find the name, you may wish to delete the salutation altogether, an option that has become more acceptable in modern correspondence. Do not use the traditional "Dear Sir" if you don't know the name of the person you're writing to; women now occupy many professional positions and might reasonably object to the assumption that all such positions are held by men.

If you are corresponding with a person whose given name is not readily identifiable as male or female — for example, K. Barnett, Terry Ferguson, Raj Bhanot, Saran Narang, or Mai Li Chiu — you may wish to write the full name in the salutation: "Dear K. Barnett" or "Dear Mai Li Chiu." Unless you are on very friendly terms with the person you are writing to, note that it is never proper to address him or her by first name in formal correspondence. Such familiarity has gained a measure of acceptance in American society, but a Canadian reader may well experience it as rude or forward. In Canada, "Dear Saran" or "Dear Mai Li" remains an inappropriate way to address a person you do not know well.

5. Subject or "Re" Line This useful device has been borrowed from the memorandum. It has become an important part of the letter, since it forces the writer to observe the rule of putting the main information first and allows the reader to identify the main point immediately. This line should be brief and to the point, and should indicate clearly what the letter is about. It usually consists of a single phrase or two.

6. Body This portion of your correspondence contains the main information you wish to communicate, in as clear a form as possible. Identify the subject matter at the beginning, giving a brief outline of the situation or problem. Follow with some pertinent details, carefully selected and organized so that the reader may easily understand your message. Finish with a specific statement that outlines what you expect of the reader. The body of the letter is single spaced and divided into brief paragraphs for ease of reading. The number of paragraphs can vary, as can the length of the letter, depending on the complexity of the subject matter. Some letters are two or three pages long, but most are one page. Whatever the length of the letter, its message should be easily grasped one reading. If your reader must reread the letter several times simply to understand it, it is poorly composed and ineffective.

7. Complimentary Closing This can be any one of a variety of forms; the most common nowadays is "Sincerely" or even "Yours sincerely." "Yours truly" is not used very much anymore, though it isn't wrong. Whichever you use, be sure to note its correct spelling. If you are very well-acquainted with your correspondent, you may even wish to use a more familiar closing, such as "Cordially" or "Best wishes" or even (if you are very friendly) "Cheers." Do not use these for formal correspondence, however. If you are in doubt, simply use "Sincerely."

8. Organization Name Occasionally, a writer using organization letterhead will signify that correspondence is written on behalf of his or her employer by placing the organization name, in block letters, immediately below the complimentary closing, above the writer's signature. This precaution is observed to clarify responsibility for legal purposes. At one time, it was safe to assume that anything written on the organization's letterhead was written on behalf of the firm, but frequent use of letterhead for personal correspondence has made this assumption impractical. Modern writers may take this extra measure to emphasize that the contents of the letter are indeed a matter of agency business. It is not necessary to include this line in your letters, but if doing so is a common practice in your organization, by all means do it.

Yours sincerely,
COMMUNITY DISTRESS CENTRE

Aidan Terry

9. Signature This is the name of the writer only; it should not include any nicknames, titles, or degrees. A professional should also use a consistent signature, not Jennifer in one letter and Jen or Jenny in the next. Choose one form of your name (preferably not a diminutive, and certainly not a nickname) and use it consistently for your professional correspondence.

10. Typed Name and Titles Since many signatures are unreadable, a courteous writer types the name in full beneath the signature. If you wish to include any degrees or titles, type them along with your name. (This information is not, you will remember, part of the signature.) If your name is gender-neutral or potentially misleading, you may wish to make it easier for your correspondent to reply to you by indicating the honorific you prefer. If you are a woman and sign yourself as J. MacLennan, for example, you should not be surprised or offended if some correspondents make the incorrect assumption and address you as "Mr." Very often you will also wish to include your position in the organization you represent.

Terry Lansdown (Mrs.)
Client Services

Nancy Black (Dr.)
Chief of Staff

Saran Narang (Ph.D.)
Editor in Chief

Soo Liang Chan (Ms.)
Assistant Manager, Human Resources

11. Secretary's Notations As with the inside address, the secretary's notation is useful for record purposes; it is sometimes important to know who typed the correspondence, whether any enclosures or attachments were included, and/or whether any other people received copies. The notations appear in the lower left of the page and are as follows.

/jml	Secretary's initials — some organizations use this form to indicate that the secretary actually composed the correspondence on behalf of the writer, though this is not the case in every firm.
DFC/jm	Writer's initials/typist's initials — may be written this way to indicate that the secretary (jml) typed what was written by someone else (DFC).
encl:2	Enclosure notation — indicates that two items were enclosed with the package.
attach:3	Attachment notation — similar to enclosure notation, but items were appended to the letter with a clip or staple. This example shows that there were three such items.
cc. D. Brown R. Vandeven	Correspondence notation — these people received copies of the correspondence. The notation "cc" stands for carbon copy, the method used for creating copies of documents before photocopiers became indispensable office equipment. Although no one now uses carbon copies, the notation "cc" continues to be used whenever

copies, however generated, are sent to individuals other than the addressee. This notation might also appear as "pc" for photocopy. In either case, its meaning is the same.

12. File Number A code consisting of a combination of letters and numbers may appear at the lower left or, more commonly, at the upper right of the page. This is a file number that assists the organization in filing correspondence in the appropriate location.

Figure 3.10 shows a letter in standard full-block format; the parts are numbered to correspond with the list above.

The Parts of a Memo or E-Mail Message

Although the letter and memo serve similar purposes and may carry similar kinds of messages, a memo is intended to remain inside the agency or institution, and this fact affects its structure. It has no need of an inside address, return address, or salutation; instead it has a relatively standard heading made up of four parts. The labels *To*, *From*, *Date*, and *Re* (or *Subject*) are usually arranged vertically at the top left-hand side of the memo. Most e-mail programs have adopted the *To-From-Date-Subject* format of the memo. The program automatically fills in the date and the e-mail address of the sender; the sender inserts the e-mail address of the recipient, along with a brief subject title.

The other sections of the memo or e-mail message are similar to the parts of the letter, as explained below.

1. To The *To* line takes the place of the salutation and identifies, by name and title, the person or persons to whom the memo is directed. In an e-mail message, the *To* line consists of the e-mail address rather than the name of the recipient. The e-mail addresses of any additional recipients may also be added here.

2. From The *From* line identifies, again by name and title, the person who wrote the memo. In the case of a message sent by e-mail, your program will automatically fill in your e-mail address on any message sent from your account.

3. Date The *Date* line states the date on which the memo was written; you may wish to use a numerical dating style in a memo, but as we discussed above, numerical dating can cause confusion, and you should probably avoid it unless your employer recommends it. You do not need to supply the date in an e-mail message, since the program itself will automatically record the date and the time of the message, which will be displayed when the recipient reads the message.

figure 3.10 This sample letter shows the parts of a letter in full block format; the numbers correspond to those in the list of parts, above.

[1] 980 Main Street
     Saint John, NB
     E1G 2M3

[2] January 21, 2002

[3] Michael Cea, Manager
     Friendly Face Youth Services
     453 Rue Montagne
     Montreal, PQ
     H3R 6Y8

[4] Dear Mr. Cea

[5] Re: Full Block Letter Format

[6] This is an example of the full block style; note how all the parts begin at the left margin. Paragraphs are not indented, and lines are skipped between them.

Also, you will notice that this letter is single spaced, as all letters should be. Note, too, the optional use of open punctuation in this letter — this means no punctuation at the end of the salutation or the complimentary closing. Of course, if you wish, you may use a colon after the salutation and a comma following the complimentary closing.

[7] Sincerely
[8] COMMUNITY AWARENESS ON LITERACY

[9] *Ruth MacLeod*

[10] Ruth MacLeod
     Director

[11] cc. Ian Hauen, Ryker Sheepskin Products Ltd
     SC/jm

[12] 00-01-SD

52 EFFECTIVE COMMUNICATION FOR THE HELPING PROFESSIONS

4. Re or Subject Line The *Re* or *Subject* line identifies for the reader exactly what issue the memo or e-mail message addresses and what you wish to say about that issue. This crucial line of your memo should contain the main point you have identified in your rough draft with the key words, "The main thing I want to tell you is that...." Professional people are busy and will not want to scan the entire memo or e-mail message to find the gist of it. Often they decide whether to take the time even to read the message by glancing at the subject line, so make sure yours is specific.

This line is especially important in an e-mail message; regular users of e-mail can receive as many as twenty or thirty messages every day. Most don't have time to carefully read all of these, and some even delete those that look unimportant without reading them at all. If you want to make sure your message gets read, supply a subject line that makes clear to the reader what the message involves.

5. Message The body of the memo, without a salutation, follows the headings. It may be separated from them by a solid line if you wish. Like the body of the letter, it contains the main information you wish to communicate, in as clear a form as possible. It is single spaced and deals with the situation or problem as specifically as possible. The body of the e-mail message is similar to that of the memo, although many people like to personalize this impersonal form of communication by adding a salutation. If your e-mail message is to someone you know well and with whom you're on friendly terms, this salutation may be as familiar as "Hi, Gail." If you are corresponding via e-mail to a professional colleague or client, you may wish to use the same form of salutation that is used in the letter: "Dear Franco," or even "Dear Dr. Berruti."

Like a letter, a memo or e-mail message may deal with issues of varying complexity. Memos used for simple issues are usually less than a page long, but the memo format may also be used for a short report dealing with more complex situations. (Reports are covered in Chapters 4 and 5.) Whatever its purpose, the memo or e-mail message, like the letter and report, provides specifics to support the main point given in the subject or "re" line. However, because these messages are often very short and to the point, they risk sounding curt or abrupt in tone. Be especially careful to observe courtesy in a memo or e-mail message in order to avoid offending your reader.

Finally, you should avoid contributing to the flurry of unnecessary memos. Use a memo only for information that might be considered "official"; a casual message may be better delivered by telephone, by e-mail, or by a brief personal note.

6. Initial or Signature No complimentary closing is required on a memo, but it may be initialed or signed if you wish. Though a signature is not absolutely necessary, it is becoming more common to sign memos. However, since your name appears at the top, there is no need to type it again under your signature. An e-mail message, of course, cannot as yet be signed, though you may wish to type your name at the end of the message. For this reason, e-mail is not yet used for very formal correspondence or for reports and letters that are legally binding.

7. Notations Since memos serve the same purposes as letters, they make use of the same notations, especially secretary's initials and carbon copy designations. If it is appropriate, copies may be sent to superiors or other interested parties within the organization. For example, a supervisor who writes a memo commending an employee for work well done might direct a copy to the personnel file; the head of a departmental committee might direct a copy of a meeting announcement to the department head to let that individual know that the committee is getting on with its work. Memos, like letters, may also contain file numbers for easy reference. E-mail messages may be sent to several people simultaneously; if so, their e-mail addresses appear in the *To* portion of the message rather than in a copy notation at the bottom of the page.

Letter and Memo Format

Letters may employ one of three formats widely used in Canada: semiblock, full block, and modified semiblock. The full-block format is the type illustrated in Figure 3.10. The semiblock style is the oldest pattern and although it is still widely used, it is gradually being replaced by the full block style. Modified semiblock is a transitional form, a blending of the other two styles. Memos, with clear-cut headings at the top of the page, have a simpler format than letters and so are generally easier to construct.

Another feature of an attractive and readable layout is the font you select from those available in your word processor program. In general, a serif font (such as Times or Roman) is easier to read than a sanserif font (such as Helvetica). Script fonts, especially in smaller sizes, are also difficult to read, as is gothic lettering. Most computer fonts are proportionally spaced, which means that thin letters (such as "i" or "t") take up less space on the page than do wide letters (such as "w" or "m"), just as they would if the document were typeset. These fonts also automatically place an extra space after a period, so that sentences are separated by a slightly larger space than words within a sentence. However, a few fonts (such as Courier, which is designed to resemble a typewritten font) are monospaced, which means that every letter — no matter its width — takes up exactly the same amount of space on the page. If you have selected such a font, you must add an additional space after the period, as used to be the case for documents typed on a typewriter. Compare the following examples for visual appeal:

Times   The quick brown fox jumps over the lazy dog. The lazy dog does not respond. The fox disappears through a hole in the hedge.

Helvetica   The quick brown fox jumps over the lazy dog. The lazy dog does not respond. The fox disappears through a hole in the hedge.

Courier   The quick brown fox jumps over the lazy dog. The lazy dog does not respond. The fox disappears through a hole in the hedge.

Whichever letter format you use, give careful attention to layout. In any piece of professional correspondence, you want clarity, and the impression of clarity is enhanced by an attractive arrangement of the letter or memo on the page. Leave generous margins — at least 1" on all sides — and place the printed material as near as possible to the vertical centre of the page. Try not to crowd your letter or memo too close to the top of the page; unless it is very brief, you should space your letter so that approximately half of the print falls within the lower half of the page.

As the reference guide in Figure 3.11 indicates, the main difference in letter format is in indentation: in *full block style*, everything, including paragraphs, begins at the left margin of the page. It is the most modern form of letter and the simplest to set up. Paragraph divisions are indicated by skipped lines. In *semiblock format*, the return address, date, complimentary closing, signature, and typed name are indented so that they begin at approximately the centre of the page. Each paragraph is also indented one tab stop (which is usually preset at 1/2" in most word processing programs); paragraph divisions may also be (but do not have to be) indicated by a skipped line if the writer prefers. This format has a more balanced appearance, but is also more difficult to type.

Modified semiblock is laid out exactly like the semiblock style, except that the paragraphs are not indented. The return address, date, complimentary closing, signature, and typed name are lined up to the right of centre, just as in the semi-block style. All of the text in the body of the letter begins at the left margin, and paragraph divisions are always indicated by a skipped line, as they are in the full block style. Though the full block style is now the most commonly used letter form, you should not use it if your employer prefers another. Use whichever format your employer prefers.

The layout of the *memo* is not as clearly defined as that of the letter. All memos contain the standard four-part heading of To-From-Date-Subject, but the arrangement of these parts may vary, depending on the preference of the writer. The memo's heading section is normally arranged at the left margin, usually in the order *To*, *From*, *Date*, and *Subject*, or *Re*, though there is some variation to this standard order. Several common variations are displayed in Figure 3.11. The paragraphs in the body of the memo may be indented, as in the semi-block letter style, or not, according to the writer's preference. Paragraphs that are not indented should be separated with a skipped line.

You may also have noticed that the examples in this book use different punctuation styles. Some use an "open" style, with no punctuation marks at the end of the salutation or complimentary closing; others use "closed" punctuation, with a colon following the salutation and a comma after the complimentary closing. Either punctuation style is acceptable in any of the formats, but do not mix open and closed styles within a single letter.

figure 3.11 A handy Reference Guide for memo and letter formats.

Memo Formats

MEMORANDUM
DATE:
TO:
FROM:
SUBJECT:

MEMORANDUM
TO: DATE:
FROM: SUBJECT:

MEMORANDUM
TO:
FROM: DATE:
RE:

Letter Formats

Full Block Letter

Semiblock Letter

Modified Semiblock Letter

points to remember

1. Use a letter or memo if the information you are communicating must be retained on file, or if the information is of formal importance in the organization.
2. Do not use e-mail for messages that are confidential or for important information that must carry a signature.
3. Apply the Six C's of professional writing to all letters, memos, and e-mail messages.
4. Letters, memos, and e-mail messages can either be requests or replies and can contain good news or bad.
5. Make sure your letter contains all the appropriate parts, whether you are sending it by fax or by conventional mail: return address, date, inside address, salutation, subject line, body, complimentary closing, signature, typed name, and notations.
6. In a memo, the *To*, *From*, *Date*, and *Re* or *Subject* information appears first.
7. Always be positive in tone and attitude.
8. Provide all relevant details.
9. Recognize reader needs, expectations, and knowledge.
10. Say all you need to say and then stop.
11. Always avoid sarcasm.

sharpening your skills

SECTION A

The following situations require letters; some of them will carry good news and some will carry bad news. In writing them, observe all the elements of style and format discussed above. Add any details that might make your letters more convincing.

1. The mayor and city councillors of your city have finally proposed to refurbish the old City Recreation Park, which has been all but abandoned and allowed to run down in recent years. Nothing is definite as yet, but the proposal involves creating a sports field, swimming area, and playground, and providing supervised activities for children during the summer months. You recall playing and swimming at the old park as a child, and you hope that these plans will be carried out. Write to the mayor lending your support to the proposal.

2. You and a friend have recently found yourselves in competition for a plum job in your field. You feel certain that you are the better qualified candi-

date, since your grades are slightly better than your friend's, and you have a full year more experience in this kind of position. Nevertheless, you have just learned that your friend has been offered the job, while you have received a polite letter of rejection. You are happy for your friend, but disappointed for yourself. Write a letter of congratulations to send to your friend. Invent any details you need.

3. You are nearing graduation and have been conducting a job search. You are lucky enough to have been offered two positions. The first is with the agency where you served your placement; the other is a more promising position with a government facility. The placement position offers better pay initially, but the government position has better prospects for promotion and benefits over the long term, and after carefully considering the two, you have decided to accept the position with the government. Write the letter to your placement supervisor thanking him for the offer, but politely refusing the job. Invent any necessary details.

4. You have heard that a former professor of yours has just been nominated for the Distinguished Teaching Award at your college. Write a letter of support for her or him (identify a professor of your choice) that may be added to the professor's dossier for the awards committee's consideration.

5. Write to a former instructor or employer, requesting permission to name that person as a reference in a job application.

6. You are the former instructor of Pat Yorgason, who has just written to you asking for a letter of reference. It has been three years since Pat was in your class, and you have taught three hundred students per year since then. You never knew Pat well and after all this time you can't picture a face to go with the name; all you can recall is the impression of an indifferent student. A check of your records confirms that impression: Pat's grade in your communication class was C–, but otherwise nothing much jogs your memory. In fact, you have taught lots of "Pats," and you can't even recall whether this one is male or female! You don't feel that you are the best choice to write a recommendation for this person. Write a letter to Pat politely explaining why another referee might be a better choice.

Pat Yorgason
PO Box 75
Melfort, SK
T0K 0K0

7. You are a volunteer at the local food bank. Donations are down this month, and you have volunteered to draft a circular calling for donations to distribute at the local mall. Speedi Print has offered to pick up the cost of duplicating five hundred circulars. Write the circular encouraging people to donate to this worthy cause. Be sure to tell them what, where, and how to donate.

8. Write a letter of thanks, on behalf of the food bank, for the donation of the duplicating costs for the five hundred circulars in Assignment #7, above. The address is 1765 Shoreline Drive, Glace Bay, Nova Scotia B6J 7Y8. The manager's name is Margaret Thomson.

9. Recently you deposited in person $300 into your bank account. A week later, on checking your balance at the bank machine, you discover that the $300 has not appeared. When you visit the bank, the teller, Baghwan Dua, discovers that the money has been placed into another customer's account. The person has the same surname as yours, but the account numbers are significantly different. Dua arranges to correct the error, but he is quite unapologetic and even implies that the mistake is somehow your fault. Write to the manager of your bank, Ramona Chief Calf, to register your complaint.

10. You are a long-time member of the Block Safety Association in your town, and as such you are on the Board of Directors. Your group has decided to hold an Open House to attract new members, and you would like to involve the local police and the RCMP in the event. You have decided to invite representatives from both groups to give talks on Personal Self Defense, Streetproofing Your Kids, Home Security Measures, and CrimeStoppers. The Community Liaison Officer of your local RCMP detachment is Ovide Vendredi. On behalf of your organization, write a letter to Constable Vendredi inviting him to participate in your Open House. Be sure to give him the dates, times, and location of the events, and ask for his assistance in setting up any or all of the above presentations.

11. You are involved with an organization known as "The Good Bears," a unique charity that operates an annual toy drive for underprivileged children. Its philosophy is simple: that all children should have a hand-crafted teddy bear or other cuddly toy. Your volunteers actually make the bears and other animals to be donated to needy children. You also accept cash donations. You have been asked to write a public service announcement for this organization to solicit contributions of home-made or purchased bears. Your organization will supply a simple pattern free of charge to those who wish to donate the labour and raw materials to make a bear.

12. You have worked in Leisure and Family Services of your town for five years. You enjoy your job, but your spouse has recently been offered a position in Winnipeg. You too have applied and been accepted for a position in that city and will be moving at the end of June. You have submitted your resignation to the personnel department. You have always been on the best of terms with your supervisor, Elaine Girrior. She has been supportive of you throughout your employment with the firm and has provided you with promotions and recognition for any special achievements you have had. She has also encouraged you to take additional training and has recognized your potential to move into an administrative position. You have just recently done so and are

sorry to have to leave the agency, even though your new position promises to be very rewarding. You wish to communicate your thanks and respect to Elaine Girrior, and you decide to write her a formal thank-you letter. Without becoming too sentimental, but communicating your warmest wishes to her, write the letter you would give to Elaine Girrior on your departure.

13. It has been a long-time goal for you to serve your placement term in the Rocky Mountains in Alberta. Your dream has come true in that you have received an offer of work for next semester from Recreation, Health, and Safety Services of the Waterton-Glacier Resort. Unfortunately, your mother has fallen ill and you won't be able to take the job. You recognize that delaying your acceptance is unusual, and an alternative arrangement is unlikely, but you very much want to have the experience of working in the mountains. Write to your new employer asking whether you can delay taking the position for six months, until your mother recovers. Your contact is

    Sandra Terry, Manager
    Waterton-Glacier Resort
    Box 26
    Waterton, AB T2W 1A6.

14. You are concerned over recent public outcry against halfway houses. A petition has been circulating in your area calling for the closing of local halfway houses, inspired in part by a serious assault committed by one of the inmates. As a human-services professional, you believe the halfway houses are a beneficial part of the rehabilitative process, and you do not want to see them closed down due to public outrage over an incident you consider to be an exception. Write to your MP indicating your views and urging him or her to take action against such proposed closings.

15. A recent fire in your home destroyed a number of your personal effects. Among the items lost are your educational records, particularly your college diploma. You are currently employed with Cedarton Family Services, but are considering a career move, and you will need the certificate as proof that you graduated from college. Write to the office of the registrar at your college, giving all of the details they will need to locate your file, and inquire whether they will be able to replace your diploma.

16. At its upcoming Open House, your agency is featuring a lecture on teenage suicide by the noted psychologist Dr. Mel Blank. This session is open to the public, and you hope to encourage much community participation. Write a letter to the program chairs of all Community Services programs at your college, inviting them to attend and to bring their students. Be sure to indicate the date, time, and place of the session.

17. Write the public-service announcement and covering letter for the above session on teenage suicide. Include all the details the media will need to announce your session on air.

18. The letters on pages 62 and 63 (Figures 3.12 and 3.13) contain weaknesses. Evaluate them according to the criteria you have learned and be prepared to rewrite them more effectively if your instructor directs you to do so.

Section B

Write the following memos, bearing in mind all you have learned about professional writing style and format. Add whatever details are required to make your memos convincing. If your instructor directs you to do so, submit your assignment via e-mail.

1. Along with three other members of your class, you are interested in forming a student club for majors in your program. In order to be allowed to hold events on campus, your club has to be ratified by the Students' Union. Ratification requires a membership list of at least fifteen people. Write a memo, addressed to all students in your program, to be posted on the department bulletin board encouraging students to sign up for your club. Be sure to include a listing of the advantages of such an organization, the deadline for ratification, fees or start-up costs, and a number where you can be contacted. If you plan to post or circulate a sign-up sheet, mention that as well. Send a copy of your memo to the chair of your department.

2. Your department chair has been arranging mock job interviews for the students in your program in order to give them experience in interviewing. The interviews are to be conducted by professionals in your future field who have agreed to come to the college to participate in the exercise. Your program chair has impressed upon all of you how important these practice interviews are. Yours is set for next Thursday at 2:00 p.m. Since you made this appointment, however, you have had a real job interview scheduled for 2:30 p.m. that same day. You can't make it to both interviews. If you are successful in the actual interview, the job will give you experience directly related to your college program. Write a memo or compose an e-mail message to your program chair with a copy to the interviewer, Allan Goren, cancelling your mock interview appointment and explaining why you can't be there.

3. Your class is having problems with a particular instructor. You wish to meet with him as a class to discuss the difficulties. On behalf of the class, write an e-mail message outlining the specific nature of the problem and requesting a meeting with your instructor to solve it. If you are actually submitting your message electronically, be sure to direct it to your communication instructor. Watch your tone especially in this one!

4. Three months ago, you were granted permission by the director of your agency to attend a conference on Drug Awareness and Intervention Techniques being held in London, Ontario, this week. You will be absent from your office Thursday and Friday. Write a memo to your direct supervisor, Alsa Wender, reminding her of your absence and pointing out that you

figure 3.12 This letter violates the principles of a letter of congratulations. What impression does it make on the reader?

2100 Allendon Crescent
Peachvale, Ontario
L7B 3Z9

July 30, 2001

Ms. Monique Martineau
90 Main Street
Oshawa, Ontario
M6K 3D4

My dearest Monique

I have just heard the news from Tobias Johnson that your book *Teen Violence: Healing the Wounds* has been accepted by Prentice Hall.

I know just how you feel — I wrote a book myself, you know, and I'm sure I'd have publishers just knocking the door down if I finished it. (They can be so tasteless, can't they?) But it seems that nearly everyone you talk to is writing a book these days, it almost makes you think you should find something original to do!

However, it is an accomplishment, dear — and who knows? Maybe someday you'll be shaking my hand as a fellow published author!

Yours very sincerely

Donna Skreyuw

Donna Skreyuw

figure 3.13 How easy will it be for Dr. Calvin to respond to this request? Why?

75 Snayall Drive
Couchgrass, Manitoba
R1A 3C6

October 30, 2000

Professor L.M. Calvin
Science Division
Northwoods College
Box 456
Bruce Mines, Ontario
N0E 04O

Dear Professor Calvin:

I am writting you this letter to please ask if you would kindly act as a reference for me?

I took your class when I attended the college about 6 years ago. Now I want to go back to school in a similar program at Pineridge College here in Couchgrass.

Could you send your letter directly to them? It would be very much appreciated.

Yours truly,

M. Jones

M. Jones

have rescheduled major appointments, and that your remaining duties will be handled by your co-worker, Brian Beine, during your absence. You are driving to London Wednesday, and staying from Wednesday night to Friday night at the Tamada Inn in London, at 519-288-1454, in case of emergency.

5. You are in charge of collecting contributions from your co-workers for the local Fire Department's Charity Clothing Drive for families who have lost their possessions due to fire. Write an e-mail message to all employees encouraging them to contribute some of their gently-used clothing to this good cause. Be sure to provide your readers with a clear motivation to donate and suggestions for the kinds of donations needed. Add information about the deadline date and the location where readers can drop off their donations for delivery to the clothing drive. Send your message to your communication instructor via e-mail.

6. In the institution where you are employed, one of your normally complacent residents suddenly reacts violently. By the end of your shift, you have managed to calm him down, but you are uncertain of the cause of the outburst. You suspect an adverse reaction to a new medication just prescribed for him by the institution's physician. Write a memo to your colleague on the next shift describing the problems you encountered. Based on your knowledge of the field, you may wish to recommend any precautions or approaches needed in dealing with this person.

7. You have been running a literacy workshop with a group of community volunteers whose help has been invaluable to you. The first group of "students" is nearing completion of the program, which will continue with new people who need assistance. You want to extend some appreciation to the volunteers for their assistance with an evening get-together (perhaps a wine and cheese party). You have also designed a certificate of appreciation which you would like to have printed and awarded to each volunteer for her contribution to the program. Write a memo to your supervisor, Wade Grandoni, outlining the details of the evening you are planning. Though you have enough money in your budget to pay for the evening, you need his permission to hold it at the centre.

8. You are currently out on a job placement through your college program. You are an unpaid volunteer, but you are required to complete this placement successfully in order to graduate. The purpose of the placement is to supplement your classes with as broad an experience of your future job as possible. Unfortunately, your supervisor at placement, Donalda Allen, seems reluctant to give you any real responsibility, and you find yourself limited to doing menial tasks unconnected to your school training. Inventing appropriate details as necessary, write to your program chair explaining your difficulties and requesting that he or she approach Mrs. Allen to arrange for you to be given more responsibility. Submit the message to your communication instructor via e-mail.

9. Read the situation description given in Assignment #8. In response to your memo, your program chair has spoken with your placement supervisor about the nature of your placement duties. Your chair has told you that Mrs. Allen was very cooperative, and explains that you can expect to be given additional responsibilities starting this week. However, when you go to placement, Mrs. Allen is distinctly unfriendly to you and instead of giving you more relevant duties, merely assigns the usual drudgery. When you attempt to carry out the tasks, she finds fault and complains about your attitude. When you try to speak with her about what your chair told you, she loses her temper and accuses you of lying and of going behind her back to complain. You attempt to defend yourself, but the situation escalates and she "fires" you from your placement. Bearing in mind that the two are friends, that your program chair believes Mrs. Allen to be reasonable, and that you need to complete a placement to finish your program, write to your chair explaining the situation and requesting a new placement assignment. Because of the seriousness of the situation, you decide to send your message as a memo rather than an e-mail message. You will need to use tact in dealing with this situation.

10. One of your instructors has arranged for five students from your program to attend a conference in your field, where you will be taking part in a panel presentation. This is an exceptional opportunity for you to make some contacts and meet some important professionals in your area of study, since very few students have an opportunity to present papers at a conference. Unfortunately, the conference falls during exam week, and conflicts with your final examination in a course from another department. It's not your best course, and your interactions with that instructor have not been altogether pleasant. You'd rather not inconvenience this particular instructor, but at the same time you don't want to miss the chance to go to the conference. In order to arrange an alternate exam time, your college requires that you make your request in writing to the dean. Write a memo to the dean of your college, Dr. Rod Serling, with a copy to both your instructors, explaining your situation and requesting an adjustment to your examination schedule. Be sure to provide justification that will satisfy both the dean and the instructor whose exam you will be missing.

11. It's unbelievable, but your instructor, Maury Huknows, slept in and was late for the final exam in your most important program course. As a result, the start of your three-hour exam was delayed for 45 minutes, and you were unable to finish. You have approached your professor, but he seems unwilling to make any allowances for your difficulties: he insists the exam should only have taken two hours anyway, and points out that several members of the class managed to finish all the questions in the time they had. You believe you should have had the whole three hours, and you are certain you would have finished the examination if you had had the full time allotment. Write a memo to the dean of your college, carefully outlining your situation and recommending a course of action: you can request either that you be allowed to re-take your final exam in a full three-hour period, or that you be

graded for the full percentage of the exam on the questions you were able to finish in the time period. Be sure to watch your tone carefully and to justify your case in terms that will satisfy both the dean and your instructor.

12. Your supervisor, Blanche White, is retiring after 25 years with your agency. You and your co-workers have planned a retirement party to be held on a potluck basis at your home. There has been a collection for a gift, and the group has decided on a silver serving tray engraved with Blanche's name and years of service. All the arrangements for the party are complete. Write a memo to your co-workers with the details of the party, which is to be a surprise for Blanche, who believes that she has simply been invited to your home for a private dinner. Caution everyone to maintain secrecy.

13. You have recently been hired part-time at the West End Group Home. You like the work, it pays well, and it is pertinent to your studies. Your supervisor, Gail Forswynd, is pleased with your skills and training, and would be interested in hiring four more students from your program. She asks you to write a message to your peers explaining the situation and inviting them to apply. Most of the shifts required are evening and overnight shifts. Each student should submit a resume, a covering letter, and the names of three referees directly to Gail. Compose your message on e-mail and send it to your communication professor.

14. You have been working on a pilot project in your agency which involves providing a series of workshops for single mothers on basic job search and interview skills. As part of this program, you have also arranged to include a short seminar to acquaint the women with computers. Most of these undereducated and underprivileged people have never worked with computers and are nervous about encountering them in the workplace. They are anxious to have the chance to learn the basic skills they will need for their future employment, and are enthusiastic about the seminar. You are also looking forward to the seminar, which was your idea, and you have arranged to hold it at your local high school this Friday from 9 a.m. to 4:30 p.m. Unfortunately, the computer instructor has telephoned you today to reschedule, due to an equipment failure that will not be corrected until next week. You agree to the new arrangement for a week from Friday, and have been able to arrange for another seminar, entitled "Grooming for the Job Interview," in the time slot for this Friday. Write the occurrence report you forward to your supervisor, Sala Schimanski, advising her of the rescheduling. Again, put the most important message at the beginning.

15. The memos shown in Figures 3.14 and 3.15 are weak for one reason or another. Read them through critically to see what improvements you might be able to suggest. Be prepared to rewrite them more effectively if your instructor requires you to do so.

on-line exercises

1. One challenge for any writer is to attract and hold the reader's attention. In "Want Me to Listen to What You Have to Say?" Ernest Nicastro demonstrates how to turn a weak letter into a more appealing, positive document by involving the reader. You will find his advice at **salesdoctors.com/response/respon02.htm**. Nicastro comments specifically on sales letters, but his article nevertheless offers useful advice for writing any persuasive document. In this chapter, we have dealt with promotional letters: how well does Nicastro's analysis fit the requirements of an effective promotional document? What is Nicastro's main piece of advice to writers of persuasive letters? How does he apply that advice to improve the weak sample on his page? Using the same process as the one Nicastro demonstrates, analyze and rewrite one of the weak samples in this chapter.

2. Read John J. O'Callaghan's "How To Get Free Publicity Through Press Releases And Short Articles" at **salesdoctors.com/patients/1pr3.htm**. Although O'Callaghan's advice is directed toward business people, the pointers he provides for writing a press release are valuable for any service provider who wishes to promote the programs offered by his or her organization. After reading O'Callaghan's article, answer the following questions. Submit your responses to your instructor by e-mail.

   a. Why does O'Callaghan insist that you write your own releases and articles?

   b. Why does he suggest (item #9) that you use a fictitious name? Is this practice ethical?

   c. Find three pieces of advice that O'Callaghan provides that are not contained in this textbook. Does he contradict the textbook, or is his advice an expansion of principles found in the book?

   d. Which of O'Callaghan's directives seems the most striking or surprising to you? Briefly explain why.

3. Go to the Chapters Canadian online bookstore at **www.chaptersglobe.com**. Use the browser to locate the book *The 3 Rs of E-Mail: Risks, Rights, and Responsibilities*, by Diane Hartman. When and where was it published? What is its ISBN? Locate at least three other related titles, and record the name of the author, the title of the book, the place and date of publication, and the ISBN. Write your list of sources into a bibliography and e-mail the list to your instructor.

figure 3.14 Convoluted wording makes it difficult to pick out the important information from the memo. How would you improve it?

Community Distress Centre

PO Box 3550
Calgary AB T3N 5H6
1-800-568-9547

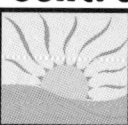

To: All Members

From: Ivana Petrovic, Social Committee Chairperson

Date: July 29, 2001

Re: Arrangements for Annual Centre Employee Picnic

This is to inform you that the arrangements for this year's annual agency picnic are final and complete at long last. After lots of hard work and planning by this committee, it was decided that it will be on Saturday, August 6.

As you know, we needed to ask for volunteers to lend us various types of equipment for playing sports and games, and we also had to arrange for barbecues to be brought to the site. Luckily we have lots of willing volunteers who can help us out with these requests and they have agreed to bring their equipment for us all to use.

If you are one of those generous people who have agreed to volunteer to us any sports or games supplies or a barbecue or any other kind of item we will be needing, those who have done so are asked by your dedicated committee to arrive one half hour early. The entertainment subcommittee and the food committee, including myself among many other dedicated individuals will be on hand by 10 am to get things rolling right along.

The picnic begins properly at 11, though you can plan to arrive with your family anytime between 10 and 11, unless you are one of our volunteers mentioned above. As has been the case with our many previous successful annual agency picnics, this one is to be held as usual at Ellsworth Conservation Park.

If you need directions how to get to the park, just contact me or anyone else on the social committee. Plan to bring everyone in your whole family for a super fun-filled day.

See you all there.

figure 3.15 What common error renders this simple message ineffective?

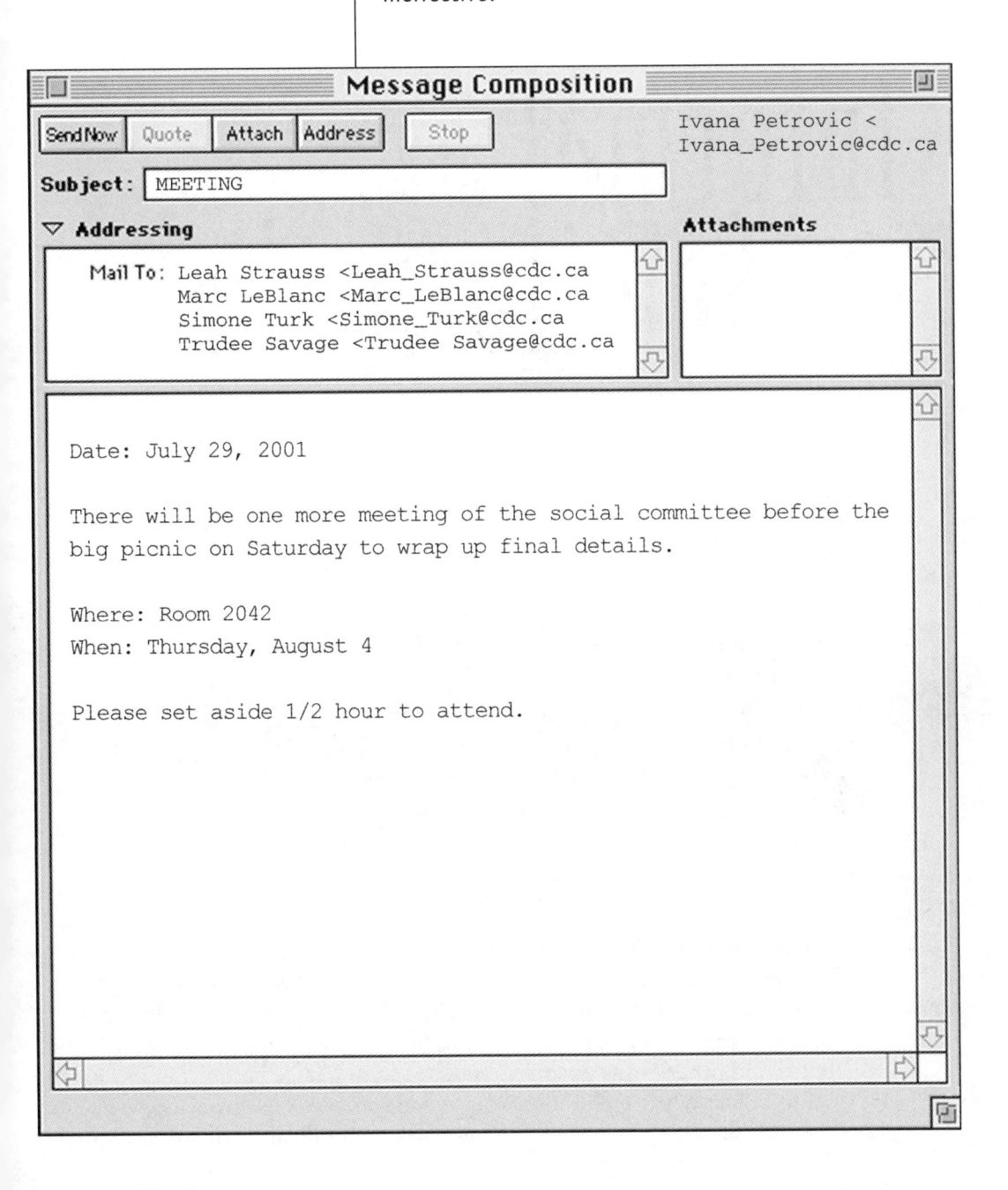

```
═══════════════════ Message Composition ═══════════════════
[SendNow] [Quote] [Attach] [Address]   [Stop]      Ivana Petrovic <
                                                   Ivana_Petrovic@cdc.ca
Subject: [MEETING                              ]
▽ Addressing                                    Attachments
    Mail To: Leah Strauss <Leah_Strauss@cdc.ca
             Marc LeBlanc <Marc_LeBlanc@cdc.ca
             Simone Turk <Simone_Turk@cdc.ca
             Trudee Savage <Trudee Savage@cdc.ca

Date: July 29, 2001

There will be one more meeting of the social committee before the
big picnic on Saturday to wrap up final details.

Where: Room 2042
When: Thursday, August 4

Please set aside 1/2 hour to attend.
```

chapter 4

Informal and Semiformal Reports

| LEARNING
| OBJECTIVES

- To learn the parts of all reports: summary, introduction, discussion, conclusion(s), recommendation(s), and appendices.
- To learn the most common report situations in human-services occupations.
- To recognize common report formats and to know how to select the format appropriate for the report you are writing.
- To know how to use the Report Writing Planner to plan your report and select appropriate information.

Of all the tasks performed by a community-service professional, writing reports on the job is one of the most important. Human-services occupations are typically notorious for the amount of paperwork they involve — regular client reports, incident reports, memos, minutes, funding proposals, entries into a daily log book, and other forms of correspondence form a large part of the routine responsibilities of these positions. Your reports provide a record of interviews and transactions with your clients, and provide continuity of information about the clients' history should personnel or circumstances change. The reports you write as a routine part of your job may also be significant if you hope to be promoted within your profession. In a large organization, your superiors may know you only through the reports you write. If you wish to advance in your chosen career, you will need to report accurately, carefully, and clearly.

Furthermore, if you are employed in a government position, whether in corrections or social work, recreation or child care, a family distress unit or a suicide prevention line, your reports will also be a matter of public record; in other words, they are legal documents. As such, they may be used as evidence in a court case or be required in an investigation, inquiry, or inquest. For all of these reasons, your reports require careful attention to detail and clarity.

Why Write Reports?

Reports are written for a variety of reasons, but their primary function is to pass on information to supervisors and co-workers. Routine incident reports provide an account of what occurred and a record of the action that was taken at the time of the incident. They also provide a means for staff to communicate with others on the next shift about incidents or situations that might require further attention.

Reports also provide a permanent record of events. In a correctional institute, a group home for teens, a child-care facility, a community distress centre, or a recreation facility for the elderly, careful records are part of the institutional history. Most of the time these function as a kind of diary of the institution, of individual clients, or of a chain of events leading to a particular action or result. Often, however, reports may constitute an important foundation for future decisions or action. Particularly in corrections and social work, and to a slightly lesser extent in other community-services occupations, reports have the status of legal documents whose purpose is to record the details of interactions with clients in accord with statutes or government policy.

Reports also constitute an important part of the total function of an institution or agency, since upper levels of the bureaucracy get a comprehensive view of things from the information supplied in the routine reports of individual caseworkers. The larger the bureaucratic structure, the more significant are reports from various sectors or individuals in the day-to-day functioning of the whole organization. As a front-line worker dealing with clients in a group home, a correctional facility, a crisis centre, a women's shelter or child-care agency, you are in a position to observe patterns of behaviour that may signal a potential problem. In some situations, your careful reporting could even save a life by alerting officials to the need for intervention. Reporting unusual behaviour, or tracking a pattern of behaviour, could help prevent violence, escape, or suicides, uncover a need for psychological or substance-abuse counselling, or reveal a situation of spousal or child abuse.

Finally, reports provide the information necessary for managers to make effective decisions by reporting actions and details as objectively as possible. A well-written report distinguishes between observed facts and inferences or opinion; analysis and judgements are clearly labelled as such. By reading such objective reports from a variety of sources in the institution over a period of time, a manager can be assured of acting in the best interests of clients and personnel.

As a human-services professional, you will be required to write numerous reports and to read the reports of others; when you are faced with piles of paperwork on the job, you will appreciate the skills of conciseness, completeness, and accuracy. Since writing reports will be such an important part of your professional life, you should cultivate these skills while you are still in training for your future career.

The Parts of a Report

Like other professional writing, in fact like all other kinds of writing, a report must have a beginning, a middle, and an end — an introduction, a discussion, and a conclusion. But along with these three basic parts, all reports (no matter how simple or complex, no matter how short or long) contain a summary, which precedes the report, and may contain an additional two parts: a recommendation or set of recommendations, and one or more appendices. The following are the six standard parts of a report, in order.

Summary

Since reports are longer than most other professional communication, and since community service professionals are very busy people who often carry heavy caseloads, the report writer includes a brief statement that gives an overview of the situation or problem dealt with, the general findings, and the specific action recommended. After reading the summary, the reader should know what to expect from the introduction, discussion, conclusion, and recommendations. The substance and the direction of your findings should be clear from the report summary. Further, the language of the summary (along with that of the introduction, conclusion[s], and recommendation[s]), should be straightforward and clear enough to be understood by the least expert of the intended readers. The length of the summary varies with the length of the report, and though there is no set length, you can think of the summary as being approximately one-tenth as long as the report itself. For example, a ten-page report may have a summary of approximately one page, while the summary of a formal report fifty pages long may be five pages. A short informal report using memo or letter format may have a summary consisting of a subject line and a brief initial paragraph.

Introduction

The introduction to a report states as clearly as possible the problem or situation being examined and any necessary background information; it may also set out the writer's approach and assumptions, and the limits of the report. In short, it prepares the reader for the discussion of the possible outcomes or solutions offered in the report.

Discussion

The main body, or discussion, of the report sets out the writer's method (including the criteria used to evaluate possible solutions) and the steps that led to the recommendations and conclusions offered in the report. It may describe possible solutions that have been rejected and show why, according to the writer's criteria, they were judged to be unacceptable. Exactly what you include in this section of the report will depend on what situation you are dealing with. However, if you have detailed technical or specialized data, you would include it in this section. In general, the discussion section of a report is aimed at the most knowledgeable of your expected readers.

The discussion is the longest and most detailed part of your report. It is made up of a number of shorter sections, each with its own heading. The word "discussion" itself rarely appears as a heading; instead, it is a broad term that is used to denote everything in the report between the introduction and the conclusion. The headings that are used in the discussion section are specific to the contents of the report. For example, a report that evaluates a government training program might use these section headings:

Program Description
Prerequisites
Advantages of the Program
Costs
Limitations of the Program
Resources

Conclusion(s)

Depending on the situation you are writing about, there may be several possible outcomes or only one. Your conclusions represent the logical results of the investigation or presentation you have dealt with in your discussion. The conclusion lays out any judgements that can be made based on the facts presented in the discussion. Your conclusion should present no surprises for your reader, who has been led by your discussion to expect what appears there.

Recommendation(s)

In the recommendation section you will provide what you consider to be, according to your evaluation criteria, appropriate action in response to the conclusions you have reached. You may have one or several recommendations to make. Recommendations normally outline the action that the reader of the report should take, and occasionally your recommendation will even list the actions you intend to perform yourself.

Appendices

An appendix is anything that is attached to a report. It is not considered a part of the report itself, but it provides additional support or explanation for points in the discussion. Any relevant supporting information that, for reasons of space or complexity, has not been dealt with in the discussion section of the report may be attached to the report as an appendix. The purpose of the appendix is to assist your reader in fully understanding your information. There may be one appendix or several appendices, and while not all reports have them, any report may do so. Formal reports are more likely than informal ones to have appendices attached.

In choosing a report format, you should be guided by the complexity of the problem or issue — that is, how much detail and/or research is required — and the intended audience or readers of the report. Most of the reports you will write on the job will be informal or semiformal.

Reports, like other effective communications, should be carefully planned. Before you begin to write, consult the Report Writing Planner (Figure 4.1) on page 75. Use it to identify the important elements of your message and the probable needs and expectations of your reader. Jot down the main information to be covered in each part of your report, keeping your reader's needs in mind as you work. Consider carefully the way in which the points in your discussion can be presented, choosing your words with care as you work. Then write your rough draft, beginning with the summary statement. The phrase "The main thing I want to tell you is that..." may help you to focus your rough work, but remember to delete it in the final version of your report.

Report Situations

In the initial chapters of this book, you learned the importance of the Six C's of effective professional writing: completeness, conciseness, clarity, coherence, correctness, and courtesy. These qualities of effective style remain as important in a report as in any other job-related correspondence. However, in work settings involving the application of government standards or regulations, routine report writing takes on an added element of legal responsibility. In such a case, the correctness and completeness of the information you provide is not only desirable, but crucial, since your report forms part of the legal record of the agency.

Reports may be written in a variety of situations and for a variety of purposes. However, the most frequent types written as a matter of daily routine can be classified into one of the following categories.

Incident/Occurrence

The incident or occurrence report is probably the single most common type of report written in the human services. An incident report records any significant

figure 4.1 Use this Report Writing Planner to identify your main message and your reader's needs and expectations.

REPORT WRITING PLANNER

Before beginning your report, answer these questions as fully as possible.

1. What is the topic of this report?

2. What is going to be done with this report? Why is it needed? Who asked for it?

3. Who are your readers? What are their interests in this subject? What background information is already known to your readers and what will you have to fill in so that your report may be understood and acted on?

4. What is your main message? What will your summary statement be?

5. Briefly outline your introduction. Remember to provide the appropriate background information.

6. Outline your discussion. Provide any relevant main points and details.

7. Outline your conclusion(s) and recommendation(s).

event that occurs during a routine working day. In a facility such as a home for the aged, a correctional institution, or a group home, incident reports cover any atypical occurrence even if it seems minor at the time it occurred; over a period of time, a series of minor incidents may point to a significant pattern of behaviour. This report is primarily an informative one that outlines details of the event as completely and fully as possible.

In Chapter 1, we discussed the elements of a complete message. You may recall the questions — when, where, what, who, why, and how — that were recommended as a guideline to ensure that you have included all the information your reader needs. Answering such questions is even more important in a routine incident report than in other situations; complete information will make future decisions and actions easier and more effective. Keeping these prompts in mind will help to ensure that nothing is left out of your report.

- *When?* Record the exact day, date, and time of the incident.
- *Where?* Describe the location in as much detail as necessary for officials to reconstruct the incident should it be necessary to do so.
- *What?* Explain exactly what occurred from the moment you became aware of the situation until its completion. What did you hear? What did you actually see? What action did you take?
- *Who?* Identify those who were directly involved in the incident and those who were present at the scene.
- *Why?* It may not be possible in every circumstance to answer this question, but if possible you should include such information in your report. If the statement of motive or cause is a result of your own inference, you should label it as such in the report.
- *How?* You may not be able to answer this question with certainty, but in some situations (for example, an escape from a correctional facility or a suicide attempt in a group home) it may be crucial information if future occurrences are to be prevented.

In addition to the standards of completeness that apply to all of your professional correspondence, the incident reports you write should adhere to a further standard of objectivity because they are part of the legal record. When reporting an accident, injury, or unusual occurrence in the workplace, you should refrain from making unwarranted inferences. The report writer should record only what happened and avoid speculation about who was at fault or what caused the mishap. A useful guideline for writing such reports is the formula "I was, I saw, I did."

"I was" records where you were and what you were doing at the time of the incident. It sets the scene for the reader, allowing a clear understanding of circumstances surrounding the occurrence.

"I saw" records exactly what you personally observed; it does not involve judgements or inferences you have made about the circumstances. For example, you may have had your back turned when you heard a loud crash. Upon turning, you discovered a broken window, and saw one of your group-home residents running from the scene. Even if it seems clear to you that he broke the window, you should realize that this is a conclusion you have drawn from the circumstances. You should not write that information in your report unless you saw the action for yourself.

"I did" tells of the actions you performed in response to the incident: did you handle the situation yourself? If so, did you need to use physical intervention? What exactly did you do? Did you call in your supervisors, medical personnel, or the police? Record every detail of your actions with respect to the incident so that others will be able to understand clearly what occurred.

An effective incident report records only information that the writer knows for certain to be accurate. Keeping to the "I was, I saw, I did" formula will assist you in maintaining objectivity in your incident reports and will ensure that your report records as fact only what you actually observed.

Accident/Injury

An accident or injury report is a special kind of incident report written when an accident or injury has occurred in the workplace. Like the incident report, it records the details of the accident, the action that followed, and the treatment that was provided. It follows the same pattern of information as that provided in the incident report: it identifies the day, date, time, and location of the accident, the series of events that took place, the observations of the report writer, and the resulting action. Because an accident or injury in the workplace is a serious occurrence, it may involve a police investigation, a workers' compensation claim, or an insurance claim or investigation. The writer of an accident or injury report must be sure to include all known details as accurately and as clearly as possible. This report, like the occurrence report, should answer all pertinent questions — when, where, what, who, why, and how — and follow the formula "I was, I saw, I did."

Misconduct/Breach of Regulation

Another specialized type of incident report is the misconduct report, which is employed primarily in correctional facilities; similarly, a breach of regulation report may be necessary in group homes or crisis centres when a client or resident has acted in a way that might endanger the safety of other residents. A misconduct report in a corrections facility might result in charges being brought against an inmate; a breach of regulations in another setting might mean the client is ejected from the program. As with other types of incident reports, these reports are legal documents which may be required in a court case or an inquiry. For these reasons, misconduct or breach of regulation reports also demand careful attention to detail and accuracy.

A misconduct report, like an incident or accident report, must provide the information necessary for readers to understand the circumstances surrounding the occurrence. It follows the same pattern of information as that provided in the previous types, with one exception: in addition to the day, date, time, and location of the event, the misconduct report identifies the specific regulation violated by the inmate, parolee, or resident. It provides not only a statement of the regulation but identifies, by number, the relevant section and subsection of the ministry regulations. Like the previous types of incident report, the misconduct report describes the details of what took place, the observations of the report writer, and the resulting action. Like them, it should answer the questions when, where, what, who, why, and how, and follow the "I was, I saw, I did" formula.

Assessment/Evaluation

An assessment or evaluation report, unlike the various types of incident report, does more than record information. In contrast to the incident report, in which the writer refrains from offering inferences or judgements, the assessment report calls upon the writer to make a judgement or offer a professional opinion of a situation, an action, or a client. Assessment reports draw upon the experience and training of the human-services professional in order to evaluate what action, treatment, or intervention are needed.

Assessment reports involving a judgement of clients or inmates are typically written upon the client's first encounter with the agency or institution, and become part of that client's file. Similar reports may be filed periodically thereafter, particularly if the social-service worker notes any significant changes in the attitude or action of the client.

Evaluation reports may also be specially commissioned as part of the investigation of a proposed course of action or an existing situation. In this case, the writer is asked to assess the likely outcome of a proposed policy change or to investigate the nature of a problem and suggest possible solutions. (A sample evaluation report, in semiformal format, is included in Figure 4.2, on page 83.) The evaluation report may be used whenever more information is needed, either on its own to evaluate an existing situation or proposed action, or as a follow-up report to evaluate the recommendations made by another report. Rather than analyzing causes and effects, it usually measures a solution or a situation against a set of criteria in order to determine the suitability or unsuitability of that solution or situation. Its conclusions are based on a careful comparison between the initial criteria (usually identified by the person who commissioned the report) and the suggested action or solution.

Unlike an incident report, which outlines the facts of the case and describes the action already taken, an assessment report calls for the writer to apply professional judgement, and usually involves recommendations for future action.

Progress

A progress report is a kind of assessment report that details the movement or development of a long-term project or program over a period of time. Progress reports are of two types. The first, the *periodic report*, is delivered at regular time intervals — every two weeks, for example, or for very long-term projects, every few months. In a college or school, students receive periodic reports of grades at the completion of each semester. An agency's annual report is another example of a periodic progress report.

The second type, the *occasional progress report*, is delivered whenever some significant stage in a project is completed, and the time interval between reports may vary. For instance, if I am overseeing the construction of a new facility, I may write reports only when significant stages are completed; since each part of the project takes a different amount of time to complete, my reports will be delivered at irregular time intervals.

Progress reports are part of the record-keeping function of an agency or organization. In the human services, a progress report is a form of assessment report on a given client's progress through treatment, rehabilitation, or other program; parole officers, social workers, rehabilitation specialists, and other human-services personnel write regular progress reports for each client assigned to them. Progress reports are used for other purposes besides tracking clients; they may also be used to assess a new program, method, or system. As well, the regular assessments you receive from your supervisor on the job are also progress reports.

Proposals

The proposal is usually initiated by the writer and is intended to persuade the reader to do what the writer thinks should be done. Although a proposal might suggest a new program or a change that the writer thinks his or her agency should adopt, the most common kind of proposal written in the human services is a funding proposal directed to external agencies or government ministries. It may request money for a new project or additional funding for a project that is already in operation.

A proposal might also be developed in response to a request for a service; for example, I might respond to the local school board's request for a training session for teachers on identifying children at risk for drug abuse or child abuse by writing a proposal to my superiors for such a session. Because a proposal is intended to solicit authorization or funding for the writer's project, it must be sufficiently detailed and convincing to gain the reader's acceptance and approval; like other reports, it must answer the significant questions of when, where, what, who, why, and how.

Investigative or Analytical Reports

The investigative report, which is usually commissioned or requested by someone other than the writer, examines and/or analyzes a particular problem or question within the agency or ministry. It is usually called for by someone higher up in the bureaucracy, and may even be the result of a government inquiry; a recent example would be the Krever Report on the tainted blood scandal in the Canadian Red Cross. An investigative report usually evaluates causes and effects, frequently offers solutions to the difficulty, and may even apportion blame. Its conclusions are based on careful research, such as results from controlled scientific experiments or data collected from testimony, interviews, surveys, or questionnaires. Such reports are generally beyond the scope of the daily routine for most human-service workers; nevertheless, their recommendations may have implications for the way your agency carries out its mandate.

Research Reports

The research report, like the investigative report, examines a particular question of importance in the field or the agency. However, the research report differs from the investigative report in that it does not seek to identify solutions to an existing problem in the organization. Instead, a research report is used to gather information helpful to the agency in developing a new procedure, policy, or organizational structure. This kind of report presents the findings from your research; it may or may not offer recommendations based on its results. As part of your college program, you may be assigned a research report of this type, in which you consult research sources in order to determine the importance of a particular issue to your field of study.

All reports require some kind of research; however, most rely on evidence drawn from the workplace itself. By contrast, a research report draws on material from outside sources — government documents, books and professional journals, articles in the popular press, Internet sources — in order to assist managers and administrative officers in making informed decisions about the future of the agency or organization.

The credibility of such a report depends to a large degree on the thoroughness and authority of your research sources. For this reason, all sources you consult, including Internet sources, should be properly documented, according to standards appropriate to your field of study. Once you have determined that the information you have collected is reliable and authoritative (an issue of particular importance in dealing with Web sites), you should be sure to record all the information your readers would require to locate the cited sources for themselves if they should need to do so.

Documentation information for print sources should include information about author, title, place of publication, publisher, and date. For Internet sources, you should identify the author, the name of the posting or Web page, and the date of the posting, along with the electronic address (URL). A style manual will provide you with clear guidelines for recording this information, along with samples of layout. Here are four examples using the documentation format of the Modern Languages Association:

Print Sources
A book:
MacLennan, Jennifer. *Effective Communication for the Helping Professions*.
   Scarborough, ON: Prentice Hall Allyn and Bacon Canada, 2000.

An article or chapter in a book:
MacLennan, Jennifer, and John Moffatt. "Language and Personal Identity." *Inside Language: A Canadian Language Reader*. Scarborough, ON: Prentice Hall Canada, 1999.

An article in a book edited by someone else:
Irwin, Lori. "The Real and the Imagined: Students as Teachers in the Rhetoric Classroom." *Public Speaking: Strategies for Success*. Canadian ed. Eds. David Zarefsky and Jennifer MacLennan. Scarborough, ON: Prentice Hall Allyn & Bacon Canada, 1997.

Online Sources
A page or entry on an Internet site:
MacLennan, Jennifer. "What Students Say About the Study of Rhetoric." 19 January 1999. Online. <http://www.engr.usask.ca/dept/techcomm/studntsay.htm>.

An e-mail message:
Moffatt, John. "Life under Deadlines." E-mail to Jennifer MacLennan. 20 January 1999.

Standardized Report Forms

Reports may be presented in any one of several styles. Although some of these are lengthy and comprehensive book-length formal documents, most of the reports written by human-services personnel are short and highly standardized, and usually are submitted on prepared forms. Standardized forms make the job of managing routine information easier for both reader and writer. Instead of having to invent a report structure for each client interview or incident that occurs, you can organize your responses using the appropriate form provided by your agency or organization.

Report forms ensure consistency in cases where large numbers of reports containing similar information must be kept by many people as a matter of routine. In some cases, the information may be entered directly into a computer file which automatically records the information in a report form. For example, if you work for an agency that helps unskilled people find work, you may have to prepare regular client status reports identifying the applicant's background, qualifications, and record of job interviews. Since you would regularly handle several applicants at once and have to keep track of all of them, and since the other placement counsellors would be doing the same, your agency would probably find it useful to prepare a standardized form for the information. Insurance claim forms, student grade reports, workers' compensation forms, intake assessment forms, registration forms, hospital charts, and even job application forms are some common examples of standardized report forms. Other types that are usually standardized in human-services occupations include occurrence or incident reports, accident or injury reports, and performance reviews.

All of these forms are designed to prompt the writer to provide the information pertinent to each type of report. Nevertheless, to ensure that your information is complete, you should keep in mind the questions outlined above — when? where? what? who? how? why? — in order that all the necessary details are included.

Nearly any kind of report that is made out on a regular basis can be organized into a standard form. Because the kind of information required is always the same, a form guarantees that each person applies the same standards and collects the same details. In this way too, much repetitious work is eliminated. Figure 4.2 shows a sample occurrence report form of the sort that might be used in a government facility; Figure 4.3 shows a performance evaluation report form.

Formal, Informal, and Semiformal Reports

Although many routine reporting tasks can be standardized on forms, not all reports are presented in this way. In some situations, you may be required to generate your own structure, as well as the information required to "flesh out" the body of the report. Reports may be presented in any one of several formats. Reports may be *informal* or *formal* in their structure, or they may strike a balance between the two as is the case in the *semiformal* report. An informal report resembles a memo or letter that has run to several pages, whereas a formal report may look more like a book manuscript or a long formal essay, complete with its own cover and table of contents. Length and layout are the most visible differences between formal and informal reports: the informal report is usually short, with an average length of three to five pages; it is also less detailed, has fewer distinct parts, and a less elaborate layout. An informal report may make use of headings to assist the reader in locating information, but because it is frequently under three pages long, such headings are not always necessary.

In writing your reports, remember that format is meant to serve function, just as it does in the standardized report forms used for repetitive tasks. Choose a format that delivers your message most effectively. Generally, the longer and more complex the report, the more formal it will be, and the more likely it will be to use headings and other organizational devices to assist the reader in understanding the material presented. You should choose a format that delivers your message most effectively. The formal report format allows clearer organization of large amounts of material, while short reports may be better presented simply. We will deal with formal reports in the next chapter.

As you may already have guessed, reports are not strictly divided into informal or formal types; occasionally you will find that you must write a report that, while important enough to warrant more formal treatment, is not really long enough to require all of the elaborate formatting of the formal report. Since the organizational structure of the formal report, with its table of contents, special

figure 4.2 A sample occurrence report form, such as might be used in the Ministry of Corrections for any province in the country. Note that the report is addressed to a specific official, and provides space for identification of the place, date, and time of the incident. Note also the space for the summary of the report contents and the space provided for the signature of the reporting officer. Each page of such a report should carry the signature of the writer.

Ministry of Corrections
OCCURRENCE REPORT

[ ] Young Offender   [ ] Inmate

To Superintendent _____

Institution _____

Date _____   Time _____

Subject/Nature of Report _____

_____

_____

_____

_____

_____

_____

_____

_____

_____

_____

_____

_____

Signature of Reporting Officer _____

CHAPTER 4 / INFORMAL AND SEMIFORMAL REPORTS

figure 4.3   A career progress report is a periodic assessment report which may be completed annually, semi-annually, biennially, or quarterly, depending on the job in question.

Career Progress Report

Evaluation for the period: _____ _____ to: _____

EMPLOYEE'S NAME: _____ Department: _____

Position Duties: _____
_____
_____
_____
_____

Additional Responsibilities Since Last Assessment: _____
_____
_____
_____
_____

Achievements: _____
_____
_____
_____
_____

EVALUATION SUMMARY	Superior	Competent	Development
Overall performance	[ ]	[ ]	[ ]
Job-related goals	[ ]	[ ]	[ ]
Development of others' goals	[ ]	[ ]	[ ]
Relationship goals	[ ]	[ ]	[ ]
Potential for advancement	[ ]	[ ]	[ ]

MERIT INCREASE RECOMMENDED   [ ] yes   [ ] no

figure 4.3 (Continued)

Narrative Statement of Assessment: _____
_____
_____
_____
_____
_____
_____
_____

Suggestions for Professional Development: _____
_____
_____
_____
_____
_____
_____

SUPERVISOR: _____ Date: _____

Signature: _____

Employee's Comments: _____
_____
_____
_____
_____

I have read this summary and enclosed comments and discussed them with my supervisor.

Employee's Signature: _____ Date: _____

headings, and fancy cover can overwhelm a short report of under ten pages, and a memo or letter format could seem an overly casual treatment of your information, you may wish to use a third style of report, called the semiformal report, which combines aspects of the informal report and the formal report styles. Rather than opening with a memo or letter-like format, as the informal report does, the semiformal report usually has the title, author's name, and date at the top of the first page; it is also more likely than the informal report to use headings to separate report sections. The semiformal report is not really a distinct type, but is a variation of the informal report. It is used in place of the memo or letter format when you wish a more formal appearance for your short reports. In this book we will use the term "informal" to refer to letter or memo reports, and the word "semiformal" for short reports that use a more formal style on their first page and that incorporate some other formal features in a report of under ten pages.

Although your employer may sometimes require a specific format for reports, often you will have to select your own format. How do you know whether to choose a formal, an informal, or a semiformal format for your report? Asking yourself the following three questions may help you to decide which is best.

1. *What is your purpose?* If you are addressing a relatively minor issue, your report will most likely be informal; if the situation is important, your report will be semiformal or even formal.
2. *Who is your audience?* The more distinguished or the wider your audience, the more formal your presentation should be. A brief document to your immediate supervisor that no one else is likely to read will probably be informal; a detailed proposal being sent to the agency director and advisory board, or outside the agency, is likely to be formal.
3. *How detailed is your analysis?* The more complex the problem or issue and the more detailed and thorough your presentation, the more carefully you will have to organize your information, and the more you will require the titles, headings, table of contents, and support materials of the formal report.

In choosing a report format, you should be guided by the complexity of the problem or issue — that is, how much detail or research is required — and the intended audience or readers of the report. Most of the reports you write on the job will be informal or semiformal.

Informal Reports

If you need to write a brief report about something for which there is no standardized form, you may choose to present your information in an informal report. Compared to the formal report, it has a more casual format. For instance, it does not have a title page and table of contents. It may be written without enumerated sections, references, or appendices, although any of these could be included if they were needed. Unless your employer provides a standardized form, the informal report format is commonly used for regular progress reports, incidence reports, evaluative reports, and proposals. If you have been commissioned by your boss to write a short report for his or her eyes alone, chances are you will be writing an informal report.

Informal reports are typed on one side of the page only, observing standard margins: 1" at top, right, and bottom, and 1½" at left. The informal report begins as a memo or a letter. The standard format of the memo (*To, From, Date, Subject*) or letter (return address or letterhead, date, and inside address) identifies the primary reader, the writer, and date. The subject or "re" line states the primary recommendation the report makes. If the report is longer than one page, subsequent pages are typed on plain paper. Remember that informal reports, like all other types, may be double or single spaced, according to the practices of your employer.

An informal report, depending on how long it is, may contain section headings. If so, skip two lines and begin each new section immediately following the previous one, on the same page. Compare the following list of report parts with the sample informal report that follows.

Contents of the Informal Report

Memo or letter opening
Statement of recommendation(s) contained in subject or "re" line
Brief summary statement
Introduction
Discussion: Background to issue or situation
              Outline of important facts and details
              Possible outcomes, results, or solutions
Conclusion
Recommendation(s)
Appendices (optional): Charts
                         Supporting data
                         Diagrams

Sample Informal Report

The Situation:

Ky Ngo works for the Ministry of Community Services in your province. Each year, the deputy minister, Daena Tobias, invites the employees in her sector (about 100 people) to an elaborate evening dinner meeting. The gathering usually features an informal meeting followed by dinner and an after-dinner presentation featuring an interesting and well-known speaker. This year, Ky Ngo was responsible for selecting and hiring this speaker. He has been able to hire Dr. Dan Ryan, a renowned stress expert from Vancouver and the author of *Sharing the Load: Strategies for Stress Management*, to speak on methods of dealing with stress in the workplace.

From previewing his presentation, Ngo knows Ryan to be a dynamic speaker, and everyone in the division is looking forward to hearing his presentation. Ngo made the arrangements two months ago; the dinner is one week from Friday. Late Thursday evening, just before leaving the office, Ngo receives a long-distance telephone call from Dr. Ryan's agent in Vancouver. Unfortunately, Dr. Ryan has come down with a severe case of strep throat, complicated by laryngitis. He is unable to utter a sound, and his doctor has advised him to cancel all of his speaking engagements for at least a week. He will thus be unable to appear at the ministry dinner.

Despite the lateness of the hour, Ngo immediately contacts an acquaintance who is a member of the local library board, which maintains a "Speaker's Bureau" listing of local experts who will speak to community groups for a nominal fee. Ngo's friend, Gabriella Mezei, is sure that another competent speaker can be found to replace Dr. Ryan. She recommends Dennis Johnson, who has successfully led seminars for the library board on effective morale-building. Gabriella agrees to contact Johnson on Ngo's behalf; she is sure he will accept the engagement, and she promises to contact Ngo the next morning with Johnson's answer. Before finalizing the arrangements, Ngo decides to attend a talk being given by Mr. Johnson the following evening.

In planning his report to Daena Tobias, Ky Ngo considers the details of the situation; to offset Tobias' disappointment at being unable to secure Dr. Ryan's services, he offers a comparison of costs for the two speakers. Figure 4.4 shows the report Ky Ngo writes to the deputy minister, Daena Tobias, alerting her to the situation and advising her of the impending arrangements with Mr. Johnson. The appendix detailing comparative costs is attached.

Semiformal Reports

Regular progress reports, incidence reports, evaluation reports, and proposals may also be presented as semiformal reports. The primary difference between the informal report and the semiformal report is the more formal appearance of its first page: instead of using memo or letter format, the semiformal report displays the company name, report title, author's name, and date at the top of the first page, as shown in the sample semiformal report below. It too is typed on one side of the page only, observing the same standard margins as the informal report, and may be double or single spaced, depending on the preference of your employer.

The semiformal report format is used whenever your reports require a more formal appearance than a memo or letter allows. It is also generally a bit longer than the informal report, running usually between five and ten pages, though it can be used for reports up to twenty pages long. Its contents are usually divided into short sections headed with appropriate titles.

Unlike the informal report, where the summary of recommendations is presented in a "re" or subject line followed by a brief summary statement at the beginning, the semiformal report has a title rather than a subject line and presents its summary in a short paragraph at the beginning of the report.

Because the semiformal report is a variation of the informal report, the distinctions between them are not entirely clear-cut; in some cases, the same material can be presented in either format, depending on the circumstances. For a very short report, your choice of format will be influenced primarily by your purpose and

figure 4.4 Ky Ngo chooses to present his report in an informal memo format rather than semiformal format. Why does he choose not to use the department's occurrence report form?

MINISTRY OF COMMUNITY SERVICES
Interdepartmental Communication

TO: Daena Tobias, Deputy Minister

FROM: Ky Ngo

DATE: January 12, 2001

RE: Replacement Speaker for Ministry Dinner

At 5 p.m. yesterday, I received notice that Dr. Dan Ryan has been forced to cancel his speaking engagements for the next two weeks, due to a severe bout of laryngitis. Unfortunately, this means that he will be unable to address next week's annual dinner, as we had scheduled.

Upon learning yesterday of Dr. Ryan's cancellation, I made tentative arrangements for a substitute speaker, Dennis Johnson, whose specialty is morale-building. I have been assured by the chair of the Library Speaker's Bureau that he is a fine motivational speaker who will provide us with as stirring a talk as Dr. Ryan's. Before finalizing the arrangements with Mr. Johnson, I will be previewing his presentation at a Library Board meeting this evening. If he proves to be an acceptable alternative to Dr. Ryan, I will finalize the engagement details following the meeting tonight.

I realize that everyone was counting on the opportunity to hear Dr. Ryan's presentation, but in light of the circumstances we are fortunate to find a suitable substitute on such short notice. In addition, we will realize a substantial cost saving for transportation and accommodation, since Mr. Johnson is a local resident. I have attached a cost comparison for your information.

I trust that these arrangements will be satisfactory.

Ky Ngo

.../2

figure 4.4 (Continued) Details such as these, which provide additional information not directly necessary to the body of the report, may be included as attachments or appendices.

2

TOTAL COST OF PRESENTATIONS:

Dr. Ryan: *Mr. Johnson:*

Speaker's fee	$1,000.00	Speaker's fee	$600.00
Return airfare	799.00	Mileage	30.00
Hotel accommodation	210.00		
(2 nights)			
Meals & expenses	200.00		

| TOTALS | $2,209.00 | | $630.00 |

your audience's needs. The more important these are, the more likely you will choose a semiformal style over the informal one. If the report is over ten pages long but the issue presented is fairly straightforward and direct, the semiformal format is more appropriate. If your report is likely to be more than ten pages and is divided into many complex sections, you should consider using a formal format.

Contents of the Semiformal Report

Report title, author's name and title, and date at top of page one
Summary
Introduction
Discussion: Background to issue or situation
            Outline of important facts and details
            Possible outcomes, results, or solutions
Conclusion
Recommendation(s)
References/Bibliography (optional)
Appendices (optional): Charts
                        Supporting data
                        Diagrams

Sample Semiformal Report

The Situation:

Sigurd Orsten works for the Ministry of Community Services. Recently, her division received a position paper outlining a plan to institute mandatory drug testing in all divisions of the public service in your province. The deputy minister, Daena Tobias, has asked several members of the Ministry of Community Services to evaluate and respond to the position paper. Figure 4.5 shows the report submitted by Sigurd in response to the government's position paper.

points to remember

No matter what kind of report you are writing, you must prepare thoroughly and organize carefully.

1. Identify your main message ("the main thing I want to tell you is that...").

2. Identify your purpose (in general, to inform or to persuade).

3. Identify your reader by needs, expectations, knowledge, or goals.

4. Develop your points fully.

5. Observe the Six C's.

6. Answer the questions *when? where? what? who? why?* and *how?* in each report.

figure 4.5 A semiformal report offers a more formal appearance than that of the informal memo report, and is therefore more suitable for complex analyses or issues. An evaluative report often includes recommendations such as those shown in the sample.

MINISTRY OF COMMUNITY SERVICES
Interdepartmental Communication

Drug Testing in the Public Service:
A Solution, or a Bigger Problem?

Sigurd Orsten
Administrative Assistant

SUMMARY
Drug testing as a means of maintaining effective job performance is a thorny issue at best, and to create an equitable and effective policy, a number of difficulties must be addressed. This report outlines the potential problems with widespread drug testing in the public service, and recommends a rigorous selection process and a meaningful performance-appraisal system, with voluntary treatment in place of widespread testing.

INTRODUCTION
The implementation of widespread drug testing is one response to the perceived problem of drug abuse in the workplace. Presumably its goal is to weed out those whose performance is impaired by drug use, but such policies give rise to questions of ethical and practical consideration. Is such testing necessary? Does it work? Who would be tested? What would be done with positive results? This report looks at some of the most obvious problems and difficulties associated with the issue of drug testing in the public service.

THE PROBLEM OF DRUG USE
Although most people are familiar with stories about widespread drug abuse, no solid body of evidence exists to indicate that drug abuse presents a problem for the public service. The Ministry of Community Services must be careful not to act rashly to institute such a policy until the extent of the problem is known. Second, the basis of the government's concern in the drug testing issue must primarily be efficient on-the-job performance. The question of the morality of drug use, whatever an individual's personal convictions, cannot form the basis

. . ./continued

figure 4.5 (Continued)

2

for such a government policy, any more than the government can dictate what, if any, church an employee attends.

Third, will testing identify substance abuse *on the job*, or will it be used to detect drug use after hours? Will it distinguish use from abuse? Will it identify illicit drugs alone, or abuse of legal substances as well?

WHOM TO TEST

Any policy must address whether drug testing will be administered across the public service, from management to clerical staff; or selectively, on a random basis; as part of performance appraisal or for screening, or both. Will employees whose performance has been consistently satisfactory be expected to submit to drug testing? Or will it be administered strictly to new employees or applicants? Will the test be administered only where there is probable cause indicated by poor performance or unusual behaviour? Will other possible sources of trouble be ruled out first? No system would be considered totally equitable, and broad application of testing, with its accompanying implication of distrust, would certainly affect employee morale.

THE NATURE OF THE TESTS

The invasive nature of the test itself is bound to create resentment. Currently drug testing is performed by urinalysis, and to avoid any possibility of cheating, the procedure would have to involve surveillance during urination. Most Canadians would balk at such a measure, but if surveillance were not a factor, the test could be rendered invalid due to cheating by any individuals who feared the test result. Under such circumstances, the testing would certainly be considered an invasion of privacy, presenting both legal and political problems.

As well, there may be some question as to the reliability of current tests due to careless or inconsistent handling of samples. Without a high degree of reliability, testing could not be used as a widespread measure.

OTHER IMPLICATIONS

The Union of Public Service Employees is unlikely to accept testing as a part of a contractual agreement. As well, we must consider whether drug testing would be in violation of the constitution. Is it, strictly speaking, lawful?

Of course, there is still the question of the huge cost of such a measure, and the morale problems created by the "Big Brother" image of management who must police staff, even those who have proven themselves over years of service.

. . . /continued

figure 4.5 (Continued)

3

Finally, what steps will be taken for those who test positive? Would permanent employees be fired automatically, or would they be expected to find treatment for themselves? Would a time limit for "drying out" be set, with re-testing to follow? Would such a person be sent to a mandatory rehabilitation program? If so, who would run such a program? Would forcing people into rehabilitation really be effective?

CONCLUSION

The Ministry of Community Services, like all government ministries, must use caution in instituting any drug-testing policy. Financial and other costs of a blanket policy are staggering, and at present there is insufficient evidence that such a policy is warranted or effective. Other methods, such as a meaningful performance appraisal system, which could address performance difficulties, might be as effective in detecting drug problems as a widespread drug-testing program, would certainly be more conducive to good staff-management relations, and in the long run would produce more effective working relationships. As well, an efficient screening process would help to select stable and reliable employees at the outset. The Ministry should avoid the "Big Brother" image associated with widespread drug testing. Any such system, if implemented, would have to be studied carefully and tailored to fit the specific needs of the Ministry of Community Services.

RECOMMENDATIONS

Until more evidence of the need for a drug testing program is available, I recommend that the Ministry of Community Services

1. Develop comprehensive appraisal and screening procedures, maintaining a positive interaction between staff and management.
2. Conduct further study to determine the extent of any drug-related problems, and the need for interventionist drug-testing procedures.
3. If poor performance due to drug abuse is found to be a significant problem, institute a voluntary treatment program for employees who need support.

7. Follow the "I was, I saw, I did" formula for writing incident, accident, or misconduct reports.

8. Wherever appropriate, use the standardized forms supplied by your employer or instructor.

9. In choosing a report format, you should be guided by the complexity of the problem or issue — that is, how much detail or research is required — and the intended audience or readers of the report. Most of the reports you will write will be informal or semiformal.

sharpening your skills

The following report situations vary in complexity and requirements. Choose *one* of them and write the necessary report. Whatever report you are writing, be sure to observe all of the rules we have discussed and add any specifications you need to make the report convincing. Before beginning to write, you may wish to use the Report Writing Planner (Figure 4.1) to outline your two principal elements: reader and main message.

1. You are in charge of a placement student at your agency, and are required to provide feedback to the college regarding the student's performance. Your brief report should comment on the following:
   a. the student's duties and responsibilities;
   b. the number and titles or responsibilities of the staff;
   c. the student's expertise and command of community service principles;
   d. the student's general attitude and behaviour;
   e. any special strengths the student has demonstrated;
   f. any areas of the student's performance that need improvement;
   g. your overall evaluation of the student's competence.

   You may use as a model someone at your own placement (do not use the person's real name), or you may model your evaluation on yourself. You should provide concrete and specific details and examples, recommending at least one area for improvement.

2. You have been sent by your program chair to investigate a placement opportunity at an organization in your area. You may use your own placement agency or any other organization with which you are familiar as a model. Write an evaluation of the facility, including a discussion of
   a. the agency's basic services and facilities;
   b. the effectiveness and expertise of the staff;

    c. the general atmosphere of the place, or the reception that clients receive;
    d. any outstanding strengths you have noted;
    e. areas that could use improvement;
    f. your overall assessment of the agency as a placement opportunity for students in your program.

3. You are on placement at the West Side Recreation Centre. This afternoon at about 3:00, while you were supervising some children in the gym area, one of the children, ten-year-old Ian Scrundlchaver, tripped while running across the deck of the pool and fell, knocking loose one of his teeth. Running is not permitted in the pool area, and it is your responsibility to supervise, but your attention was diverted because you were assisting another child, eight-year-old Andrea Hansen, with her flotation device. According to the nurse on duty, Martha Black, to whom you immediately took Ian, the tooth is still rooted (though loosened) and should not fall out. Ian was crying but is otherwise unhurt. You are required to make a report of any accidents or injuries in case of possible legal complications. Write the occurrence report you will file with your supervisor, Burton Urquhart, noting as many of the details of the incident as possible.

4. As a human-services professional, you will be required to write numerous reports on both short- and long-term projects. Some of these will take the form of periodic or occasional progress reports, including reports on your own performance in the job. In most instances, you will have to evaluate your achievements and your failures along the way, indicating how you plan to overcome any obstacles you have met with. This semester, you are enrolled in a professional writing course, and it is now mid-term. Your task for this assignment is to prepare and submit a short (informal) report to your instructor outlining and evaluating your own progress in the course. The report will include such topics as your initial objectives or expectations, your achievements thus far, any failings or obstacles you have encountered and what you have done (or plan to do) to overcome them, the work that has yet to be done, and your expected grade or performance. You will want to supplement your report with evidence such as mid-term or assignment grades, course projects, and topics covered. Keep in mind that you are not evaluating the course *per se*, but your own commitment to and progress in the course. Essentially what you are preparing is a self-evaluation report such as you might occasionally be expected to prepare for annual performance reviews on the job.

    Although the assignment is intended to focus on your professional writing course, you may wish to use another of your courses instead. If you want to do this, get the approval of your instructor.

5. As an officer in a correctional facility, you are on morning shift from 0700 to 1500 hours, assigned to Unit #2. You are in charge of 15 inmates, as-

sisted by C.O.2 Shane Nishi. Shift change-over was completed at 0705 hours, when you walked down the range and told all inmates to get up and clean their cells. At approximately 0715 hours you walk the range again, and you note that inmate Doug Rombough, #28814 in cell #5, is still in bed. You stop outside the cell and call to Rombough, but he does not respond. Rombough has two notations recorded about similar morning behaviour, so you are not unduly alarmed. You enter the cell to rouse Rombough. He is lying on his back in his cot. You call the inmate's name a second time, but he still does not respond. You shake him but he remains unresponsive. You lean over to check and discover that the inmate is not breathing. You note a scent of vomit. You clear the airways and apply rescue breathing. After several seconds, you are able to restore breathing, but it is very shallow; a check of the inmate's pulse shows that it is very weak. You place Rombough in the recovery position, and you call to C.O.2 Nishi, who has accompanied you on the range but not into the cell, to return to the staff station and summon medical aid. You stay with Rombough. As you await medical aid, you conduct a routine search of the inmate's cell; you find an empty container that smells of alcohol. You know that some inmates have been concocting a potent moonshine from kitchen scraps. You confiscate the bottle. Rombough is taken to the medical unit at 0715 hours by C.O.2 Jim Britten and C.O.2 Jacques Angleterre, where he is examined by Dr. D. Seierstad, M.D. Write an accident/injury report detailing the events of the morning.

6. On January 4, 2001, you are on morning shift from 0700 to 1300 hours at the Hillside Detention Centre, assigned to Unit 2. Although you have never had any difficulty, you are aware of some ongoing trouble with inmate Thomas Cook, #28814. On several occasions he has been reluctant to rise in the mornings and has twice had misconducts for his refusal to get up. His attitude is often abusive when he is given the order to rise. Today, however, he is up and ready promptly with his bunk and cell in order. He even greets you as you walk down the range. This cooperative behaviour is unusual for Cook, but he seems to be genuinely trying to revamp his behaviour. You think this positive change should be noted. Write the necessary incident report.

7. You are alone on night shift (11 p.m.–6 a.m.) at the Downtown Group Home, which houses six teenaged residents. At 11:15, you conduct a routine bed check, your first of the night. When you look in on 15-year-old Randy Szigli, you notice that the window of his room is wide open. The outside temperature is -2° C, and the room is very cold. You enter the room and close the window. Turning from that task, you notice that the shape under the covers seems too small to be Szigli. A closer look reveals that the bed is in fact empty; pillows and clothing have been stuffed under the blankets to resemble a sleeping body. Szigli is not in the room.

You check the rooms of the remaining residents; all are asleep. A check of the rest of the house reveals that Szigli is not in the building. You immediately notify your supervisor, Rebecca Silverheels, and Constable Berny Zukewsky of the local police. On the advice of Ms. Silverheels, you awaken the resident with whom Szigli spends most of his time, 14-year-old Armando Giron, to ask him about the missing boy. Giron claims to know nothing about the other boy's whereabouts, so you send him back to his room without awakening any of the other residents.

At approximately 3:50 am, Constable Zukewsky returns Szigli to your care. The teen is sullen and quite clearly exhausted, so you send him to bed without interrogating him. Write the report that you leave for your supervisor in the morning.

online exercises

1. If you are preparing a research report, you may wish to begin with the "Searching the World Wide Web" page at Purdue University's On-Line Writing Lab, **owl.english.purdue.edu/files/128.html**. Choose a topic relevant to your studies, and try searching it using two or three different search engines. Compare the results of your search; what differences did you find in the kinds of sources that each engine produced? Did one seem to be better for your purposes than the others? Prepare a short informal report of your findings to turn in to your instructor. If your instructor directs you to do so, discuss your findings with the class.

2. Travel to the Web site for the Media Foundation, publishers of *Adbusters* magazine, **www.adbusters.org/information/foundation.html**. Search the site to find out as much as you can about the mandate and purpose of the foundation, including ways in which an interested person might participate in the Media Foundation's campaign of resistance to the commercialization of culture. Present your findings to your instructor in an informal report. Your instructor may also direct you to present your findings in an oral briefing.

chapter 5

Formal Reports and Proposals

LEARNING OBJECTIVES

- To learn the basic format of a formal report and how to select the appropriate format.
- To understand the purpose and focus of a formal proposal.

A formal report may be used for any number of purposes. Annual reports, research reports, some progress reports, evaluation reports, proposals, and feasibility studies are some types. Generally the formal report is more complex and detailed than the informal or semiformal report. It tackles more difficult problems, analyzes them in greater depth, and presents thorough evidence to support its recommendations. It is usually much longer than either of the other report forms, being anywhere from ten to several hundred pages. You should use a formal report format if your subject matter is of great significance to your organization, if your readership is likely to be large or important, or if your findings are extensive. Usually a project resulting in a formal report will involve several or all of the above considerations. For example, a lengthy report from your department to the director that makes important recommendations for major department changes will most likely be formal.

The Parts of a Formal Report

A formal report, especially if it is to be sent outside the organization, is meant to maintain the institution or agency's professional image. As such, it must be attractive and polished. It should be error-free and written on one side of the page only, with standard margins of 1" at top, right, and bottom of the page and 1^1/$_2$" at the left side. It may be single or double spaced, according to your agency's practice. Its pages are numbered, usually in the upper right corner. It normally has a formal cover that bears the agency name, report title, author's name, and date and it is usually bound. The parts of a formal report are as follows.

Cover

A cover usually encloses a formal report. It can either be purchased plain or specially designed. If you are buying a cover, avoid those with gaudy pictures or designs. A plain-coloured, good-quality cover is preferable. The cover, like the work inside, should make as professional an impression as possible, and one in grey, black, or white makes a more dignified impression than a wildly coloured one. Avoid cheap, poor-quality report covers. Spending a little more for a good cover will make a better overall impression. If your cover is a specially designed one on which the title of your report appears, choose the title carefully to reflect the content: informative, but not too long or too brief. A subtitle may help to clarify the material presented within the report.

Letter of Transfer or Transmittal

A letter of transfer or transmittal should be attached to the outside of the report cover or bound inside the cover just ahead of the title page. The choice is a matter of preference, and in writing your report you should follow the practice of your organization. The letter is a formal one from the writer (you) to the person or persons to whom the report is addressed. It should briefly outline the reason for the report and point out some of its important findings or features. Like all professional letters, it is single spaced. If your report is to stay inside your organization, you may wish to use a memo form in place of this letter; if it goes to readers outside the institution, write a formal letter on the letterhead of your organization or agency.

Title Page

The title page, containing the name of the organization or institution, the title and subtitle of the report, the name(s) and title(s) of person(s) who commissioned the report, the name(s) of author(s) and their title(s), and the date, comes next. If you are provided with a title page format by your employer, use that; otherwise use the format of the sample title page shown in this chapter. The formal report should contain a title page whether or not the title appears on the cover. Do not number your title page.

Summary of Recommendations

The summary of recommendations usually precedes the table of contents; it is a brief overview of all of the important parts of the report and should include condensed versions of the introduction, discussion, conclusion, and recommendation(s). After reading your summary, even your least knowledgeable reader should have an idea of your findings and your approach. This section is numbered with lower case Roman numerals, in the bottom centre of the page.

Table of Contents

The table of contents, a detailed listing of the sections of the report (which may or may not be numbered) and the pages on which these are to be found, comes next. Like the summary, this page is not considered part of the actual body of the report, and so is not numbered as part of the text. Numbering of the pages of the report usually begins at the introduction.

Introduction

The introduction begins the report proper, and is numbered as page one, usually in the upper right corner of the page. It not only introduces the subject matter of the report, but it prepares the reader for the report's particular focus and its findings. It also outlines any necessary background information, states the problem or issue, describes the situation, and sets out any limitations that might have been imposed on the investigation or analysis, as well as giving specifics about the direction that the analysis has taken.

Discussion

The discussion, or main body, of the report follows. It sets out the writer's method (including the criteria used to evaluate possible results, solutions, or outcomes) and presents a detailed analysis of the problem, issue, or situation that led to the conclusions and recommendations offered in the report. It should outline the important facts of the situation, including relevant history, details, and examples. As well, it should itemize any possible outcomes or courses of action, indicating the one that has been recommended and detailing the reasons for rejecting the others. The discussion of the formal report, like that of the informal report, is broken into subsections, each with a specific heading reflecting its contents. The contents of these subsections deal with facts specific to the focus of the report. Exactly what topics you include in your discussion will depend on the situation you are dealing with, but detailed technical or specialized data, aimed at the most knowledgeable of your expected readers, should be placed here. All pertinent facts, arranged in a logical order, are presented. Remember that, as in the informal report, the word "discussion" denotes everything in the report between the introduction and the conclusion, but is rarely used as a heading in the report itself.

Conclusion

The conclusion outlines any inferences that can logically be drawn from the material presented in the report; it shows the outcome of the analysis. It briefly summarizes the findings of the report and should be a natural result or extension of the point of view presented in the discussion. It should not contain any unexpected revelations or outcomes, but should satisfy the expectations created by the rest of the report.

Recommendation(s)

The recommendation (or recommendations) spells out the action that the report writer expects will be taken on the conclusions presented. If a conclusion says "this is what I think about this situation," the recommendation says "here's what we should do about it." The recommendation may include several steps that the reader is expected to follow; if so, these should be listed and numbered individually so that they are easy to identify and follow.

Bibliography

The bibliography (a listing of works cited or references) may also be included since many formal reports involve some sort of research. This list provides the reader with the information needed either to do further reading on the subject of the report or to check the accuracy of the writer's interpretations. (Sample bibliographic entries can be found on pages 80–81 in the previous chapter.)

Appendices

Appendices are often necessary in a formal report, since the information presented in such a document is sometimes quite complex. As in the informal report, these attachments may include any supporting data that are either too cumbersome or too complicated to be included in the body of the report. Some examples might include charts, supporting data, or diagrams.

The parts of the formal report are usually arranged in the order listed, and each of the parts (introduction, subsections of the discussion, conclusion, and recommendations) normally begins with its own title on a new page, almost like a chapter of a book. Starting at the introduction, the pages of the report are numbered; depending on your agency's policy, page numbers may appear in the upper right corner, or centred either at top or bottom of each page.

Remember that part of the effectiveness of a formal report, as of any professional communication, depends on its visual appeal, so it is important that your report looks professional. Although informal reports may sometimes be handwritten, a formal report must always be typed. Follow an accepted format carefully and take great care that no spelling, grammatical, or typing errors mar the quality of your report. Do not make corrections to a formal report in ink or pencil; instead, reprint the page. Always make corrections using the same font as you used for the rest of the report.

Formal reports also make use of frequent paragraphing and employ headings and subheadings to assist the reader in following the reasoning of the writer. But it isn't simply a neat and professional format that gives a formal report its visual appeal: most formal reports also use visual aids to present their messages clearly.

Using Visuals in a Formal Report

A well-written formal report should contain straightforward, readily understandable explanations. Sometimes visual aids can make your explanations even clearer. Such visual aids include photographs, line drawings, diagrams, graphs, and charts. Depending on their size and immediate relevance to the text (the written material), they may be placed either within the body of the report or in an appendix at the end. If they are necessary to the reader's immediate understanding and if they are small and simple enough, visual aids should be positioned close to the appropriate paragraph in the report, preferably on the same page. It is best to number them sequentially (Figure 1, Figure 2, and so on) and to identify them by a title and a brief caption. The report text should refer to the visual aid by figure number or title when discussing the material shown in the visual. If the visual is very complex or if it is not necessary to the reader's immediate grasp of the situation, it could be placed in an appendix. If it is very complex but necessary to the reader's understanding, the complex version could be placed in the appendix and a simplified version placed in the body of the report. Below is a brief description of when and how to use each of these visuals.

Photographs

Whenever you must describe a site, a scene, or a product to give the reader a clear idea of what the item looks like, there is nothing like a good photograph. A photograph may be colour or black and white, as long as it is clear and of good quality, with no fuzziness or unnecessary clutter in its composition.

Professional typesetting and colour separations for high-quality printing are expensive and unlikely to be an option except for items as important as the annual report of a government ministry, which is often as much a promotional document as it is a report. For small reports or for a small number of reports, you will most likely be using in-house laser printing and photocopying. You have several options, even under such circumstances. Larger agencies may be equipped with up-to-date equipment for such tasks: high-quality colour photocopiers, scanners, digital cameras, and colour laser printers can make it easy and relatively inexpensive to include photographs in your day-to-day reports, provided the results are clear enough to display the information you require. A smaller human-services agency may not own such equipment, but it is available at most copy shops. Depending on your needs and available equipment, you may find it best to have multiple prints of the actual photograph made and paste them into position in each copy of the finished report. You will have to decide for yourself how many reports you are prepared to assemble by hand like this. An advantage of this hand-assembly is that it may allow you to use colour photographs of high quality in a report that is otherwise simply photocopied. Ordinary black and white photocopying will not produce sufficiently clear prints even of black and white photos.

Line drawings

When the information a reader needs from the visual is likely to be unclear in a photograph, a simple line drawing may be a useful substitute. A line drawing may be used, for example, to show the design of a logo or the design and layout for a brochure you are about to produce. You may have seen such drawings used in advertising circulars to illustrate products when photographic illustration would be too expensive. You need not be a professional artist to do a simple line drawing, but your work must be neat and easy to read. It should be drawn with black ink and clearly labelled, and should be as uncluttered as possible. Below is a line drawings of one step in a simple design task. Figure 5.1 shows the illustration without shading; Figure 5.2 shows the same illustration using shading techniques that will reproduce clearly.

Diagrams

Diagrams are useful if your report explains how something works or is assembled. Diagrams may break down a process into steps or may show the parts or proper use of a piece of equipment. A diagram may even show the floor plan of the agency's proposed new office space. Diagrams, like line drawings, should be clearly drawn in plain black ink or produced by computer. As is the case with line drawings, diagrams are meant to assist you in communicating your message clearly. They should therefore be as simple and clear as possible. You may, if you have access to a colour photocopier or printer, use colour in your diagrams. If your report is to be reproduced in black and white, you should substitute shading for the colour in your original, taking care to ensure that any labels are still clearly legible. Figure 5.3 shows the main floor plan of the West Side Group Home.

Graphs

Graphs are used to show the relationship between variables and to display successive change or growth over time. This growth is shown by a line that slopes either upward (for an increase) or downward (for a decrease) inside the graph. The change is measured using a scale that is marked out along the vertical axis (at the left) and along the horizontal axis (at the bottom) of the graph. The

figure 5.1 A line drawing is useful for illustration when a photograph is unavailable or insufficiently clear.

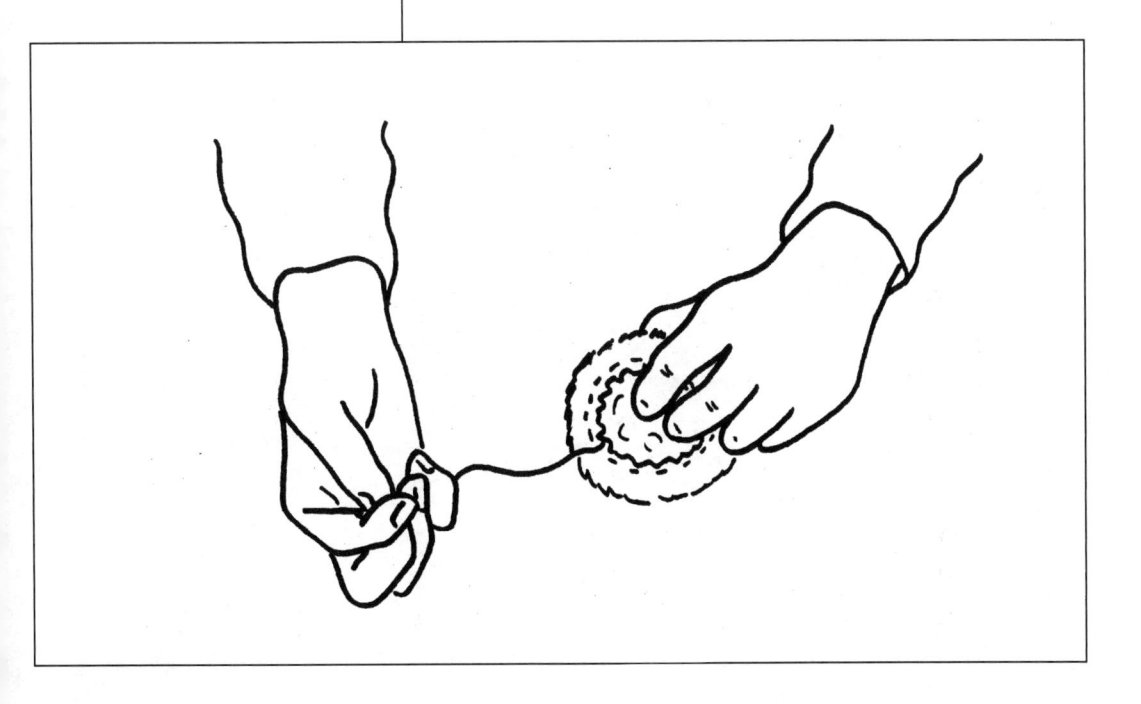

figure 5.2 A line drawing using shading. Notice how shading adds depth to the illustration.

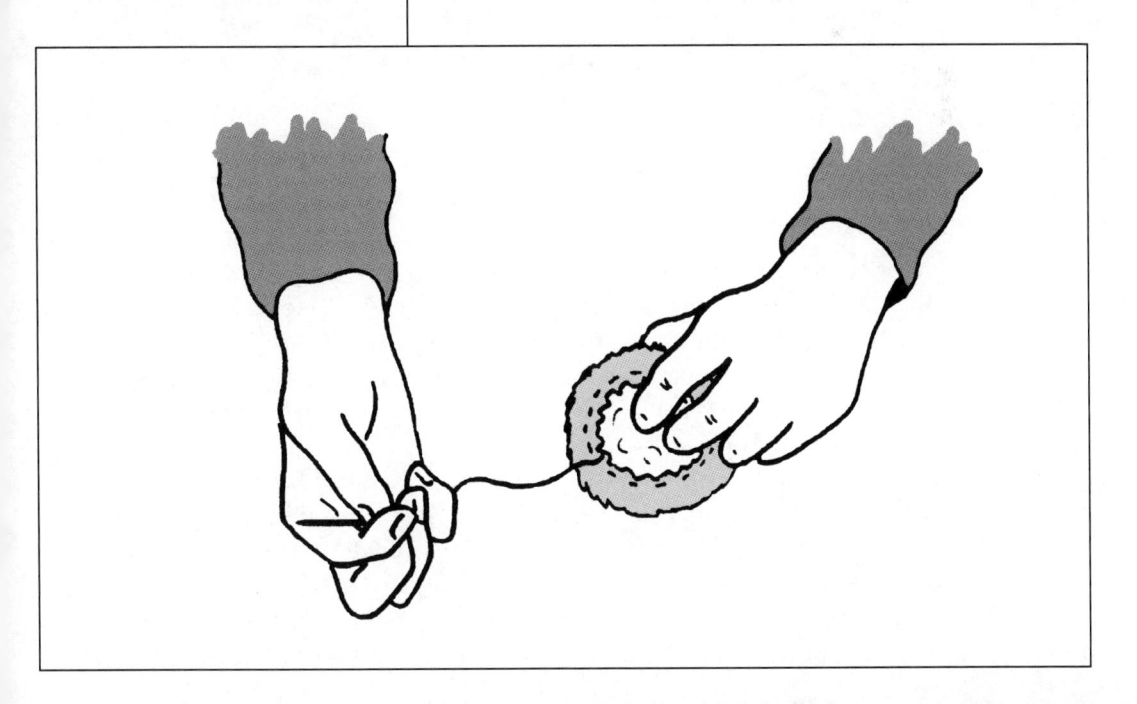

figure 5.3 A diagram such as this floor plan assists your reader in accurately visualizing your meaning and may help prevent misunderstandings.

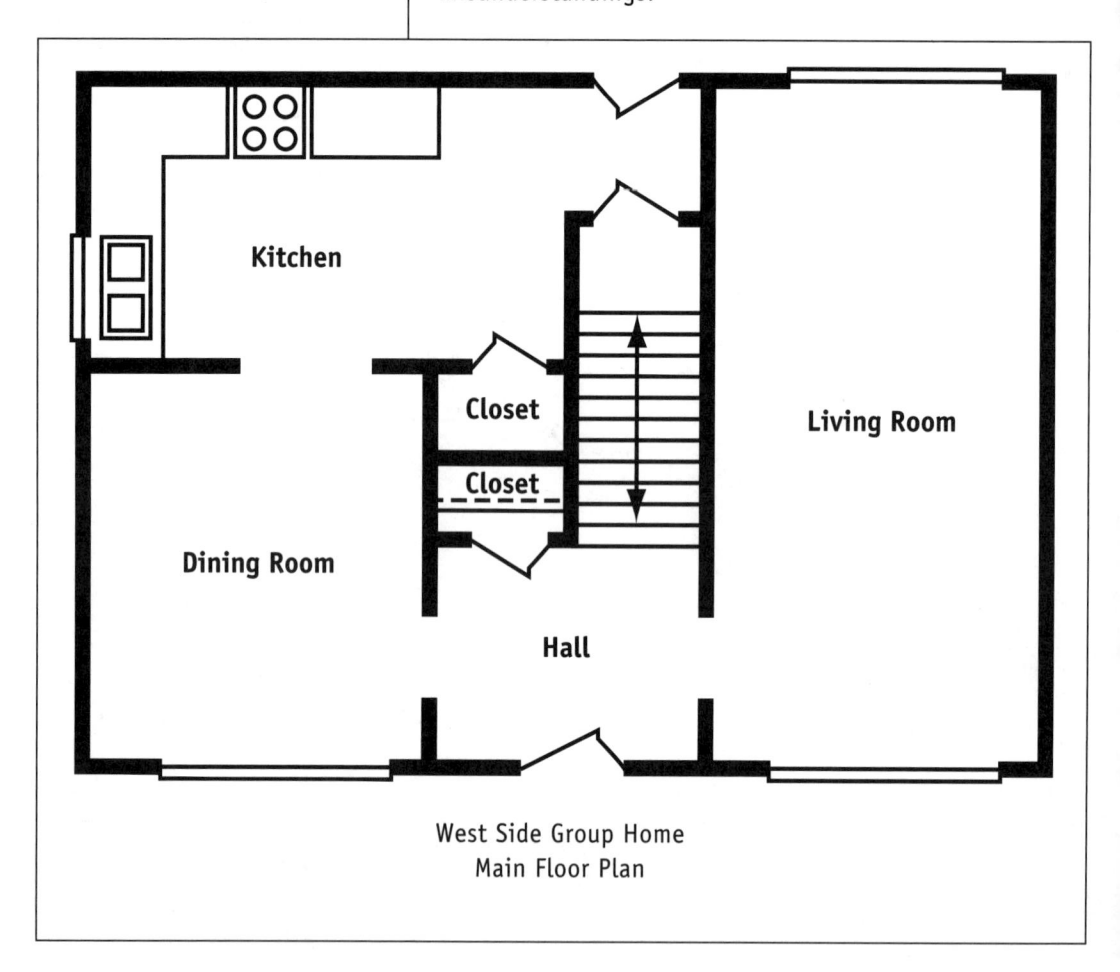

West Side Group Home
Main Floor Plan

notches along the horizontal axis (bottom) of the graph represent time periods (days, weeks, or months), while the notches indicated on the vertical axis (up the left side of the graph) represent growth units (pounds, number of items, or profits). For example, you could use a graph to track weight gain or loss, showing the time interval along the bottom and the weights along the left side. Graphs may also show a comparison of two or even three growth lines, but any more than three or four is confusing. If, when you keep track of your own weight loss or gain, you also record a friend's progress on the same graph, you are using it comparatively. Like line drawings and diagrams, graphs can be produced on a computer. In fact, computer-generated graphs are often preferable, since for most of us it is usually easier to achieve a professional-looking result on a computer than by hand. Some programs allow for elaborate shading, colouring, and three-dimensional effects, all of which can enhance the appearance and clarity of your report.

However, although fancy graphs and diagrams are attractive and can be fun to create by computer, it's sometimes easy to get carried away with visual effects and lose sight of their primary purpose. It is tempting at times to include fancy visuals just because they look attractive rather than considering whether they really serve to communicate information clearly. A graph is meant to provide an easy way for the reader to visualize significant information. If you decide to create and include graphs in your report, ask yourself honestly whether they will do the job you want them to do. Some graphs, although attractive to the eye, can actually complicate rather than clarify information the reader needs. Graphs that force the reader to puzzle through complicated information are ultimately detrimental to the impact of the report. Remember that graphs, whether in colour or black and white, are meant to give the reader a quick overview of information that can be easily compared. Don't try to make a graph do too much. If you use a graph to show comparisons in weight loss or gain, drug dosages, mood swings, absenteeism, or costs of training, for example, you should use a different colour to represent each of the items compared (absenteeism in four different departments, client loads for three different counsellors, costs of two different training programs, weight loss for four individuals). To compare items in a graph that must be photocopied on a black and white copier, use lines of varying thicknesses or a combination of broken, dotted, and solid lines. The graph in Figure 5.4 shows the weight-loss patterns of three people over a six-week period.

Charts

Charts come in many different forms, but the most common are bar charts and pie charts. Bar charts are used to compare a single significant aspect of two or more items; each bar on the chart represents one of the items being compared. The length of the bars may be easily compared and give the reader a quick impression of the difference among items. Bar charts may be drawn vertically or horizontally. The vertical bar chart (Figure 5.5) compares total numbers of callers to distress lines in the same metropolitan area during the first three months of the year.

Pie charts (as in Figure 5.6) are used to show percentages or parts of a whole: how a budget is spent, the percentage of employees who have college diplomas, the breakdown of total agency expenditures.

Proposals

In reports, as in all professional writing, the writer must develop the skill of identifying the reader's needs, expectations, and interests. As we saw in the section on fundraising appeals, this skill is crucial especially in persuasive writing. A proposal is a report that persuades the reader to adopt or change a policy, take an action, or implement a new program. The main parts — summary, introduction, discussion, conclusion, recommendations, and any appendices — are the same as for any other report, and as in other reports, the headings in the discussion section reflect the specific subject matter of the proposal. All reports are challenging to write, but a proposal is more so because, as the writer, you must not only provide all necessary information, but also influence your reader to accept the project or suggestion you're putting forth. In order to move your reader to action, you must focus on the advantages of the proposal you are offering.

Proposals may be initiated by you or they may be invited by someone else; your approach will differ slightly depending on which is the case for you. If the idea for the proposal originated with you, you will want to do the following.

- Identify your suggestion immediately (remember, "the most important thing I want to tell you is that ...").

figure 5.4   A graph enables the reader to compare easily the relative weight gain (or loss) of three individuals.

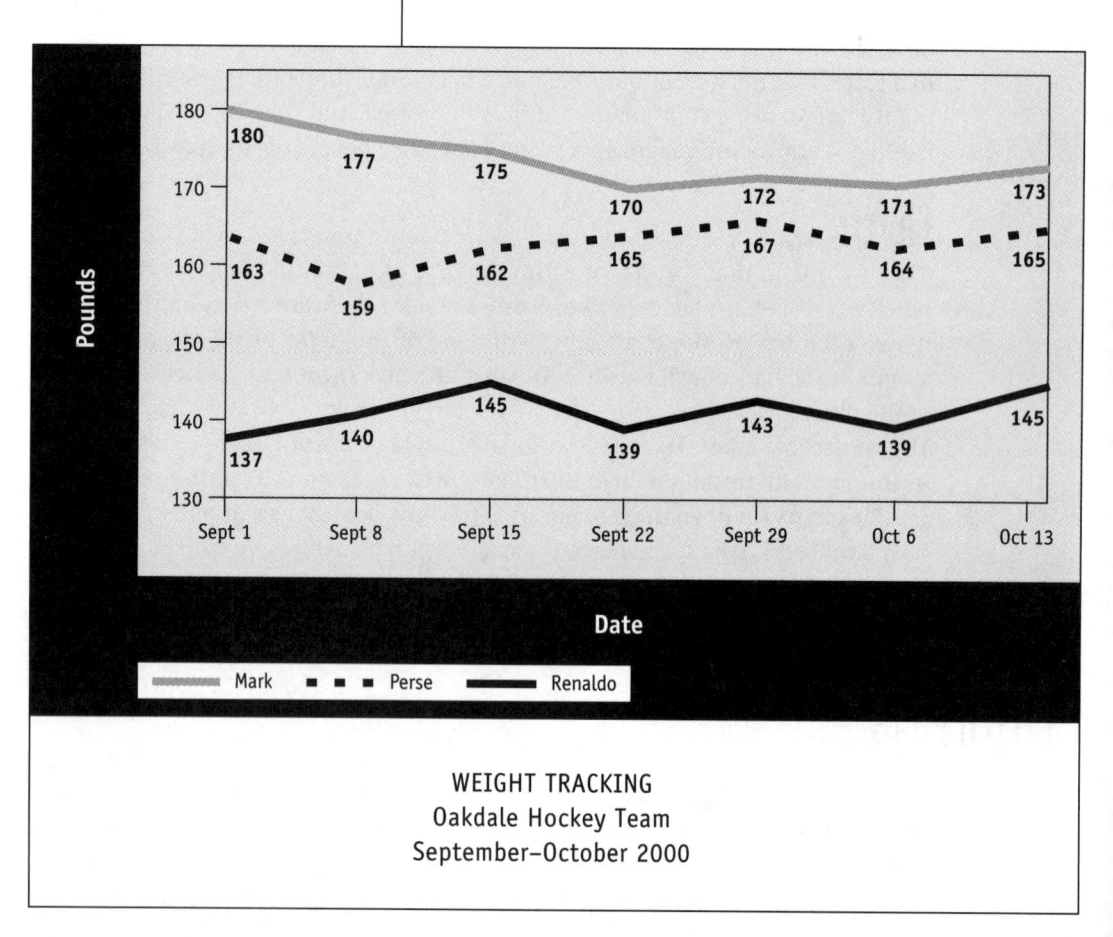

WEIGHT TRACKING
Oakdale Hockey Team
September–October 2000

- Spell out the advantages of the proposed change. If it will save the reader time, work, or money, or if it will increase sales, efficiency, or profits, show how.
- Make it easy for the reader to implement the proposal. Give all pertinent details of the situation and point out any existing resources that can be put to use. Try to anticipate any questions your reader will have and answer them in advance.
- Keep an enthusiastic, positive tone, even when outlining disadvantages. Although you will naturally feel that the advantages of your proposal outweigh any disadvantages it may have, your reader may initially have other ideas. Your task is to make that reader share this positive view of your proposed action.
- Indicate as accurately as possible what implementation will cost, but do this after you've presented all the advantages of your proposal. People may be more willing to spend money, time, or effort after they have been convinced of the importance of a project.

figure 5.5 A bar chart can be used to compare the numbers of calls to a distress line over a particular time period.

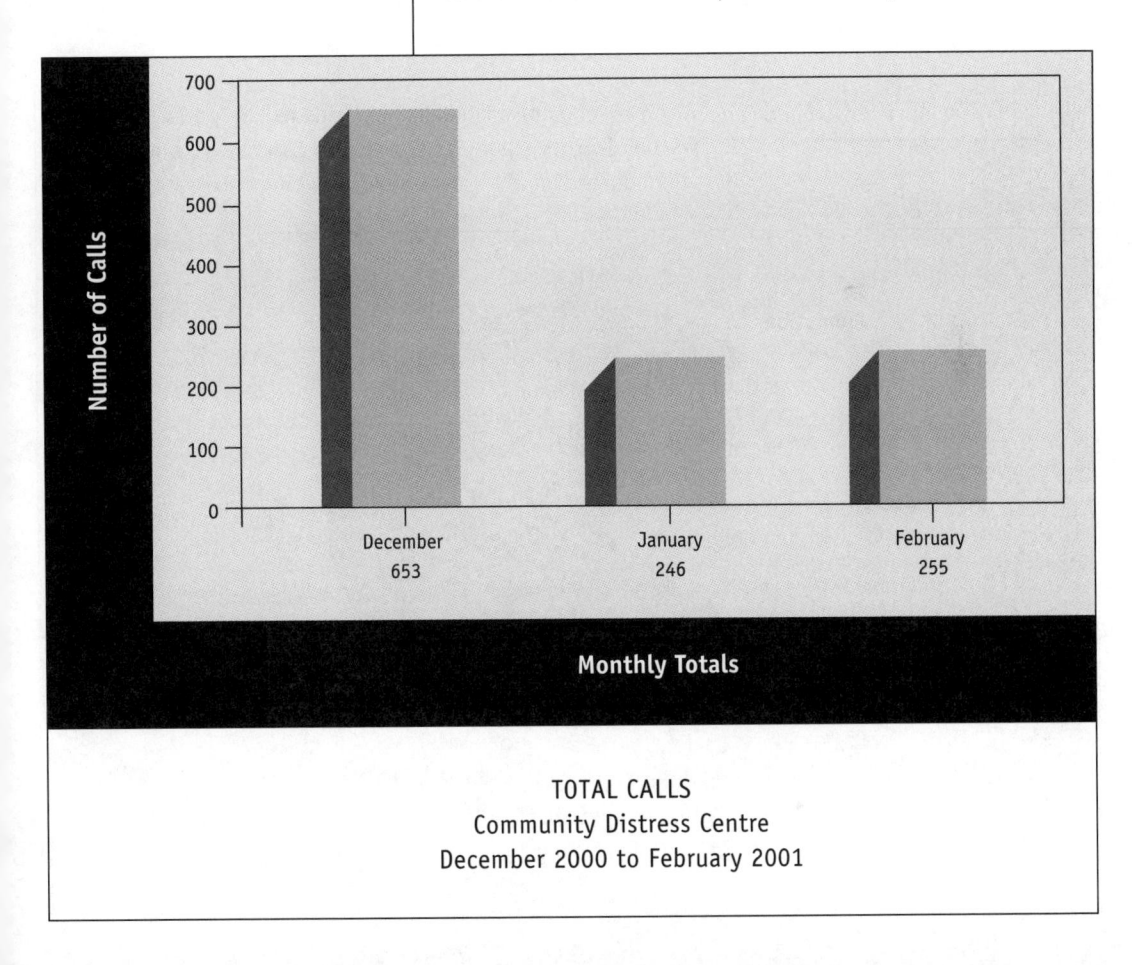

Month	Number of Calls
December	653
January	246
February	255

Monthly Totals

TOTAL CALLS
Community Distress Centre
December 2000 to February 2001

- Indicate the steps that must be taken to bring about the results you propose. Remember that to help your reader accept your project, you must show how it can be done.

Above all, with a proposal, you must demonstrate that you really know what you're talking about and have done your homework thoroughly. You may know that your proposal is sound, but unless you can convince your reader that you have thought the project through and have anticipated any problems, you will not gain his or her confidence, approval, or money. Don't expect a reader to act on faith if your presentation is incomplete or unclear. Do your research.

Occasionally, you will be invited to submit a proposal that outlines how someone else's suggestion may be implemented. As with original proposals, you must still present all the information the reader will need to evaluate your suggestions, but in this case the proposal will differ slightly, since you will be responding to requirements that the reader has outlined for you.

- Since your proposal was requested, you are more likely to have your reader's interest at the outset; however, you will still need to emphasize the advantages of your proposed way of doing things, showing that it is the best means of reaching your reader's desired objectives.

figure 5.6 A pie chart shows the relationships of the parts to the whole. In this example, the reader can see at a glance what percentage of total budget is spent on salaries.

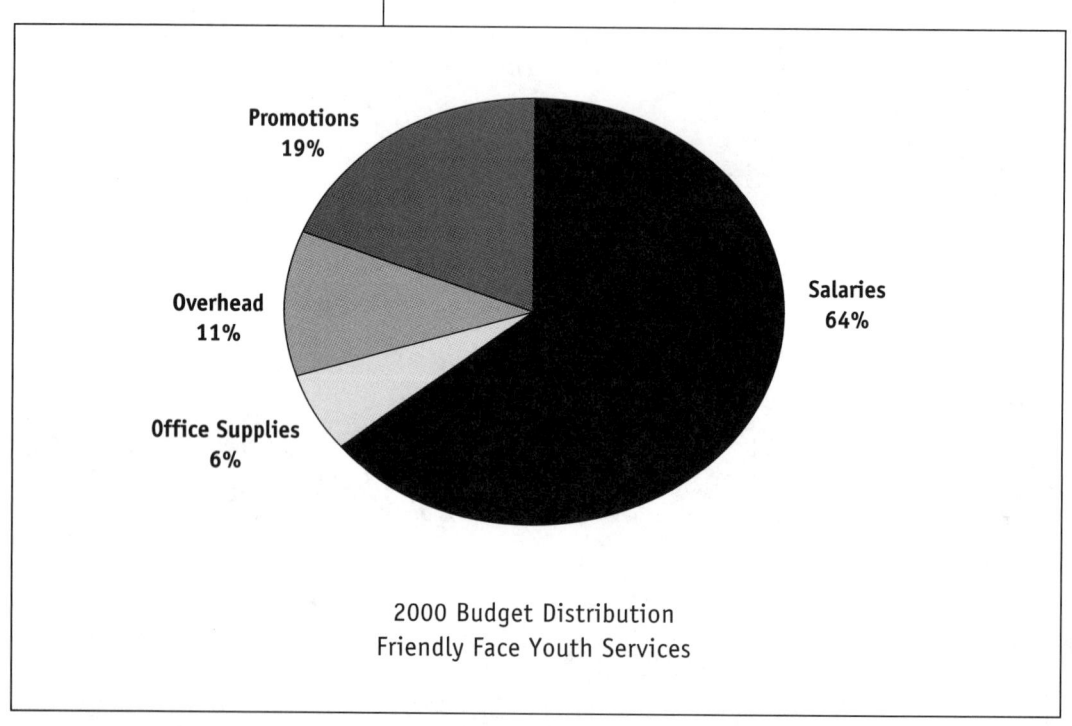

Promotions 19%
Overhead 11%
Office Supplies 6%
Salaries 64%

2000 Budget Distribution
Friendly Face Youth Services

- Because the reader has requested a proposal designed to meet specific needs, you must make sure that the details of your proposal match those requirements.

Remember that a proposal, whether originated by you or requested by someone else, must be especially persuasive to convince a reader to implement the very good idea you've presented.

Sample Formal Report

The sample formal report illustrated in Figure 5.7 on page 112 is a proposal, but the format is similar to that of any other type of formal report.

points to remember

Once again, no matter what kind of report you are writing, you must prepare thoroughly and organize carefully.

1. Identify your main message ("the main thing I want to tell you is that...").
2. Know your purpose (inform or persuade).
3. Remember your reader (needs, expectations, knowledge).
4. Develop your points fully.
5. Observe the Six C's.
6. Be sure to format your report carefully and use appropriate headings.
7. Use visuals to clarify, not complicate, the information in the text.

sharpening your skills

The following report situations represent some for which you could write a formal report or a proposal. Using the report preparation form in the previous chapter to outline your approach, follow your instructor's directions to write *one* of these reports.

1. The Ministry of Community Services encourages employees to reinforce and renew their skills through its program of "Continuing Competence." Some people in your department are considering returning to college to enter the program that you are now completing. Daena Tobias has requested a report from you comparing programs at colleges in your area. For this assignment,

figure 5.7 This formal proposal demonstrates both effective persuasive report writing and proper formal report format.

MINISTRY OF COMMUNITY SERVICES

Innovations in Training

A Proposal

for

Improving

Our Report Writing

Workshops

Jennifer Varzari, Coordinator

Training and Development

October 27, 2002

figure 5.7 (Continued)

MINISTRY OF COMMUNITY SERVICES
Interdepartmental Communication

TO: Daena Tobias, Director

FROM: Jennifer Varzari, Coordinator
Training and Development

DATE: October 27, 2002

RE: Proposed Training Program in Report Writing

I have attached a proposal for a new Report Writing training program for new employees, which I discussed with you in our meeting of October 1. The proposal provides a detailed description of the new program and some samples of the support materials we will need to implement the project.

My department is prepared, upon receiving your approval, to go ahead immediately with the design of a manual, and we expect to be able to begin the new training procedure as early as March 2003, in time for the spring intake of new employees.

We would be happy to meet with your advisory group to discuss this proposal and answer any questions you might have. We appreciate your interest in our suggestions and your ongoing support for innovative approaches to training our employees.

figure 5.7 (Continued)

SUMMARY

A combination of training modules and workshops would be a more efficient means of supporting our personnel in report-writing techniques than the learn-on-the-job method we are now using. Since the employees produce reports regularly, and since we depend on them for information to support Ministry decisions, we want to ensure that our employees are properly trained in Ministry procedure. We propose to implement a new series of workshops to help bring our new employees up to speed quickly and efficiently.

Such a system will make everyone's job easier, since it will ensure that the information you need to make informed and effective decisions will be carefully and efficiently collected and communicated, in accord with existing legal and procedural standards.

My department is in a position to organize and implement such a program within the next six months, should you agree to its value to the efficient fulfillment of Ministry function.

figure 5.7 (Continued)

Table of Contents

Introduction. 1

Proposal Description 2

Benefits of Workshop Training in Report Writing 3

Contents of the Training Manual 4

Preparation and Resources. 6

Conclusion. 7

Recommendations. 7

Appendices

       A. Cost Breakdown for Manuals/Support Materials
       B. Survey Results

figure 5.7 (Continued)

1

INTRODUCTION

We currently offer our personnel no training, as such, in report writing. New employees are expected to learn the specific techniques and formats required by the Ministry of Community Services "on the run." For routine reports that do not involve legal considerations, this is as effective a means of training as any, but where specific legal or procedural issues are involved, as is frequently the case in MCS reports, on-the-job learning is neither the most efficient nor the most effective means of dealing with report training.

The Ministry of Community Services needs employees who are competent, efficient report writers, and who are sensitive to the legal and political implications of even routine reports. Most of the new employees we hire have strong basic language skills, but few have training in the requirements of Ministry report writing. The current system is not meeting all of our needs as fully as training workshops would.

At present, new employees must use their own judgement or approach co-workers for advice on sensitive issues. Many employees have expressed frustration at the confusion and inefficiency of the on-the-job method of training. As well, senior administrators spend too much time screening and editing sensitive materials prepared by employees who have not yet become accustomed to the Ministry's reporting protocol. All agreed that a training workshop would benefit both newer and experienced employees by bringing new people "up to speed" more quickly and effectively. Eighty-seven of the one hundred employees we surveyed for this proposal indicated that they would like to have had explicit training on Ministry guidelines for report writing; only one felt that the on-the-job method needed no improvement.

Though our current method eventually sensitizes employees to the legal and political ramifications of their reports, it does not offer sufficient support for the learning process. Our proposed training program will offer employees the help
hey need to become proficient reporters of Ministry information.

figure 5.7 (Continued)

PROPOSAL DESCRIPTION

Instead of the on-the-job method currently used to train new employees, the Training and Development Department would provide new employees with a two-day seminar on report writing. The workshop system would involve two trainers each spending sixteen hours in a workshop session, with approximately fifteen employees participating (16 ¥ 2 = 32 hours). Workshops would be offered as required, most likely following the spring intake of new employees. Initially, the new system would involve a greater time commitment from our trainers, but ultimately would waste less time than the current system that relies on support from co-workers and supervisors.

Our employees themselves recognize the need for improved training. Of one hundred employees surveyed, fifty-four indicated that they spend over half their working time on writing, and most (70 percent) felt that they relied heavily on others for editorial guidance. An even greater number (79 percent) felt that they needed more training and experience in mastering and implementing Ministry guidelines for report writing.

Clearly, training our employees in the methods and expectations of MCS would cut down on the time needed to produce written materials and would improve the quality of work.

figure 5.7 (Continued)

3

BENEFITS OF WORKSHOP TRAINING IN REPORT WRITING

This system offers distinct advantages over the current system. The time spent consulting with co-workers on the basics of report writing and the time spent extensively rewriting submissions would be significantly decreased. (We would not, of course, eliminate or discourage the practice of employee co-operation). The advantages for participants, training and development staff, and the Ministry are as follows.

PARTICIPANTS:
1. will receive more practical instruction and more individualized attention from the trainers;
2. will receive immediate and relevant feedback on actual writing they are doing for the job; and
3. will receive training in the standards and requirements of MCS report writing.

TRAINERS:
1. will be in close contact with new employees and more intimately involved in the daily demands of reportage within MCS;
2. will be able to address specific individual writing problems that can't be effectively handled on the job; and
3. will be able to track more effectively successful training procedures and techniques.

THE MINISTRY:
1. will gain better-trained writers who produce more efficient reports;
2. will experience a reduction in the number of reports that must be extensively rewritten to accord with legal or political constraints;
3. will benefit from the general morale boost that is felt across the company as confidence in writing is increased; and
4. will benefit from the improved relationships among staff as they work more closely with the Training and Development Department.

figure 5.7 (Continued)

4

CONTENTS OF THE TRAINING MANUAL

The bulk of the information needed to produce the training manual for new employees has already been prepared by the Training and Development Department; supplementary materials are currently being developed. Below is the projected Table of Contents for the manual.

Introduction
    The role of reports in MCS
    The basic principles of writing reports
    Reader and purpose

Report Writing Guidelines
    Legal considerations
    Political sensitivities
    "I was, I saw, I did"

The "Unnatural" Order of Professional Writing
    Identify your main message
    "The main thing I want to tell you is that..."
    The report writer's priority list

Style of Professional Writing
    The Six C's
    Conciseness and clarity
    Keep it simple

figure 5.7 (Continued)

Report Style
    Focus
    Follow your priority list
    Main report parts

Report Formats
    Informal
    Semiformal
    Formal
    Standard report forms

Choosing the Appropriate Report Type
    Report situations
    Occurrence/incident
    Evaluation
    Investigation
    Progress
    Proposals

figure 5.7 (Continued)

6

PREPARATION AND RESOURCES

PRESENT RESOURCES
Oscar Katz, Gwynne Nishikawa, and Heather Scott have already begun preparing a collection of exercises and tips for use in the Report Writing Workshop. As well, Gwynne and I have been working on a supplementary manual for participants in the workshops, which should be completed within a month. Some additional materials would have to be developed to round out the package as a reference manual, and these should include a series of guidelines for achieving mastery of specific MCS requirements.

These learning materials can be set up attractively and printed on the printing department's laser equipment. In-house photocopying and coil binding would enable us to produce economical manuals at approximately $5.00 each (cost breakdown attached as Appendix A), not much more than the present cost of printing individual handouts. The manuals could be distributed to new employees on their joining the company, in advance of their first meeting with training personnel.

IMPLEMENTATION TIME
We estimate that the manual and supplementary materials could be prepared within two months, in time to begin the new training procedures for employees hired in the spring.

figure 5.7 (Continued)

7

CONCLUSION

Though workshop training is not practicable for all of our new-employee programs, we believe it is essential for training in report writing and editing, and that it will ultimately make our employees more efficient and competent.

Once the new system is in place for report-writing training, we can chart our success by follow-up studies and comparisons with the results of the present method. As well, we might consider making the new manuals and approach available to other government agencies through our Resource Sharing Program.

RECOMMENDATIONS

I recommend that the new approach to report-writing training be implemented on a pilot basis as of March 2003, for a one-year trial period. At the end of this time, Training and Development personnel will conduct a study to determine the success of the project and the feasibility of extending it permanently.

figure 5.7 (Continued)

APPENDIX A:
Cost Breakdown for Manuals/Support Materials

We recommend having the manuals printed in runs of 50 copies, which would help to maintain the cost at under $5.00 apiece; manuals will be 48 double-sided pages long.

First Print Run Cost for 50 Copies

Laser 'typesetting'	$0.10/page	$4.80*
Photocopying	$0.05/two-sided page	120.00
Binding	$2.50 each	<u>125.00</u>
Print Run Total		$249.80
Per Copy Total		$5.00

*One-time only cost; subsequent print runs will come in slightly cheaper, since the same typeset originals can be used again.

figure 5.7 (Continued)

APPENDIX B:
Survey Results

We used a questionnaire to collect information from one hundred employees who have joined the Ministry over the last four years. The completed questionnaires are available for viewing in Jennifer Varzari's office.

1. How much of your working time is spent writing (including reports, promotional material, copy, correspondence, or other job-related materials)?

    Fifteen respondents spend more than 75 percent of their working time writing; a further thirty-nine spend over half their time on writing activities; thirty-nine said 25 to 30 percent of their time is spent writing, and seven indicated under 25 percent.

2. Did on-the-job learning provide sufficient support to help you master MCS report-writing standards in a reasonable time?

    Seventy-nine respondents felt that it did not give them enough experience to bring them up to speed quickly; ninety-nine said they would have appreciated more structured guidance; only one indicated satisfaction with the current method.

3. Do you currently rely on editorial guidance from others in your department? To what extent would you say this is so?

    Seventy respondents indicated a heavy reliance — 75 to 100 percent of the time — on guidance from superiors or co-workers; the other thirty indicated a range of reliance from 5 to 50 percent of the time. Most, however, showed that the extent of this dependence decreased as mastery of Ministry expectations increased.

4. Would you have found it beneficial to have attended a workshop on Ministry report-writing standards and techniques?

    Forty-six of the respondents indicated interest in attending a workshop now, should one become available; ninety-nine said that they would have found a workshop highly beneficial when they first joined the Ministry.

figure 5.7 (Continued)

Appendix B, Continued

5. In your view, should training in Ministry report writing be made available to new employees?

> All one hundred respondents said yes. Eighty felt that they would have relied less on peer or superior editorial input if training had been provided.

you should investigate program offerings at three Canadian colleges. Write up your findings into a formal report addressed to Daena Tobias. Your report should outline for these prospective students all they will need to know regarding the basics of the program (including admission requirements, duration, courses, any practicum or co-op experience or special courses, and the policy on advanced standing or experiential learning credit), as well as the general facilities offered by various institutions (student services, library facilities, recreational facilities, and any special assistance for mature students). You will also want to draw up a study of costs. Evaluate the programs according to their appropriateness for the personnel in the Ministry of Community Services and recommend the one you feel is most applicable.

2. One of the responsibilities of the case workers in your CS agency is running Basic Job Readiness Training workshops for clients. In your office of ten, each person runs approximately three workshops per week (on average). Recently, your supervisor, Gord Putz, has received some negative reports on the quality of the workshops — not so much their content, but their delivery. Putz suspects that many of the trainers could use some additional training in public-speaking skills. At any rate, their workshop participants have identified flaws in the presentations, such as dull and lifeless delivery, "memorized" spiels, and general lack of confidence. Putz would like you to investigate the situation and offer some suggestions as to how these individuals can improve their report presentations. You have decided to investigate the available resources and have discovered three that seem most appropriate for your people:

- Dale Carnegie Foundation Training;
- Toastmasters; and
- public-speaking course offered by your local college.

You should investigate the three options, outlining approximate course content, emphasis, duration of the courses, and cost of each. You have considered preparing an in-house training program, as well, and will evaluate the advantages of that program. Gord Putz has indicated that he wants something done fairly soon and at a modest cost.

3. You work in the Community Distress Centre in Saskatoon. At a recent meeting of CACDC (the Canadian Association of Community Distress Centres) in Montreal, several members expressed concern about the lack of contact among personnel at the various locations across the country. Most of the staff at the distress centres are volunteers, and because their work requires anonymity, most can discuss their volunteering only with others at their own centre. All of the centre coordinators agree that a sense of community and shared purpose would really help to boost morale, particularly at some of the smaller centres, where volunteers feel especially isolated.

You are aware that some organizations publish in-house magazines or newsletters as a means of drawing everyone into the "team," and you believe that a similar newsletter might provide a stronger sense of community among distress centre volunteers. Articles would focus on topics of interest to volunteers, and might include tips for handling suicide or other serious calls for help, reports of individual experiences on the distress line, spotlights on advances in different regions, social activities among various centre groups, and even profiles of volunteers in different cities.

You believe that a newsletter would go a long way toward improving the morale of all CACDC volunteers, and you are willing to take on the task yourself. You want to produce a modest but professional-looking pamphlet of approximately four pages, to be distributed approximately four times per year. Using software available at your local centre, you have figured out that you can produce the copy quite inexpensively. The centre's agreement with a local printshop would ensure that copies could be printed for approximately five cents apiece, with a circulation of approximately 2000. Such a newsletter would be immensely more attractive and readable than the memos currently distributed by CACDC, and would provide volunteers with a forum through which they could build a strong sense of community.

Write the proposal to the President of the CACDC, Dot Brown, encouraging her to authorize you to produce this newsletter. Send a copy to the director of your centre (your communication instructor).

4. Choose any topic in the broadly-defined area of professional communication as the focus of your formal report. If you prefer, you may work with *one* of the topics on the list below rather than selecting your own. Drawing on all available research sources, survey the current trends in thinking on the topic you have chosen. Write a formal report that answers the following questions.

   a. Briefly, what major trends appear to be current in this area of communication? Is there a particular emphasis seems to be especially important?

   b. Has there been any significant change in focus or direction of conventional thinking on communication in the profession, as a result of new technologies?

   c. What impact has this trend or these developments in technology had on the practice of your profession?

   d. What conclusions can you draw from your research into this topic? What are the implications of this information for others who wish to pursue careers in your field?

   Here are several topics that have received attention in the recent past, though you are certainly not limited to these. You may choose your own topic if you find something of greater interest to you.

   Cross-Cultural Communication in the Human Services
   Personnel Retreats
   "Opting Out"
   Information Superhighway
   Distance Education by Internet

"Outsourcing"
Ethics in Professional Communication Practice
Communication Coaching and Consulting

Your research should include a minimum of ten sources, and may include interviews or World Wide Web sites as well as library journals and books.

online exercises

1. At the page entitled "Guidelines for Writing an Engineering Report," **civeng.carleton.ca/Courses/UnderGrad/1996-97/82.497/Report-Guidelines.html**, posted by Carleton University's Department of Civil and Environmental Engineering, you will find advice on the preparation and organization of a formal report. Although the advice on this page is adapted specifically to the needs of engineers, formal reports in all disciplines share several common characteristics. Read the advice carefully, and then answer the following questions:

   a. What is the "cardinal principle" of all report writing?
   b. What is the role of the reader in shaping the contents of the report?
   c. Which of the Six C's of Professional Communication seem to be most important to the writers of this Web page? How do you know?

   Send your responses to your instructor by e-mail, or submit them in the form of a short report.

2. Among the features of Prentice Hall Canada's Web site is a page called *Guidelines for Submitting a Proposal*. You will find these guidelines at **www.prenticehall.ca/general/manu.html**. List the ways in which the instructions on this site resemble the instructions given in this chapter, and the previous chapter, for preparing a report. Why do you think the publishing house has made this information available to prospective authors?

3. At **198.103.98.138/commish/misse.htm** you will find the Mission Document of the Correctional Service of Canada, which is presented in a formal report format. After you have looked through the document, answer the following questions.

   a. To what extent does the report conform to the format discussed in this chapter? Is there any way in which it departs from this format? Why might this be so?
   b. What is the purpose of the Mission Document? Why does the Correctional Service need such a document? Who is its intended audience? Does it have the same meaning for those who work for CSC as it would likely have for the general public? Why or why not?

chapter 6

Oral Reports and Presentations

LEARNING OBJECTIVES

- To master the four common types of oral presentations: impromptu; manuscript; memorized; and extemporaneous.
- To learn how to prepare an oral report and how to deliver your message effectively and confidently.

More and more often, human-service professionals are called upon to present materials orally, whether in workshops, seminars, or staff meetings. Inexperienced speakers often find these public-speaking situations unnerving, and may try to avoid them whenever possible. However, anyone who wants to advance to a position of authority in an organization will sooner or later have to face an audience.

An oral report or briefing, like a written report, should be carefully thought out, well organized, and clearly presented. No matter how uncomfortable you are at the thought of public speaking, you can give an effective speech or presentation if you prepare and organize your materials carefully, and practice effectively. You will find that your fear will actually fade if you gain control over your subject matter and focus on communicating your message to your audience.

One big difference between oral presentations or reports and the written variety is the advantage of meeting your audience face-to-face. Though it may be intimidating to stand before a group of your peers or your supervisors, you should remember that it's also a lot easier to establish rapport with someone who is in the same room with you than it is to engage and motivate the readers of a written report. If you can think of the opportunity for oral communication as an advantage rather than a burden, you will find it easier to prepare for the experience. In order to take full advantage of the opportunity to speak directly to your audience, you will need to think about your speech as communication rather than simply a performance. Like all effective professional communication, oral communication depends on making a connection with your audience and staying focused on your purpose. When you are preparing an oral presentation you should also think about the context or setting in which your report will be given.

1. Consider your audience To whom are you speaking? Are you delivering material to your peers? Your subordinates? A group of visitors? The Board? What is the audience's interest in your project? How much information do they already have? What do they want or need to know? How much depth do they expect? As you consider these expectations and needs, adapt your report presentation as closely as possible to your audience's expectations. Recognize that some things you consider important may have to be left out if they are not as significant to your audience.

2. Focus on your purpose Why are you giving this presentation? What, exactly, are you expected to accomplish? Should you give a quick overview of your project, or should you present an in-depth analysis of your work? Are you expected to outline, support, or justify what you've been doing? Do you have to persuade your audience to accept a new point of view or course of action? Will you be subject to questions from your listeners? What are your own expectations? At the planning stage, you will need to shape your speech to reflect the task it is meant to accomplish.

3. Identify the speaking context One of the things that makes oral communication different from written work is the fact that it is presented face-to-face in a physical setting. The size of your audience, the room in which you are speaking, and the limits of time are among the factors that will constrain you in planning your speech. How much time will you have to make your connection with the audience? If you have prepared a forty-five-minute presentation only to find that you have been allotted three minutes, you'll have a difficult time — though not as difficult as if you're in the reverse situation! Make sure you know how much time you're expected to fill. Where are you giving your presentation? How big is the room? What facilities are available? How far will you be from your audience? Will you be using a microphone? Overhead cameras? If you're expected to give a three-minute overview of your project, you may have to do that standing next to your desk as the visitors are paraded through; a forty-five-minute comprehensive outline will probably be presented in a meeting room or boardroom.

Types of Oral Presentations

Oral presentations vary not only in length and formality, but also in the style of delivery. There are four main types of speech delivery, but not all are suited to every occasion. Be sure to choose the one which is most appropriate for the requirements of your situation.

1. Impromptu An impromptu speech is given on the spur of the moment: the speaker is called upon to speak without warning and without any prepared notes. This type of presentation is most commonly used as an exercise in public-speaking classes or groups, or it may occur when a party guest who wasn't expecting to be honoured is called upon to say a few words. For obvious reasons, the impromptu speech is usually short (under two minutes); a topic that is suitable for such a speech is one on which most anyone could speak without having to prepare. The speaker isn't expected to provide new information; at best, she may simply give us a new way of looking at something we all know. This style of delivery is not suitable for any occasion where the speaker is expected to be prepared to give a presentation.

2. Manuscript A manuscript presentation is written out and read word-for-word from the printed document. It is the result of extensive research and thoughtful organization by the speaker, and is most appropriate in situations where there are legal considerations (a lawyer or politician issuing policy would probably use this form) or where exact wording is important. This kind of speech is rarely effective for persuasion, since it is difficult to maintain audience engagement when you're focused on a manuscript in front of you instead of on your audience. If you aren't focused on them, you won't hold their attention, and if you lose their attention, you can't hope to move them. As well, written discourse just doesn't sound like spoken discourse — and reading from a manuscript tends to deaden the speaker-audience relationship. Even if you are very accomplished at reading aloud (most people are not), you may have trouble keeping your audience's attention during this kind of presentation. Despite these warnings, you may be tempted to resort to a written manuscript in your talks. However, if you have ever had to listen to someone read an essay or a paper aloud, you know how hard it can be for an audience to pay attention. It's just plain boring to listen to such a speaker, and that's not a style you should want to emulate. To keep your audience with you, you need to focus on communicating clearly with them and making a personal connection.

3. Memorized A speech can also be prepared in advance and memorized, but this is also not good speaking practice, because a memorized spiel will typically fail to engage the audience. If you've written something and then memorized it, it will sound like exactly that — your focus will be on the text in your head as you reach for exact phrasing, and not on the audience in front of you. As well, since you're reaching for exact wording rather than for ideas, a slip of memory will leave you gasping. You may not be able to recover your train of thought without repeating phrases you've already spoken. Finally, as you focus on remembering word-for-word what you were going to say next, you lose the contact that's vital to the communication exchange. There is little likelihood that you will be using a memorized speech unless you are acting in a play. Otherwise, memorization is not the way to achieve the audience connection you desire.

4. Extemporaneous In this, the most versatile and useful form of oral presentation, the speaker works from an outline written on a card and expands the details from memory. An extemporaneous presentation is superior for most purposes because it allows you to respond to the immediate needs of your audience and so establish a bond with them. Don't make the mistake of thinking that an extemporaneous speech is unprepared or "ad-libbed"; it isn't. It requires detailed planning and organization ahead of time, but the delivery has a natural, spontaneous, engaging quality. It is by far the most flexible of speech delivery styles, and of the four types listed here, it is the one that you will find most useful.

Preparing Your Presentation

Like all good reports, extemporaneous presentations require meticulous planning, preparation, and practice. When well done, they appear comfortable and natural — so much so that they may fool an inexperienced observer into thinking they are completely spontaneous. One of my students, a very accomplished speaker who has mastered the art of extemporaneous speaking, recently gave a presentation in a senior class. One of her classmates, misunderstanding this highly polished presentation, astonished her by remarking, "I can't believe that you were able to wing it like that, and it came out so well!" This student prepares meticulously, researches thoroughly, and practises repeatedly, but her inexperienced classmate saw only the natural, comfortable delivery of an effective extemporaneous speech. That's what your audience should see also.

When preparing an extemporaneous speech, you must clearly identify your main message and your audience, but to make the presentation really work well, you must create and maintain an effective relationship with your audience. Your oral and visual delivery will help to ensure that your audience responds to your speech, but your real effectiveness as a speaker will rest on the only written material you will bring with you to the front of the room: your notecard.

Instead of reading from a manuscript, or delivering a memorized monologue, a speaker delivering an extemporaneous speech speaks naturally about her knowledge of the topic, gleaned from her research and preparation. Her speech has a clear, explicit structure, and a clearly identified purpose. She carries *one notecard* on which she has written only enough, in a scratch outline form, to jog her memory of the points she wants to make.

An extemporaneous speech is never written out fully, even during the preparation stages; it is developed as an outline only, and that outline is pared down, as you practice through the material, until it is simply a cue to memory. Once you have arrived at your final bare outline, you should jot it lengthwise on a notecard no larger than 3" × 5". Unless your speech is very lengthy (longer than twenty-five minutes), you should be able to fit sufficient information onto a single card. You may use both sides of the card, but don't be tempted to write down too much detail. Preparing your notecard well is one way of ensuring that your presentation will be successful, since it is the only text you will have with you at the front of the room. You should never read directly from the card unless you are citing quotations or statistics, and these should be used sparingly. Consult the card only as a reminder of your organization: it is a tool but not a crutch.

The words on the card should be written as large as possible, in bold ink; you may wish to use highlighters or coloured ink to colour-code your main points. If you wish to include a brief quotation in your speech, or cite statistics, these may also be written on the card.

Why should you use a card rather than a page? A card is preferable first of all because its small size forces you to write down only main points, expanding the details from memory (that is, extemporizing) as you speak. The card is meant to prompt you, and give you something to rely on should your memory fail you because of nervousness.

In addition, you can palm a 3" × 5" card quite easily, so that it is inconspicuous in your hand. By contrast, a full page is too large to be used unobtrusively and can actually serve as a distraction to your audience. It can rattle and shake if your hands tremble, communicating your nervousness to your audience and emphasizing it to yourself. Do yourself a favour: write your extemporaneous speech outline on a card.

Before turning to the process of preparing the speech and making the card, we will spend a little time discussing topics for your speech.

Choosing a Topic

Clearly, one of the first things you must do in preparing for a speech, whether it's in the classroom or the boardroom, is to select and properly focus your topic. In some cases, your professor may assign you a topic, or your choices may be limited by the projects you're working on in your job. Whether you are assigned a topic or are freely choosing for yourself, you should be careful to pick a subject or an aspect of the assigned topic that is interesting and important to you. Effective presentations require careful research and preparation, and those tasks will be easier for you if you've chosen a topic that interests you.

Also, if you're fascinated by your subject, your enthusiasm will show in your presentation, making it more dynamic. Speakers who choose subjects that bore them usually bore their audience with dull, lacklustre performances. Remember: no topic is by nature boring; it becomes so only in the hands of an under-prepared, unenthusiastic speaker.

Let's assume that you have been assigned a speech in a class, but no topics have been assigned. Your instructor has given you the freedom to choose your own topic and approach. How do you choose something interesting for both yourself and your audience? First, you should strive to give your speech a sense of immediacy for your audience; if possible, it should address something that will be important to them right now. The newspaper magnate William Randolph Hearst once said that a dogfight in your own neighbourhood is more interesting than a full-scale war half a world away. He knew the importance of giving the audience something relevant to their lives. You should keep this principle in mind, too.

Here's an example of immediacy. One of my students gave a speech designed to persuade his classmates not to use the school elevators when it was unnecessary. Because student tuition costs had taken a sharp rise just previous to his presentation, he used the costs of operating the elevators — more than a full year's salary for one extra professor — as his focal point. By avoiding the use of the elevators, he argued, the students may be able to increase the number of course offerings at the school, or prevent an additional scheduled tuition increase. This focus affected all the students in the class, and dealt with something of immediate interest and importance to them. They couldn't help but be interested.

Another student who was looking for a speech topic was walking along the main hallway of the school, past the location of a small snackbar. She noticed with some annoyance the amount of debris that littered the hallway — candy wrappers, chip bags, pop cans, and pizza boxes. As she picked some of it from the floor to put into the trash, she found herself asking silently why nobody else was doing the same. She realized she'd found a subject for a persuasive speech, and she set about to investigate it: how much time did the maintenance staff spend cleaning up garbage that messy students left behind? What other chores were neglected because the staff was occupied by this task? In what way could her student audience benefit by taking the action she was asking for? The answers to these questions, which she obtained by interviewing the head of Maintenance Services and by doing some library research on the psychology of physical surroundings, provided the basis for a powerful speech persuading her classmates to put their own garbage in the trash cans, and to pick up just two pieces of litter from the floor each time they walked along the hall.

Speech topics are everywhere. As long as there are problems to be solved, new ideas to be communicated, actions to take, there will be subjects for speeches. It's up to you to find one that you care about, are committed to, and can interest your audience in. It's possible to take any approach to your topic that you please, provided it will gain your audience's interest and prompt their action. But one thing is certain; if you can't interest yourself in your topic, you're not going to succeed in holding the interest of an audience. You'll be bored, and that boredom will be evident to your audience. The most important thing you can do for yourself and your audience is to pick something that holds your interest as well as theirs.

There's one other rule to picking a topic that you should consider: some topics have been overworked. For example, most speech instructors have heard far too many speeches on recycling and on exercise. Chances are that, if a topic comes easily to your mind, it has likely crossed the minds of everyone else in the class. Try to pick something a little different from the same few tired topics. Unless you can find some brand new information and focus on a specific connection to your audience, you will probably lose your audience in the first few minutes of your speech. Give them something unusual, original, and exciting. As an additional rule of thumb, if you heard about it on a television talk show, it's probably been overdone, and you should not choose it for your speech.

Finding a Topic When You Can't Think of Anything

Many of us have the most difficult time simply coming up with a beginning idea. Freewriting is a technique you can use to help generate ideas. Sit down with pen and paper, or in front of your computer, and start to write — it doesn't matter what you write at the beginning. You can really start from anywhere, from any thought that pops into your head. The trick is to force yourself to keep on writing — no matter what — for at least 15 minutes without stopping. Don't pause for anything. Even if you have to write something like "This is stupid! I can't think of anything to say!" you will find that pretty soon your thoughts will swing around to the task at hand and ideas will start to flow. Many people find this to be a good generator of ideas for any type of assignment where the topic is left completely open. Once you begin to generate ideas about topics, you can go over them to consider their persuasive possibilities.

You might want to try a somewhat more structured approach. Using your computer, or a pen and paper, make a list of as many topics as you can think of. Don't worry at first if the topics you're selecting seem to be too broad to make a clear speech; narrowing your topic to a specific purpose will come later. As you begin to brainstorm you should write down all the ideas that come to you, no matter how silly they may seem. You can always cross out the weak ones later. The list will likely be things that you already know about. Your list may look like this sample:

school	majors	teachers	sports
music	theatre	movies	books
dancing	art	hobbies	transportation
self-defense	clothes	education	advertising
stress!	exams	time out!	reading

Once you've got a list, ask yourself if any of these subjects contain any possibilities. You will need to find a "hook" that will catch your audience's attention and link the speech to them. Once you've got a list like this one, go through a second time and brainstorm all the sub-topics that come to you on each of the subjects. For instance, we might begin with school:

school —	teachers	cost	courses
	grades	requirements	special classes
	exams	library	cafeteria
	gym	clubs	meeting people
	drama/music performances		student newspaper

Select from your second list any topics that might offer possibilities of an interesting topic for you and your class. If you need to, generate a third list, and then a fourth — each time becoming more specific. For instance, let's take the topic of the student newspaper:

newspaper —	volunteer opportunities	movie reviews
	articles about school	quality of writing
	information about sports teams	weak reporting
	interesting editorials	columnists
	why do so many people hate it?	costs
	journalism experience	

After making such a list, one of my students decided to give a speech encouraging her classmates to read the newspaper. Another chose to speak about why the class should boycott the newspaper entirely. Another encouraged people in the class, who were communication majors, to join the writing staff at the paper, citing the experience in journalism that could be gained.

This, of course, isn't the only topic that can work this way. One of my students gave an excellent speech encouraging her classmates to volunteer for the university's brand-new late-night escort program. Another offered a speech encouraging the class to nominate a favourite instructor for a teaching award by pointing out how doing so might help to retain good teachers on staff and would pay something back to someone who had contributed in an important way to their education. Yet another student offered his classmates a method for increasing their reading speed and comprehension. By emphasizing the amount of reading they were faced with in the current semester, as well as the overall reading load in their program, he was able to convince many of them to try the method he advocated.

As a final suggestion for finding a topic, you may find it useful (if you are free to choose your own topic) to think through your experiences using the following technique. Three areas of everyone's experience can profitably be "mined" for topics. First, consider recommending to your audience a product, a book, a movie, or a magazine that you have used and liked: I have heard excellent speeches encouraging the audience to subscribe to the speaker's favourite magazine, recommending a favourite recipe, encouraging the audience to incorporate spinach into their diet. Any product that you have used that you think is good

— perhaps a metal polish for removing rust from your bicycle, or a particular brand of jeans — can be made the basis for a persuasive or informative speech.

Second, you may wish to invite your audience to participate in an activity or join an association that you belong to. The activity may be socially significant, such as volunteering at the local hospital or donating to the food bank, or it may be personally relevant, such as participating in a new sport, joining a particular student club at your college, or trying a new hobby. I have heard some great speeches on rock climbing, juggling, participating in the 24-hour famine program, and joining the rhetoric and communications society at our school. Once again, this method of topic invention is a good foundation for both persuasive and informative speeches.

Third, it's also possible to make a good and interesting speech out of challenging the status quo. Most of us take certain social attitudes for granted: walk instead of taking the elevator, recycle, get more exercise, wear a certain brand of jeans. You can catch and hold an audience's attention sometimes just by taking an approach contrary to what the audience expects. The trick to this approach is to concentrate your efforts very specifically: not simply global resistance to commercial culture, for example, but a speech on why you should NOT wear a certain brand of shoes or jeans, on why you should NOT take the stairs instead of the elevator, or why you should NOT recycle. Of course, you will still need to do your research and be sure your evidence is convincing. It's not enough simply to disagree with received wisdom; you must prove your case. However, many issues — even ones that everyone takes for granted — can be viewed from the opposite side. This approach can yield a really challenging and interesting speech if you think it through carefully.

Whichever of these methods you use for choosing a topic, or if you use another method, be sure to evaluate your choice in light of the course requirements, your own interests, the demands of the assignment, and the probable interests of your audience. Ask yourself what kinds of angles you could take on each subject, and consider where you might turn to research them further. If your presentation date is a week away, you may not want to pick a subject that will require a trip to a distant library or a lengthy wait for inter-library loans.

Making the Notecard

Below is a sample outline and notecard for a presentation that I gave on the subject of toy design, a hobby of mine and a subject on which I have written and published three books. I initially gave this presentation at the launch of the first book and have used it since in speaking to other groups on the same topic. Even though I speak in front of classes every day, I was just as nervous in giving this presentation as any speaker is in an unfamiliar situation. Here is how I prepared myself.

Before preparing the outline, I jotted down as many ideas as I could think of that might provide possible approaches to the subject. Here are some of the ideas I came up with.

General Topic	toy design
Possible Subtopics	sources of inspiration for designs
	demonstration of a simple technique
	steps in the design process
	getting designs published
	selling your designs
	writing a book on design
	how I got started designing

Focus

Once I had jotted down several possible approaches I might take, I thought about the speaking situation. When I first gave the presentation, I was speaking to a variety of prominent people from the college and the community in a large meeting room. The group consisted of about fifty professionals and community members who were not designers themselves, but had come to hear me speak about the book and the design work I was doing. They were interested in learning about the personality behind the work. Their expectations ruled out some of the topics I'd listed; for instance, these people were not interested in getting such a book published themselves. They were not really concerned with learning a technique either, and in any case, the room was too large to allow for such a demonstration, so that was out too. These people were simply interested in learning something about my design work, and my experience had taught me that there are several questions that people often ask about this hobby.

For these reasons, I selected three of the above topics: how I started designing; sources of inspiration/ideas; steps in the design process. I organized my three topics logically, and in my introduction I linked the three by mentioning that these were questions that I was commonly asked about my work in design.

Once you've focused your topic and completed your research, you should prepare a preliminary speaking outline. **DO NOT WRITE OUT YOUR SPEECH IN FULL!** Work at an outline level only, and pare that down as much as possible before you turn to your card. Use words that have enough meaning to you to remind you of what you want to discuss. You should aim for mastery of ideas, not memorization of particular words and phrases. Your card should be so pared down that it would be useful only to the person who had done the research for the speech. If it has enough information that someone who had not researched the material could present your speech, it probably contains too much. Once you've prepared your initial outline, you should start practising through the speech, adjusting anything that needs to be changed or reorganized. When you have enough mastery of your information, but before you're through practising, you should make up the final version of your card.

Use only ONE notecard, no larger than 3" × 5", for your speech outline. Remember, your card should contain only a brief outline that will serve to remind you of your main points. Each point you write down is intended to provide a cryptic signal that will trigger your memory of the materials and help you organize your comments during the presentation. It isn't meant to record details or exact phrasing.

Figure 6.1 shows an example of the notecard I used for my 20-minute presentation on toy design. The words "Three questions" that I used in my introduction reminded me of what I wanted to say to begin my presentation. Because these questions were also likely to be in the minds of my listeners, this introduction helped me capture their interest. The points listed under each section developed my presentation fully, and I displayed the actual toys as visual aids.

Preparing a Briefing

On the job you will not be as free to select your presentation topic as you are in school; instead, you may be required to speak about some aspect of your work. This kind of presentation, often referred to as a briefing, is similar to the kind of presentation outlined above, but may differ in the exact steps you follow to prepare your materials. Let's look at the outline and notecard used by Jennifer

figure 6.1 The organizational outline for my hobby presentation and the notecard that will serve as a reminder of my main points.

SAMPLE SPEECH OUTLINE

INTRODUCTION: Three Questions

I. How I Started Designing
    A. Childhood interest in toys/crafts
    B. Nephews/nieces
    C. Altering patterns becomes designing

II. Sources of Ideas
    A. Classic children's stories — witches, elves, Santa, gypsies, angels
    B. Unusual names — Madame Sosostris, Pat Hare
    C. Illustrations — birthday cards, colouring/story books

III. Steps in the Design Process
    A. Concept — show birthday card
    B. Sketch — show preliminary sketch
    C. Pattern — show pattern development
    D. Finished toy — show toy

Handwritten notecard:

Introduction
  3 Questions
I. How I started
  A. Childhood
  B. Nephews/Nieces
  C. Altering → designing
II. Ideas
  A. Classic Stories
  B. Unusual names
  C. Illustrations/Cards
III. Process
  A. Concept (card)
  B. Sketch
  C. Pattern
  D. Finished toy

Varzari in preparing a briefing for the director's advisory group on the training workshops she outlined in her proposal on pages 112–124 in the previous chapter of this book.

Because Jennifer's presentation is clearly defined by her work, she already knows the kind of approach she must take, and she does not need to jot down ideas for subjects. However, she does need to clearly define her audience, her purpose, and her speaking context, as suggested at the beginning of this chapter.

Audience Jennifer knows that her audience, the director's advisory board, has the power to recommend or veto her proposal. They are an important group in the organization, with greater authority than she, as manager of her department, is able to command. They have already received and read her proposal, and have indicated their interest by inviting her to attend their meeting to discuss the proposal and answer their questions.

Purpose Jennifer must convince the advisory group that her proposal is worth implementing. She knows that they want to do what is best for the organization, so she must show them that this project is to the organization's benefit. Because they have already read the proposal, her introductory remarks will be a quick overview of the project, emphasizing the agency's need for improved training in this area.

Speaking Context Jennifer has been allotted a half hour at the beginning of the advisory group's regular weekly meeting. They will be in a small meeting room that holds twenty people. There is no lectern; Jennifer will be seated at a meeting table with the members of the group around her. It will be a relatively informal setting, and Jennifer is expected to present a brief introductory presentation followed by questions from the group.

Jennifer will want to bring support materials with her to the meeting — the survey results, copies of the materials to be used in the training, and an outline of the procedure. She should also prepare a card to help her frame her initial remarks. As a notecard, she can use a shortened version of her proposal, but because her audience has already seen that document, she must not simply read from it or repeat materials they have already read. Given the audience's interests, Jennifer should emphasize the agency's need for report writing training, the failures of the current system, and the advantages of the new one. Below is the outline Jennifer developed for her presentation (Figure 6.2).

Delivery

Organization and preparation are, of course, very important in an oral presentation, but effect on the audience will also be determined by the quality of your delivery. We all have been bored to near distraction by speakers whose points may

figure 6.2 Outline for a briefing. Jennifer Varzari focuses on her audience, her purpose, and her speaking context.

BRIEFING OUTLINE:
Jennifer Varzari's Presentation to the Board

INTRODUCTION:
    A. The importance of employee writing competence
I. Value of report writing training
    A. Efficiency
    B. Professional image

II. Problems with current system
    A. Inefficiency
        1) Lost time
        2) Repetition of training
    B. Employee dissatisfaction
        1) Survey results

III. Advantages of proposed system
    A. Employees
    B. Company
    C. Training staff

CONCLUSION
    A. Implementation plan

---

have been interesting and even lively, but whose presence was unimpressive or distracting. In order to speak effectively, you need to take account of two major aspects of effective speech delivery — sight and sound. The key is to remember that everything in your speech should enhance and not detract from the overall impact. Often this simply means not calling attention to weak spots, but just as often it means taking special care to create definite strengths in your presentation. Your visual and vocal presence as you claim your place at the front of the room are the most important factors in successful delivery. Here are some of the elements of delivery that can make or break your speech.

Visual Presence: The Sight of Your Presentation

Many people don't realize how powerful a visual impression can be, and in an oral presentation it can be crucial. The speaker may be in front of an audience for anywhere from five minutes to two hours. The attention of audience members is concentrated on the speaker; listeners, without necessarily being completely aware that they are doing so, often take in every idiosyncrasy of the speaker's behaviour and every detail of appearance. (To test the accuracy of this point, ask yourself what small peculiarities you have noticed in your instructors — details of behaviour, expression, or dress. You'll be surprised how much you have noticed without necessarily being aware of it.) While you can't control everything about your appearance as a speaker, there are some details you can take care of consciously that will help you to present a confident and capable visual presence to your audience.

1. Dress for the Occasion Wear clothing that is appropriate to the audience and speaking situation. Don't expect to be taken seriously if you show up in a ragged pair of jeans. Even if your presentation is for a class, dress up a bit. Don't wear clothing you will feel uncomfortable in, however, and avoid pulling at or adjusting your collar, sleeves, waistband, or any other part of your costume. Remember, too, that unless you are speaking about fashion, conservative dress is usually preferable to flamboyant outfits. You want to be memorable for what you say, not for what you wear, and clothing that attracts attention away from your speech will undercut your purpose.

2. Stay Calm Approach the lectern calmly and pause briefly before beginning to speak, so as to give yourself a chance to catch your breath. Don't rush to the podium and immediately begin to speak. Give yourself time to relax and your audience a chance to get used to your presence. Likewise, don't rush away from the lectern just as your last words are leaving your mouth. Give the audience a few seconds to recognize that your speech has ended and allow for questions if it's appropriate to do so.

3. Use Appropriate Movements and Gestures to Show Emphasis You should appear calm and self-possessed. Stand straight, but not stiffly, keeping your body weight distributed evenly on both feet, using gestures to emphasize your points. As well, though you will likely feel vulnerable, don't lean on or hide behind the lectern.

You should not be afraid to move about comfortably in front of your audience, but don't fling your arms about wildly, fidget, or shift uncomfortably from one foot to the other. Such extravagant movements are likely to detract from your presentation (your audience may begin to count your unconscious gestures — Did you notice how many times she pushed her glasses up? Did you see him jiggling the change in his pockets?) If you watch carefully, you will notice that a skilled speaker neither avoids nor overuses gestures and movement. Such a person knows how horribly dull it can be to watch someone who does not move about at all and how distracting unnecessary movements can be.

4. Maintain Eye Contact The ideal situation is to meet the eyes of every member of the audience at all times — or at least to give this impression! Of course this is an impossible ideal, but if you keep it in mind, you will avoid fixing your eyes on a single spot and delivering your presentation to it. Don't, as some speakers do, stare at a point on the back wall (your audience will wonder what you are looking at so intently and turn to stare too) or look too long at your notes. Eye contact is one of the chief means by which a speaker can create a bond with listeners; it helps to maintain their interest. Don't be afraid to meet your listeners' eyes.

5. Employ Appropriate Facial Expressions People who are nervous sometimes betray their lack of confidence by giggling or grinning inappropriately, even when the speech is serious. Try to keep your expression consistent with the material you are delivering. It is perfectly correct to smile when it is appropriate, but you should appear to be in control of your facial expressions.

6. Use Visual Aids Of course, one of the most important of the visual factors of your presentation is your use of visual aids. When used effectively, these can make your presentation. Remember that they should be simple, readable, and well-timed. More about these below.

Vocal Presence: The Sound of Your Presentation

Although in these days of television, sound may not seem as powerful as appearance, it is still a very significant element in any oral presentation, since your voice is the primary medium through which your information is transmitted. As with visual presence, your vocal presence must be confident and steady; it should not detract from your presentation. There are some common flaws to which first-time speakers are subject, but with awareness and practice you can eliminate them from your presentation style.

1. Maintain a Reasonable Volume Most inexperienced speakers speak too softly to be heard. Without yelling, be sure your voice is loud enough to be heard by everyone, especially those in the back row. If you can, practice your speech in the room where it will be delivered, having a friend sit at the very back to determine whether you can be heard. If you absolutely cannot project your voice that far, try to arrange for a microphone. The members of your audience will not be attentive if they cannot hear you clearly.

2. Watch Your Pitch A common weakness is for speakers to raise their voices at the end of statements as if they were asking questions. In fact, this voice tic is a form of questioning — a plea for the audience's constant support and reassurance. Unfortunately, when used repeatedly, it can make you sound nervous and uncertain. State your points confidently, dropping your pitch at the end of each sentence.

3. Maintain a Pleasant Tone Voice quality is another factor that can influence a speaker's effectiveness. Try to cultivate a voice that is pleasant to listen to: a voice that is piercing or nasal, for example, may irritate listeners and prevent your message from getting through. As well, try to project some animation into your voice.

A deadpan delivery in a monotonous voice tone is just as annoying to the audience as a grating, nasal tone.

4. Speak Clearly Enunciate your words carefully. Many speakers swallow the last half of their words or run over them too quickly, making them hard to listen to or to understand. Check your pronunciation too, particularly of words with which you are unfamiliar. Mispronunciations of important words will harm your credibility with your audience.

5. Speak Slowly Enough Although you don't want to pause for too long between words, far more speakers are inclined to speak too quickly than too slowly. Don't rush through your material. Your audience will appreciate a brief pause here and there to allow them time to grasp your points.

6. Avoid Fillers or Speech Tags Don't say UM! (Or *okay, like, you know,* or *really.*) These can be so distracting that an audience may actually begin to count them (Did you know she said "um" thirty-seven times in ten minutes?) and thus lose the thread of your speech. Don't be afraid to simply pause if you need a few seconds to collect your thoughts; you need not make sounds all the time. If you find that you tend to use fillers when you give a speech, practice eliminating them in your ordinary speech. Consciously allow yourself to pause and take a breath instead of saying "um." If you can't always hear them in your own speech, ask your family and friends to gently alert you when they hear you saying the offending sound. It takes practice, but it is possible to eliminate fillers almost entirely from your speech.

7. Avoid Any Obvious Grammatical Errors, Profanity, Slang, or Inappropriate Technical Jargon Audiences should be intrigued by your presentation, not put off by it. Slang and profanity are never appropriate, and professional jargon should be avoided unless the audience is made up of people from the same profession. Remember that your most important task is to communicate your ideas to your audience. You cannot do this if your language is inappropriate.

Visual Aids in Oral Presentations

The impact you make on your audience can be enhanced by the effective use of visual aids. People do learn more easily and remember better when they are shown rather than told something. Visual aids are one of the most effective means of demonstrating a point to your audience. Even a large chart or overhead slide with your main points displayed for the listeners will help to fix your points firmly in their minds. Further, visual aids will not only help make your presentation clearer to the audience, but also will serve as an aid to your own memory. There are several different kinds of visual aids that you can use.

1. If you are discussing an object (such as the toys in my example above), bring it with you if it is large enough to be seen and small enough to be carried around. Having the actual object with you will help to attract and hold your audience's attention during your speech.
2. If you can't bring the object itself because of size or unmanageability, you may wish to provide a scale model, for example, a small version of the CN Tower or a large-scale model of the DNA molecule. A scale model will assist your audience in visualizing what you are talking about and make your presentation easier to follow.
3. If the object is impossible to bring and no model is available, other visuals such as pictures, drawings, or sketches may be used effectively.
4. Charts or graphs, large, simple, and colourful, can also support the speaker.
5. You may even use a blackboard or a flip chart while you speak.
6. Films, slides, and overhead projections may also be useful, but you must be careful not to let them dominate your speech.
7. If your speech discusses how to do something or how something is done, demonstrate the process step by step, using real objects, models, or clear diagrams wherever possible.

Guidelines for the Use of Visual Aids

1. Decide on the type of visual aid you will employ (model, demonstration, chart, drawing, photograph, list of main points, etc.) and prepare it in advance. If you are using a blackboard, you may wish to write most of your material before beginning your speech.
2. Whatever visual aids you choose, be sure that they are clear and understandable enough to be easily followed by your audience. Complex or overly detailed visuals will do nothing to clarify the information you are presenting and may just confuse your audience.
3. Your visuals should be large enough to be seen by your audience. A 3" × 5" photo from your album may be interesting to you, but is unlikely to be of any value to your audience members who cannot see it from their seats. Also, it is difficult to keep your audience's attention while you pass around small photos or models. You will want to keep their eyes and attention fixed on you.
4. Show your visual aids while you speak about them (believe it or not, some people forget to show their carefully prepared charts, drawings, or models at the appropriate moment because of nervousness or poor planning) and be sure to speak about them once you have displayed them. Nervous or inexperienced speakers sometimes display very intriguing-looking visuals and forget completely to refer to them during the presentation. Neither let your visuals take the place of your words nor assume that they speak for themselves.
5. Visual aids should be used sparingly — don't overwhelm your audience with so much visual material that your presentation is lost. Remember that these are aids to your presentation and should not substitute for an effective presentation. The speaker remains the focal point in an oral presentation and

all visual aids should enhance that presentation. Too much visual material can detract from your presentation, and visual aids cannot by themselves serve as a substitute for an effective presentation.
6. While showing your visuals, remember to speak to the audience and not to the picture or chart you are discussing. Avoid turning your back to your audience as you speak so as to maintain your relationship with the audience at all times through your speech. Be especially careful of this point if you are using a blackboard or flow chart as you speak.
7. Practise using the visual aid when you practise delivery of your presentation.

The Importance of Practice

Once you have organized your presentation and selected and prepared your visual aids, the next step is to practise your delivery. If you can, set up conditions as close as possible to those in which you will be speaking. Have a friend or someone else you trust listen to your presentation and give you honest feedback. If you have access to a video camera, have your presentation taped and then watch it for ways to improve. You cannot do a really good presentation without practice.

Actually deliver your presentation several times, out loud, to master your timing, your command of your material, your delivery, and your use of visual aids. You will have enough to worry about as you step up to speak, without worrying about your command of the material. You will feel much less nervous if you are well prepared and can concentrate on projecting a positive, confident image. Practise delivering your speech out loud until speaking about this topic is as natural to you as breathing, but stop before you begin to memorize particular turns of phrase. Your audience will be able to spot a memorized presentation, and the quality of your speech will suffer for it.

In addition to improving your delivery, practice will also tell you whether your presentation fits the time you've been allowed. Think about how much time you have: a short time limit means you'll have to be selective about the details you include. On the other hand, you will need to make sure that you have enough material to fill the time you have. As I write this, I have just awarded the first failing grade to a five-minute speech assignment in my communications class. The time came in at two minutes and twenty-five seconds. The speaker had done practically no research and had chosen a poor topic. Don't let this happen to you. Practise your delivery, to be sure you have estimated correctly how long your presentation will take. You don't want to be in the uncomfortable situation of running out of material, or of being cut off because your speech is too long. If your speech comes out too long, cut some material out. If it's not long enough, you will need to develop your points with further research. Don't wait until the morning of your speech to find out that you didn't prepare properly — practise in enough time to make any adjustments that are needed.

When you are practising, **do not write out your presentation in full**. If you do this, you will have a tendency to read it during practice, or to memorize it, either of which will deaden your delivery and almost certainly bore your audience. Practise from the card you intend to use when you finally give the presentation; by the time of the presentation it will be familiar to you and will serve as an additional aid to memory, resulting in a much smoother presentation.

Always practise speaking from the single note card that you intend to use in the final speaking situation.

points to remember

In summary, an oral presentation needs as much care and attention in its organization and preparation as a written report. Here, briefly, are the things to remember when getting ready for a presentation.

1. If you can, choose a topic or aspect of a topic that you are interested in and familiar with; in a professional context you will be speaking about some aspect of your work.

2. Focus your topic to suit your audience, according to their needs, their expectations, and their prior knowledge.

3. Tailor your topic and your approach to the purpose and the setting of the presentation.

4. Prepare your topic so you can cover it adequately in the time you have been allotted for speaking.

5. Select and prepare at least one appropriate visual aid.

6. Practise your delivery, practise your use of visuals, practise your timing!

7. Remember that every element in your presentation should support, and not detract from, your presentation. Avoid inappropriate gestures, mannerisms, or visual items that will distract your audience from the message.

Whether you are presenting your report orally or in writing, you must prepare thoroughly and organize carefully.

sharpening your skills

1. Prepare a briefing on *one* of the following topics, making sure it is no more than ten minutes long and employing at least one visual aid.

    a. Proposal for in-house magazine (see page 126).

b. Proposal for training workshop in report writing (see pages 112–124).
   c. Your research into your program as offered at other institutions (see page 111).
   d. Your research into a topical issue in communication (see page 127).

2. Prepare a ten-minute presentation for your classmates, employing at least one visual aid, in which you provide them with tips on *one* of the following.
   a. Incorporating visual data into a report presentation (briefing or written format).
   b. Applying report-writing organization to a specific report situation.
   c. Conducting library research for a report on any topic (identify a specific topic and show samples).
   d. Distinguishing between a proposal and an ordinary report in purpose and organization.
   e. Writing a self-evaluation report.
   f. Organizing presenting a briefing.

3. Choose a topic that you are interested in and knowledgeable about, and prepare a five-minute presentation for your classmates, employing at least one appropriate visual aid and providing some information that your audience is not likely to know already.

4. Prepare a five-minute persuasive speech in which you advocate that your audience read a book or magazine you have read, participate in an activity or hobby you enjoy, join a club to which you belong, or try a product, tool, or study method that you have found useful. Be sure to focus on your purpose (moving your audience to the requested action) and explain the benefits to the audience of doing what you suggest.

online exercises

1. Many people find public speaking very frightening, but there are steps you can take to minimize your fears. Travel to the Cosnett Associates' "Presentation Laboratory" at the Salesdoctors magazine Web site, **salesdoctors.com/cosnett/index.htm**, where you will find two postings dealing with presentation anxiety ("Presentation Anxiety I: Physiological Interventions" and "Presentation Anxiety II: Psychological Interventions"). What strategies do the authors recommend for dealing with the fear of public speaking? Which ones do you think will be most useful for you? Prepare to discuss these suggestions with the rest of the class.

2. Breathing properly can help you to speak with more ease and confidence, but how do you go about practising to breathe? Get some advice on "Proper Breathing for Powerful Speech" from broadcaster and public speaking consultant Steve Ryan. You will find his article at **salesdoctors.com/ryan/ryan03.htm**. After reading the article carefully, practise the breathing exercises Ryan recommends (you will probably want to do this at home!). Discuss your experiences with the rest of the class.

3. One of the most powerful tools you have as a speaker is your visual presence, an element that can be enhanced by effective visual aids. You will find some helpful advice on "Preparing Slides," part of the Web site *Giving a Talk*, prepared by Frank Kschischang a professor of Electrical and Computer Engineering at the University of Toronto. Locate Dr. Kschischang's advice at **www.comm.toronto.edu/~frank/nobots/guide/guide3.html**. What is the most important single quality of an effective visual aid? Why?

4. In his essay "How to Improve Your Presentation Skills," **www.smartbiz.com/sbs/arts/bly17.htm**, Robert W. Bly offers some sensible advice for public speakers on preparing and timing a speech, organizing information, and practising for effective delivery. What advice does Bly give that is not presented in this chapter? What details does he leave out that this chapter addresses? Are there any similarities between the two versions of how to prepare for a speech? What reasons can you think of for the differences between the two? Be prepared to discuss these issues with your class.

chapter 7

The Job Package

LEARNING OBJECTIVES

- To learn the types of résumés, the principles of résumé format, and what to include in your résumé.
- To learn what to include in a letter of application and a letter of recommendation.
- To practise completing an application form.
- To become familiar with typical job interview situations and questions.

As your first step from school into the real world of the professional workplace, the job application package may well be the most important professional writing you will do in college. When you are competing for your first career position in a tough job market, everything depends on the impression your application makes, so it must be as professional — and effective — as possible.

Like all other professional communication, the job application has a clear, specific purpose. In it (perhaps more than in any other kind of professional writing), you must recognize and respond to the reader's needs. The job application is a special kind of persuasive document; your task is to convince the employer of your suitability for a position in the organization or agency to which you are applying. You must focus not simply on what you have done or what *you* consider most important, but on what your prospective *employer* wants, expects, or needs to hear, and you must tailor your presentation to suit the job you're applying for. You can figure out what the employer is interested in by taking time to read the job advertisement carefully. You can then use that knowledge to shape your application so that you emphasize the experience and skills that the employer will find relevant.

In writing an application, you normally will prepare a résumé and a letter of application, and often you will be required to complete an application form supplied to you by the employer. As well, you will no doubt have someone write a letter of recommendation on your behalf, so it's important to know what such a letter should contain.

The Résumé

A résumé is a kind of biographical summary that you prepare for an employer. It outlines the information he or she would likely want or need to know regarding your suitability for a job. You can think of a résumé as "you" on paper — or, at least, the professional "you" — and keep in mind that you want to make the best possible impression. Remember that the résumé and application are the first step in establishing a professional relationship with your prospective employer. In a résumé, even more than anywhere else, all the virtues of professional writing are important: understanding your reader and your purpose, and applying the Six C's of professional writing — completeness, conciseness, clarity, coherence, correctness, and courtesy.

Visual impact (layout) also makes a big difference as to how you will be perceived. A pleasing balance between white space and print is important; a résumé should display its important information without crowding or obscuring any part. As you have already discovered, effective layout actually assists in communicating your information — it's part of your organization. As you recall from Chapter 3, another feature of an attractive and readable layout is the font you choose. Since readability is especially important in an application, you will most likely want to choose a font that is easy on the eye. In general, a serif font (such as Times) is easier to read than a sanserif font (such as Helvetica), a script-style font, or a gothic font. Choose a serif font for your résumé, and use the same font for your letter of application so that the two will be visually unified.

The résumé introduces you to the prospective employer and should make that employer want to speak with you. That is its only function, and you will be called for an interview only if it fulfils this purpose effectively. For this reason, it should make a very good impression.

Types of Résumé

There are three main types of résumé: the *functional* (or skills-oriented), the *chronological*, and the *analytical* (or crossover). The functional résumé is sometimes recommended for people who have little formal education or experience; it emphasizes employable skills instead of positions held or training completed, so it may obscure gaps in an employment or education history.

However, there are a couple of problems with this kind of résumé. First, it often contains no dates, names, or locations that can be verified, so its claims appear unsubstantiated. What is worse is that, because it is commonly used when the applicant's background is sketchy, employers may assume that a functional résumé is being used to cover up undesirable information and may become suspicious about what is left unsaid. Thus, while this format may serve the *writer's* needs — to make a lack of experience or gaps in work history less obvious — it doesn't usually provide the details an employer needs to make an informed assessment. As a result, because it does not effectively serve the needs of the reader, this kind of résumé may be set aside without much consideration. A sample functional résumé (Figure 7.6A) is included in this chapter for your consideration, though for all these reasons it may not be the best form to use.

The chronological résumé is more widely used and generally accepted than the functional: it presents your training and experience chronologically, always beginning with the most recent and working backwards. The information is organized under fairly standard headings and focuses on facts and details, without elaboration or interpretation. Employers usually prefer this chronological organization over the functional format because it shows the applicant's relevant experience and provides details of dates and names that may be verified.

Because it accommodates the employer's expectations, the chronological format is generally a better choice than a strictly functional résumé. However, neither of these is perfect. The brief bare-facts outline provided by the chronological résumé alone may not be enough to convince a prospective employer to take a closer look at the applicant. The competition for good jobs is always intense, and many employers want more of a "sense" of the applicant before the interview. For this reason, the analytical or crossover résumé (which is a blend of the chronological and functional approaches) is frequently a better choice. Because it combines the strengths of both forms, the analytical résumé accommodates both the employer's needs and the applicant's background. This is the résumé style you will learn in this chapter.

The Parts of a Résumé

A résumé contains a survey of an applicant's education, work history, achievements, and skills. Many people assume that a résumé should simply list every job-related experience you have ever had, no matter what it is, but as you know by now, simply including every detail indiscriminately is not enough. A résumé, like other forms of professional writing, is a form of communication with a very specific purpose. It is effective only if it gets you an interview, and since it is the *reader's* needs that will determine who is interviewed, the résumé should be designed and focused to meet those needs. Although the résumé does contain standard sections, its contents are to some extent flexible, and what you choose to include will depend partly on your experience and the position you are seeking. All résumés should include sections for personal information, education, employment, and skills. Experience and education are always arranged in reverse chronological order (that is, starting with the most recent and working backwards in time). A few additional categories, discussed below, may be useful if they are relevant to your background and to the new position. The following is a list of categories usually included on a résumé.

Personal Information

Always begin with your name, your address, and a phone number where you may be reached. You may also wish to include your e-mail address and a Web-site address if you have them. Do not include an e-mail or Web-site address that will soon be defunct, however; for instance, if your e-mail and Web site are college accounts that will become defunct after you graduate, do not invite your prospective employer to contact you this way if you are close to graduation. You will notice from the recommended examples that personal information should be displayed in an appealing position on the first page. You may wish to use a desktop publishing program to design an appealing personal letterhead to use as the first page of your résumé document. This type of letterhead can be very effective if well designed, but you should avoid cutesy graphics and combined effects such as boldfacing, italics, block capitals, and underlining. A slightly conservative effect is more professional than one that displays a whole range of visual effects in a single heading.

Personal details such as age, height, weight, social insurance number, state of health, marital status, and citizenship are no longer considered appropriate for inclusion on a résumé, though in the past they were commonly included and are still occasionally recommended by people who are working with outdated information. If, despite these guidelines, you wish to include such information, place it near the end of your résumé — don't take up valuable space on the front page. You definitely should not include such sensitive information as religious affiliations and racial or cultural origin, unless, of course, they have some direct bearing on the job for which you're applying. As a general guideline, leave out any personal information that has no bearing on your ability to perform the job or that may invite prejudice; if a piece of information is not a strength, don't put it into your résumé.

Career Objective

The career objective statement, a phrase or sentence that states your career aspirations, is an optional part of a résumé. If your cover (application) letter is well focused and your experience is directly related to the job you're seeking, you may want to leave out the career objective, since in that case it would be redundant. Recent graduates of a college program that has specifically trained them for the position they seek may find a statement of objective unnecessary. However, a career-objective statement can be useful if your experience is diverse; in this case, an accurate, well-worded career objective can focus your background. Here are some instances in which a career-objective statement can prove useful.

- If you are aiming at a *specific* position or type of position and are not interested in any other kind of work, you may wish to focus on this aim in your career objective.

- If you have spent some time out of the workforce — to raise a family or to travel, for example — a career objective can explain the gap in your employment history.
- If you are changing careers, this statement can serve as a link between your aspirations and your previous experience.

If you decide to use a career-objective statement, you must be clear and specific; avoid such statements as "I am seeking a challenging position that will make use of my skills and offer room for advancement." Can you think of any candidate in any job competition for whom this would *not* be true? Such a vague statement takes up room without adding anything valuable to your résumé and is better left out.

Education

For a student or a recent graduate, information about your education usually comes immediately after the personal information, because it is your most recent, and likely most relevant, experience. Once you have been working in your field for a year or two, you will likely want to place your employment history before education on your résumé, because by then it, and not your education, will have become your most recent and most relevant experience.

All dated information is given in reverse chronological order so that emphasis falls on the most recent and most relevant experience. Your educational history should include the following information, beginning with the most recent experience: dates attended; name and location of institution; diploma, certificate, or degree obtained; and some brief detail about your particular program of study. Mention grades only if they are outstanding.

List everything back to (and perhaps including) high school, but no further. As well, if you have taken more than one diploma or degree following high school, or if you have been working for a period longer than two years following graduation from college or university, you should consider leaving out even high school. Be selective: remember that the employer needs to know only what is relevant and useful in making the decision to interview you.

Employment History

Beginning with your most recent position, state your employment history in reverse chronological order, including dates, place of employment, job title, and duties. Provide a quick outline of the job, emphasizing any skills you could bring to the new position. Again, always be forward-looking, focusing on the skills that will be needed in the job you want rather than on those demanded by your old job. You may cluster similar or related jobs if you have had a series of them, or even delete some less important or irrelevant jobs. For example, if I have worked as a sales clerk in three different clothing stores over a period of two years, I may present this work as a single entry because all three positions were similar. I should list the dates from the point I began my first position until I left my last position, then provide the job title (for example, Sales Personnel) and the names of all three employers. This strategy can save valuable space on the résumé if you have a lot of information to include, and is demonstrated on the résumés of Gabe Praskach and Rachel McLardy, later in this chapter. In all cases, emphasize skills or knowledge that are relevant to the job you seek.

Skills

A segment that elaborates on your skills can be a very useful device, especially for a recent graduate who may have little directly relevant employment experience. In such a section you have an opportunity to emphasize your relevant skills, regardless of your past experience. Depending on your preference and the kind of experience you bring to the job, you may wish to retitle this segment as *Areas of Ability*, *Areas of Expertise*, *Special Skills*, or *Employable Skills* instead of simply *Skills*. Whatever its title, however, this section allows you to target your abilities to the job you're after. Employers want to know that they are hiring someone who does more than meet the minimum qualifications; they want assurance that the candidate they are considering is the best choice from among applicants with similar training or experience. For this reason, including an effectively targeted skills section on your résumé may give you the edge over other applicants of similar background. You should take full advantage of this chance to promote your unique combination of skills, but make sure this segment of your résumé is focused for the job you seek.

It can also be a good idea to cluster your skills under subheadings of some type, as demonstrated in some of the sample résumés that follow. You will notice a variety in the ways that the skills are clustered and presented in the samples; each person has selected a method that shows his or her skills to best advantage and that best suits the job sought. Like the writers of the sample résumés, you should choose the format that displays your skills and experience most effectively. Though you may place your skills section at the beginning of your résumé, most people prefer to put it at the end where it supports the information given in the rest of the résumé. The prospective employer then comes on it after reading the details of your employment and education history.

Skills are generalized abilities that may be transferred with relative ease from one situation to another, and there are three main areas in which any employer is interested. These classifications will give you an idea where to start when grouping your own skills. Claim for yourself only those skills that you can demonstrate with an example. As you list your skills, be sure you can identify and describe a situation in which you demonstrated each one. An employer may ask you for such an example in an interview.

1. Specialized Skills Nearly all jobs require some type of specialized skills necessary to the efficient performance of the job duties. These might be highly technical, such as operation of equipment (computers, for example), knowledge of specific procedures (such as CPR, client assessment, or bookkeeping), mastery of certain kinds of software packages (Web design, desktop publishing, or statistics packages), or any other specialized ability (public presentation, training skills). Do you have the skills required by the job you are applying for? You should state them clearly on your résumé.

2. Practical Skills General work-related skills can also set you apart from others with similar education or experience. Although all the applicants for a given position may be trained in the field, not all are equally competent. Employers want to be assured not only that you can do what the job requires, but that you can do it efficiently and well. In this category you might include such qualities as punctuality, conscientiousness, organizational ability, problem-solving skills, ability to work to deadlines, and efficiency. These qualities emphasize how you handle tasks in the workplace. Again, be sure you can think of a specific example from your past experience that illustrates each skill you name, in case you are asked for one in an interview.

3. Interpersonal Skills The third area of concern for an employer is how well you will get along with your clients, co-workers, and supervisors. Interpersonal skills include such abilities as tact, diplomacy, leadership, motivational skills, cooperation, and teaching ability. Essentially these skills are concerned with how well you handle your professional relationships with people. Employers do not want sarcastic or complaining people to join their staffs. As with the previous categories, be prepared to provide evidence of your effective interpersonal skills if called upon to do so.

4. Artistic Skills If they are relevant to your line of work, you may wish to include such abilities as drawing, design, painting, and photography. If you will need to demonstrate your skills in these areas, you should prepare a portfolio of your work to bring with you to the interview. Your instructors in art and design courses can show you how to do this.

References

Prepare a list of two or three names of people who are willing to provide references for you. Opinion is mixed about whether you should include these references with your résumé. Some employers I have spoken with are suspicious of an applicant who does not automatically volunteer references, even when he or she promises to supply names "upon request." Others say they are not concerned about receiving the list of references until after the first interview is completed, because they normally do not contact references until that time, and then only if the candidate is to be offered a job. Still others put no stock in solicited references at all.

In light of such divided opinion, what should you do? All of the employers I spoke with agreed that providing references will never hurt your chances, whereas *not* providing them may do so. Thus, it may be safest to provide them if you can.

References should be provided by former employers or others acquainted with your work, or by former teachers. Letters or testimonials from friends, family, or fellow students are not appropriate for a job search. Personal references are not very useful to employers, unless a character reference is specifically requested. You will find more information on references in the section on letters of recommendation (pages 189–192).

These are the common and essential sections of every résumé; however, there are some other useful categories that you may want or need to include in your résumé. Select any of these that seem appropriate for the job you seek, displaying your unique experience to best advantage. If none seem relevant to your experience or necessary for the job you want, you can certainly leave them out. If you have an accomplishment or experience that is relevant to your job search, but does not fit into any of the listed categories, you can invent your own heading. The résumé is a flexible instrument that you should structure according to your own individual needs and the demands of the job you seek.

Awards

List in reverse chronological order any awards received in school activities, giving dates, institutions, and titles of awards. If you have never won any such awards, leave out the whole category. If your awards are not school-related, you may want to place them in another category entitled *Achievements* or *Accomplishments*.

Extracurricular Activities

This category is useful only for students or recent graduates; once you have been working for two or more years, the relevance of this information will fade. List here any *significant* contributions to school-related activities; membership in academic or athletic clubs or teams, participation in student council, yearbook, or newspaper activities, and so on. If you did not participate significantly in such events or organizations, leave this category out. College experiences of this nature have greater longevity on a résumé than high school ones; as a general guideline, delete this section if it describes high-school experience more than three years old or college experience more than six years old, unless your achievements are especially outstanding or relevant to the job you seek, and have not been replaced or surpassed by anything else.

Additional Courses/Training

List courses or certification that are outside of your main education but that have relevance to the job you seek. Perhaps you are formally trained in corrections, but have also taken some night-school courses in alternate dispute resolution or mediation techniques. Perhaps you are a recreation administrator, but have training in computer programming, or an early childhood educator with expertise in Web design. Perhaps you have taken pilot's training, a first aid course, or training to teach swimming or music. If so, include this information on your résumé. You may not wish to include general interest courses unless they are in some way relevant to your job search. Once again, list in reverse chronological order the dates, institutions, and names of the courses.

Volunteer Experience

If you have held several volunteer positions and feel that they warrant consideration, you can create a separate category for them; if they are few (and relevant) you might want to include them as part of your employment history instead. (Be sure that you do one or the other; don't include the same items in two different categories on the same résumé!) If you decide to create a separate category for volunteer work, list in reverse chronological order any positions where you would, under other circumstances, have been paid for your work. Finally, list volunteer positions only if they contribute meaningfully to your résumé.

Community Service

Include membership in service clubs, organization of community events, or service in civic positions, if these contribute meaningfully to your résumé. It is usually considered best to leave out organizations of a strictly religious nature, unless the job you're seeking is religiously oriented. List dates, name, and location of organization, position title, and any relevant duties. If the organizations to which you belong are professional associations and are not unions (the Canadian Council on Social Development, the Canadian Communication Association, and the Canadian Healthcare Association are some examples), you can retitle this category *Professional Service* rather than *Community Service*.

Achievements/Accomplishments

Use this category to feature any relevant accomplishment not covered in any previous section. This section includes awards other than scholastic ones (for instance, Citizen of the Year), certification of some form (pilot's license or swimming instructor's certificate), publication of a book or article, or a special achievement in your work. Once again, in reverse chronological order, include date, name and location of institution, agency, or publisher, and nature of certificate, award, or publication. List such achievements only if they help qualify you for the job you seek, and title the section appropriately.

Layout

The appearance of the résumé — its visual appeal — is almost as important as its content. The résumé is seen by an employer before you are, and it should make a positive impression. Just as you wouldn't dream of going to an interview with a smudge on your face or an unkempt appearance, you should never introduce yourself to a prospective employer with an untidy or unattractive résumé. Few employers will be interested enough to interview an applicant whose résumé is poorly constructed; to them a messy résumé suggests a lazy or unmotivated individual — not, of course, the kind of person they want to hire!

An effective layout builds visual appeal by creating a pleasing balance between white space and printed elements, with reasonable margins on all sides (1" at top, bottom, and both sides is standard). A consistent format also lends a professional appearance, as it does to all professional communication: major headings should begin at the left margin, lining up neatly beneath one another. They should all be presented in the same format (all capitalized, for example, or all underlined). Subcategories should be indented so that they too line up consistently throughout the résumé, and they should also be consistently treated (all italicized, for example). Use consistent spacing between sections: for example, you might skip one line between subsections and two lines between major categories. This consistency is not only attractive, but, because the layout is also part of your organization, it actually helps the reader to make sense of the information you are presenting.

Use capital letters, underlining, or boldfacing to set apart important details, but use these features consistently and sparingly. In general, you should not combine underlining with capital letters or with boldfaced or italicized type. Other combinations (boldfacing and block capitals, italics and boldfacing, italics and block capitals) are permissible, though these too should be used sparingly and consistently to help your reader make sense of the information on your résumé. A little of each goes a long way and overuse will destroy the effectiveness of these visual devices. For example, if too much of the résumé is printed in capital letters, it is not only harder to read, but important information no longer stands out. If you have ever tried to read a textbook that someone has attacked overzealously with a highlight pen, you know how quickly any form of visual device loses its effect when overused.

In general, it is also not good practice to combine several different fonts in a single document, and you should especially avoid fonts that are difficult to read — sanserif, gothic, or script fonts are typically harder on the eye than a simple serif font and therefore are not so desirable in a résumé or application letter. Finally, be sure to choose a font in a readable size — 10- or 12- point type may take up more space, but is much easier to process visually. It is in your interest to design your résumé so that it's easy for the reader to find the information she needs to make a decision in your favour.

It should go without saying that visual appeal also means using a good quality printer, with sufficient toner or ink to produce sharp, clear type. Don't send out a résumé with faint print; the employer may simply discard the whole thing rather than struggle to read it. You should also send an original résumé, tailored to the job, with every application you submit. Any photocopies you do provide should be perfectly clean.

There are nearly as many varieties of résumé layout as there are people to give advice, but some are better than others. How can you tell a good layout from one that is not so good? A good résumé format is easy to scan for important information and should be appealing to look at. Here are some characteristics of an effective résumé format. The examples that follow meet these criteria.

An effective résumé format:

- Maintains consistent margins and uses white space effectively. Nothing is crowded or cramped, and everything is readable.

- Can be easily skimmed for main points. Use visual effects and indentation to make significant information easily available to the eye so that the reader can quickly get the gist of the applicant's work history without having to read every detail (though necessary details are given too, of course).
- Looks professional, but is also flexible enough to be arranged to suit an individual applicant.

Never underestimate the importance of an attractive layout; your communication instructor may be willing to struggle to read your résumé to the end, but an employer does not have to do so. In fact, many employers can cut down a pile of résumés from two hundred to a short list of ten or twenty by immediately discarding unattractive résumés — without even reading them. Remember that, at least initially, the reader of your résumé is seeking reasons to *eliminate* your application, not reasons to keep it.

The diagrams below illustrate the use of white space in the résumé layout. All the samples of effective résumés use the principles of good layout. One way to check the effectiveness of a layout is to hold the résumé away from you. A good layout is appealing to look at even if it is too far away for you to read the print, because the print and white space are balanced and the important information stands out from the rest of the material on the page. Study the diagrams (Figures 7.1A and 7.1B) and take a critical look at some of the résumé examples to see what makes an effective layout and what looks unattractive.

points to remember

1. Résumés should *always* be word processed (or, if you do not have access to a computer, at least typewritten). Choose a laser quality or a very good near-laser quality printer with sufficient toner or a fresh cartridge. Dot-matrix printers do not provide a sufficiently clear print for your résumé.

2. Always use good-quality paper, preferably white. A paper that has a textured surface is especially impressive. You should as a general rule avoid coloured paper, except possibly an ivory or grey; even pastels can seem garish in a stack of white or off-white résumés. Strong colours should certainly be avoided, since they will call attention to themselves at the expense of the information on your résumé. Most employers are cautious when making hiring decisions and are more likely to be impressed by a high-quality, well-organized résumé than by a brightly coloured one. Make your résumé stand out for its quality and save your flamboyance for after you've got the job.

3. Prepare an original résumé for each job you apply for. Since each job is different, ideally you will want to tailor your résumé to each new position. However, if you are applying for a number of similar positions, you may find it more convenient and less expensive to use photocopies. If you must send

figure 7.1A This sample shows a common résumé format, using only two main margins. Though it is neatly laid out, its lack of variety and large unbroken blocks of print draw the eye downward rather than into the block, making it difficult to scan the page easily. As a result, important information may be missed.

NAME:	GABRIEL A. PRASKACH
HOME ADDRESS:	2938 West Street Vancouver, B.C. V8H 3D4
TELEPHONE:	(604) 546 7890
BIRTHDATE:	October 4, 1978
EDUCATION:	
Sept. 2000–Dec. 2000	Completed the first half of the ADR (alternative Dispute resolution) certificate program with advanced standing at West Coast College, 299 Valley, Dr., Burnaby, B.C., V5G 4R5. Courses of study included: mediation, law and society, sociology, and communication.
Sept. 1998–May 2000	Graduate of the two year Child and Youth care Worker Program at Beothuk College, Murgatroyd Street P.O. Box 1234, Kamloops, B.C., V6N 4R7. Courses of study included social practices, writing effective reports, grammar and English composition, pysical intervention, interviewing and assessment, and law and social practice.
WORK EXPERIENCE:	
Mar 2000–Present	Full-time workshop Facilitator with Human Resources Development Canada, Vancouver ("Providing Services To Persons With Disabilities"). My duties included speaking to junior and high school students about issues involving disabilities and accessibility; I also facilitated workshops with HRDC staff and counsellors; and I liaised with Social services organizations and employers and educational institutions.

figure 7.1B This sample makes use of more varied margins and smaller print blocks. Important information stands out easily, especially if it is boldfaced or underlined.

GABRIEL A. PRASKACH
2938 West Street, Vancouver, BC V8H 3D4
(604) 547 7890

EXPERIENCE

Mar 2001–Present
Workshop Facilitator ("Providing Services To Persons With Disabilities")
Human Resources Development Canada; Vancouver, BC
- Speaking to junior and high school students about disabilities and accessibility;
- Facilitating workshops with HRDC staff and counsellors;
- Liaison with social services organizations, employers, and educational institutions.

Apr 1999–Aug 1999
Student Placement Officer (Students with Disabilities)
Hire A Student; Vancouver, BC
- Provided placement services for university and high school students with disabilities;
- Recommended changes to policies and procedures to increase accessibility for students with disabilities.

Apr 1998–Dec 1998
Career Centre Assistant
BC Career Development and Employment; Vancouver, BC
- Conducted career planning workshops;
- Researched occupational and vocational opportunities and resources.

June 1997–Sept 1997
Senior Camp Counsellor
Camp Martial Day Camp; Vancouver, BC
- Supervised 15 twelve-year-old boys;
- Planned activities and programs;
- Handled conflicts;
- Supervised one junior counsellor.

Jun 1996–Aug 1996
School-to-Work Transition Interviewer
Vancouver Association for Supported Employment; Vancouver, BC
- Interviewed students with disabilities to assist them with the transition from high school to full-time employment.

a photocopied résumé, however, make sure it is as close as possible to original quality. Don't ever send a blurred or smudged photocopy to an employer.

4. Don't try to cram too much information onto one page. Some experts still steadfastly believe that résumés should not exceed one page; for the most part, however, this old-fashioned principle can impose unnecessary constraints on an applicant. In an attempt to adhere to this standard, some people sacrifice clarity and visual appeal to fit everything in, producing a crowded, unattractive page that is difficult to read. A busy employer may be more inclined to discard such a document than to take the time to muddle through it or strain to read a smaller than normal font. As people change careers with greater frequency and bring more complex and varied experience to the job search, expectations for length and content must evolve. Most people applying for a permanent position nowadays would have difficulty displaying their backgrounds attractively on a single page. In a highly competitive job market, you must sell yourself convincingly, and there just isn't room enough on one page to do this.

    One employer, for example, told me that he had recently rejected an applicant for a permanent position because she had not provided enough detail in her résumé. He said that if he could offer the applicant any advice about the résumé, it would have been, "Put some information into it!" A well-laid-out, easy-to-skim résumé of two pages is, of course, preferable to a crowded, unreadable document of one page. You will want to keep your résumé from becoming too long, however; a new college graduate should be able to present a reasonable summary of education and experience in no more than two or three pages.

5. This may seem self-evident, but it bears repeating: a résumé should *display your strengths*, not call attention to your weaknesses. Apart from personal information, education, and experience, the résumé is a flexible instrument that can be shaped to fit your background. Use only the categories you require, retitling them or rearranging them to fit your experience and the job you're applying for. If you find that you have experience or training that does not fit the standard categories listed, invent your own and provide them with a suitable heading.

6. Remember that all dated information in every section of a résumé is always arranged in reverse chronological order, beginning with the most recent.

7. Keep your résumé current. Before computers and word processors were widely available, the job of updating your résumé was onerous because the entire thing had to be reformatted and retyped with every change. Computer technology makes revision much easier and periodic updating relatively painless. You should bring your résumé up to date every six months, even if you are not currently applying for work. Doing so will make the task easier when the time comes for you to seek a new job and will ensure that none of your

achievements are overlooked. You should also keep hard copies of your résumé, just in case your computer files are damaged in some way.

Sample Résumés

In the following pages, you will find a series of résumés accompanied by brief critiques (Figures 7.2A to 7.6). The first résumé of each pair is weak and in need of improvement; the second is an improved version.

The first set belongs to Rachel McLardy. Look carefully at both versions and at the commentary for each; can you see any additional weaknesses that Rachel could improve?

Comments: Figure 7.2A There are several problems with Rachel McLardy's first résumé. Like most strictly functional résumés, it makes a series of claims but provides no way for the employer to verify details. No names or locations are given, and the dates are too vague to be helpful. An employer is more likely to be put off than reassured by this sketchy history and will likely wonder what Rachel is hiding. This résumé was prepared for Rachel by an employment agency. It could be more attractively presented and more clearly focused to the employer's needs. Notice how much space is wasted on the first page just on the name and address information. As well, Rachel's unfocused list of skills should be edited toward the job she is applying for. In addition to its faults in presentation, the résumé also contains errors in spelling, grammar, and sentence structure which reflect badly on Rachel, even though she didn't write the résumé herself. Rachel was educated in Saint John, NB, not St. John's, which is in Newfoundland— and her lists should be arranged in parallel grammatical construction (for instance, under "Childcare" she should use verbs throughout: "prepared, provided, supervised...").

Comments: Figure 7.2B Rachel's new résumé is in analytical format, in the chronological order that employers prefer. The average employer will feel more comfortable about hiring her now; her background can be verified because she's given specific details that provide a basis for her claims. The career objective has been made much more specific and Rachel has been selective about the skills she has emphasized, bringing them into line with the job she is seeking. The format is easier to read, with important information prominently displayed. Section headings are boldfaced to make them even more prominent.

Notice also that Rachel's name appears in the centre on the front, but to the right on the second page; this keeps her name in front of the reader and also places it in a dominant position on the page. If she wished, Rachel could rearrange this résumé to put the "Areas of Skill" first. However, such an arrangement risks being mistaken for a strictly functional résumé.

figure 7.2A WEAK RÉSUMÉ. Based on what you have learned about effective résumé content and layout, evaluate this functional résumé and point out its weaknesses.

RACHEL MCLARDY
6166 Almon Street
Saint John
New Brunswick
E3R 1T9

544 9847

CAREER OBJECTIVE

Seeking a position in a people-oriented environment in which my eagerness to learn and my energetic, responsible nature will be an asset.

EMPLOYABLE SKILLS

Organizational
 – oriented and trained new staff
 – organized clothing according to styles/sizes
 – filed invoices and receipts

Communication
 – adept at verbally communicating with people
 – able to be persuasive
 – helpful and cooperative fellow worker
 – assisted in a promotional advertisement campaign

Retail
 – handled cash transactions
 – can do inventory
 – prepare and serve lunches
 – clean and neat

figure 7.2A WEAK RÉSUMÉ. (Continued)

RACHEL MCLARDY

Childcare activities
- prepared lunches
- provide pyisical care
- supervision
- drama experience

WORK HISTORY

Duncan's Donuts – 1999-00
Beauville School – 1999
Brunswick Play Corner – 1996-99
McLardy's Grocery – 1990-92

HOBBIES AND COMMUNITY INVOLVEMENT

reading, creative writing, and costume design/production

EDUCATION

Childcare certifacite St. John's, NB
American Sign langauge – 30 hour course

figure 7.2B Rachel's new résumé features her experience in a much more positive and effective manner.

RACHEL MCLARDY
6166 Almon Street, Saint John, New Brunswick E3R 1T9
544 9847

OBJECTIVE   A responsible position in a childcare facility.

EDUCATION

1999–00   **Childcare Worker**   Thomson College
           Certificate   Saint John, NB

   This twelve-month program involved extensive theoretical and practical training with regular work in the college daycare centre.

1995   **Academic Diploma**   Calvin Wesley High
                                       Oromocto, NB

CHILDCARE EXERIENCE

1999   **Lunch Monitor**   Beauville School
                                       Saint John, NB

   Supervised school-aged children during lunch period, both inside the building and on the playground.

1996–99   **Childcare Worker**   Brunswick Play Corner, UNB
                                       Small Fry Daycare, Wetaskiwin, AB

   Responsible for all aspects of care, including supervision, physical care, and direction of games and activities. As relief staffer at Small Fry, I was on call daily. While in high school (1987-89), I provided in-home childcare for three families.

figure 7.2B IMPROVED VERSION. (Continued)

Rachel McLardy /2

OTHER EXERIENCE

Present			**Hostess** (Nights)		Duncan's Donuts, Quentin Road

1990–92			**Clerk/Cashier**		McLardy's Grocery, Oromocto, N.B.

SKILLS

Childcare:
- first aid
- CPR
- physical care
- light cooking
- program planning
- wellness

Personal:
- honest
- reliable
- conscientious
- patient

INTERESTS/ACTIVITIES

Have studied art, drama, and sign language (First level, Maritime Dialect).
Interests also include reading, creative writing, and costume design/production.

REFERENCES

Gladly provided upon request.

figure 7.3A WEAK RESUME: What tips could you give Gabriel to improved the layout of his résumé?

NAME:	GABRIEL A. PRASKACH
HOME ADDRESS:	2938 West Street Vancouver, B.C. V8H 3D4
TELEPHONE:	(604) 546 7890
BIRTHDATE:	October 4, 1977
EDUCATION:	
Sept. 2000–Dec. 2000	Completed the first half of the ADR (alternative Dispute resolution) certificate program with advanced standing at West Coast College, 299 Valley, Dr., Burnaby, B.C., V5G 4R5. Courses of study included: mediation, law and society, sociology, communication, and
Sept. 1998–May 2000	Graduate of the two year Child and Youth care worker Program at Beothuk College, Murgatroyd Street P.O. Box 1234, Kamloops, B.C., V6N 4R7. Courses of study included social practices, writing effective reports, grammar and English composition, pysical intervention, interviewing and assessment, and law and social practice.
WORK EXPERIENCE:	
Mar 2001–Present	Full-time workshop Facilitator with Human Resources Development Canada, Vancouver ("Providing Services To Persons With Disabilities"). My duties included speaking to junior and high school students about issues involving disabilities and accessibility; I also facilitated workshops with HRDC staff and counsellors; and I liaised with Social services organizations and employers and educational institutions.
Apr 1999–Aug 1999	Full time student Placement officer for students with disabilities at Hire-A-Student in Vancouver, where I provided placement services to students with disabilities and recommended policies for accessibility.

figure 7.3A WEAK RÉSUMÉ. (Continued)

Apr 1998–Aug 1998   Part-time service clerk at IGA Markets Ltd. Willow Mall, West Vancouver BC, V1H 3S8. My duties included, stocking shelves, building displays, assisting customers, bagging groceries and collecting shopping carts.

Jun1998–Aug 1998   Career Centre assistant with BC Development and Employment in Vancouver BC, where I conducted planning workshops for students seeking work and career training, and I also did research into occupational and vocational opportunities and resources for students at both the high school and the college level. This job was full time on a contract basis while I was attending school.

June 1997–Sept 1997   Senior Camp Counselor at Camp Martial day camp, Vancouver CYO, 90 Stiltser St., Vancouver, BC, V8N1S2. My duties include the supervison and care of 15 twelve-year-old boys with one junior counsellor.

Jun 1996–Aug 1996   School to work transition program in the Vancouver Association for supported Employment, I was a coucillor for students with disabilities, whom I intervieed to assist them with the transition from high school to full-time work experience.

ADDITIONAL EDUCATION

I took two workshops between 1998 and 2000, on job markets and career planning from the Human Resources Development Canada centre in Vancouver.

SKILLS AND HOBBIES

I have some understanding of computers and of what it means to be disabled. I enjoy reading science fiction and murder mystery novels and listening to music becuase I have a rather large and comprehensive collection of CDs. I also play guitar.

Comments: Figure 7.3A A very disappointing résumé from someone who is actually very capable and good at what he does. The format is rather confusing and hard to read, and it contains irrelevant details. Most of Gabe's work history is in some way related to counselling and child care, as is his education. He should de-emphasize or delete the irrelevant information to show how he has prepared himself specifically for a career in this area. Notice also that his work experience, which is more recent than his education, should come first.

figure 7.3B IMPROVED VERSION. Compare this résumé with Gabe's earlier one. How is it better?

GABRIEL A. PRASKACH
2938 West Street, Vancouver, BC V8H 3D4
(604) 546 7890

EXPERIENCE

Mar 2001–
Present

Workshop Facilitator ("Providing Services To Persons With Disabilities")
Human Resources Development Canada; Vancouver, BC
- Speaking to junior and high school students about disabilities and accessibility;
- Facilitating workshops with HRDC staff and counsellors;
- Liaison with social services organizations, employers, and educational institutions.

Apr 1999–
Aug 1999

Student Placement Officer (Students with Disabilities)
Hire A Student; Vancouver, BC
- Provided placement services for university and high school students with disabilities;
- Recommended changes to policies and procedures to increase accessibility for students with disabilities.

Apr 1998–
Dec 1998

Career Centre Assistant
BC Career Development and Employment; Vancouver, BC
- Conducted career planning workshops;
- Researched occupational and vocational opportunities and resources.

June 1997
Sept 1997

Senior Camp Counsellor
Camp Martial Day Camp; Vancouver, BC
- Supervised 15 twelve-year-old boys;
- Planned activities and programs;
- Handled conflicts;
- Supervised one junior counsellor.

Jun 1996–
Aug 1996

School-to-Work Transition Interviewer
Vancouver Association for Supported Employment; Vancouver, BC
- Interviewed students with disabilities to assist them with the transition from high school to full time employment.

figure 7.3B (Continued) In his revised résumé, Gabe has changed the format and rearranged or deleted some information to emphasize his training and experience in fields related to his diploma in Social Services.

Gabriel Praskach /2

EDUCATION

2000 **Alternate Dispute Resolution Certificate Program**
West Coast College; Burnaby, BC
- Studied mediation techniques and one-on-one counselling, interpersonal communication, and report-writing. Completed half the program with honours; left to seek full-time employment.

2000 **Child and Youth Care Worker Diploma**
West Coast College; Burnaby, BC
- Program included Therapeutic Interventions; Psychological Assessment Techniques; Developmental Issues; Interpersonal Skills Development; and three Field Practicum segments.

ACTIVITIES

1998– **WorkAble Committee**
Present Human Resources Development Canada; Vancouver, BC
- Served on Accessibility subcommittee;
- Prepared detailed report on accessibility: *Removing Barriers to Access in the Canada/BC Services Centre.*

WORKSHOPS

1999 **Tapping the Hidden Job Market**
Youth Employment Centre; Burnaby, BC

1998 **Career Planning for Adults**
BC Advanced Education; Vancouver, BC

REFERENCES:

Vas Gajic
Project Supervisor
HRDC
(604) 328 7473

Brenda Bergen
Career Consultant
BC Advanced Education
(604) 430 3535

figure 7.4A WEAK RÉSUMÉ. What information has Brendina included that might better be left out? What other errors make this résumé weak?

RESUME

BRENDINA JOAN REURINK
332 Braemar Boulevard, Scsrborough, ON

PHONE: 236 7890

<u>History</u>

September 1998 to Present	Attend Warden College. Enrolled in a Correctional Services course and have a 3.4 grade point average. Included a placement.
February 1998 to December 1998	Salesperson at Paint Your World, 2543 Ellesmere Rd. Scarborough, ON – assisted customers – helped co-ordinate colours – opened and closed the store – ordered supplies – decorated displays – took inventory – closed off cash – helped with maintenance of the store – made deposits to the bank
October 1997 to February 1998	Salesperson at The Painted Room, 2543 Ellesmere Rd. Scarborough, ON – duties were the same as above
March 1997 to August 1998	Salesperson at The Painted Room, 2200 Westview Mall Willowdale, ON – duties were the same as above
September 1991 to June 1996	Attended East Lake Collegiate Institute – graduated from Grade 12 – majored in Buisness
<u>Personal Information</u>	Single Birth Date – September 21, 1978

Comments: Figure 7.4A Although Brennie has little paid work experience relevant to her college program, she has ignored the strengths she does have, including two placements and relevant volunteer experience. Instead of emphasizing the weaknesses (lack of experience, repetitive unrelated jobs in the retail sector), Brennie should capitalize on the strengths that her college program and unpaid experience have given her. She has also done little to assist the employer in making sense of her background by neglecting to separate her education and her employment experience. No employer will want to work this hard to make sense of a candidate's experience.

Even in such a short résumé, Brennie has managed to include irrelevant information: there is no need to include her birth date or marital status; indeed, these things are now considered inappropriate for inclusion in a résumé. She has also mistakenly typed "Scarborough" as "Scsrborough." As well, although Brennie has placed her education first on the résumé, the amount of space she has allotted it, compared to a detailed list of duties associated with her work at the paint store, makes her studies seem unimportant. She has done little to match herself to the needs and expectations of an employer in a correctional facility or group home.

While it is true that Brennie's limited work experience poses a challenge, it is also true that she could do more to make her qualifications attractive to a prospective employer. She needs to take another look at her experiences outside her part-time jobs and make use of the valuable placement experience she has gained from her college program. Although Brennie has struggled to keep her résumé to only a page, she has done so at the expense of showing her qualifications for the job she wants. In her case, less isn't necessarily better. Her second attempt (Figure 7.4B) is a huge improvement.

figure 7.4B IMPROVED VERSION. What additions have improved Brennie's chance of securing the job she wants?

BRENNIE REURINK

332 Braemar Boulevard, Scarborough, ON M1C 2R1
e-mail: reurbr@wardcc.on.ca
PHONE: 236 7890

CAREER GOAL: An entry-level position in a minimum-security correctional facility, preferably working with youthful offenders.

EDUCATION

1999 **Correctional Services Diploma**
Warden College; Scarborough, ON
Comprehensive program included courses in Canadian criminal justice, client care, criminology, group dynamics, interpersonal communication, report writing, and security skills. I maintained a 3.4 average throughout my studies.

PLACEMENTS

1998–99 **Bow Valley Correctional Facility**
East Toronto, ON
I worked six hours per week, partnered with a full time Correctional Officer.

1997–98 **Downtown Group Home**
Don Mills, ON
I worked two full shifts per week, including overnight. The home houses six teenagers ranging in age from 12–16.

VOLUNTEER WORK

1998–99 **Telephone Counsellor**
Scarborough Distress Centre; Scarborough, ON
I was trained to handle all manner of distressed callers, including suicides. I work four three-hour shifts per month.

figure 7.4B IMPROVED VERSION. (Continued)

Brennie Reurink /2

1996   **Metro Police Ride-Along Program**
        Toronto, ON
        I participated twice in the ride-along program, in which a civilian accompanies an officer on duty

CERTIFICATES

1999   **Firearms Safety Certificate**
1998   **CPR**
1998   **Standard First Aid**

PART-TIME WORK EXPERIENCE

1997–98   **Sales Clerk** (part-time)
           Paint Your World; Scarborough, ON
           The Painted Room; Scarborough and Willowdale, ON
           I have worked part-time throughout my school years.

SKILLS

I am reliable, dependable, and resourceful. I take my work seriously and have taken every opportunity to supplement the skills provided by my college program. I have undertaken certification in firearms safety and have taken additional courses in self-defence and physical intervention techniques. I am familiar with the Canadian criminal code as it relates to the corrections system and have developed strong counselling skills.

REFERENCES

Gladly provided upon request.

figure 7.5A WEAK Résumé. Why will this person likely be turned down for an interview?

Résumé

Personal   123 Winnetonka Way
                    Blisston, Ontario
                    555-9876

Education

September 2000   Waskasoo College
to May 2001   Social Service Program
                    Cedar Falls Campus

September 1994   Waskasoo College
to January 1995   Mini Child Care Course

September 1991   Waskasoo College
to May 1993   Correctional Worker Program
                    Cedar Falls Campus

September 1992   Waskasoo College
to May 1993   Upgrading Course
                    Allendon Campus

Field Placement

September 2001   Jersey Youth Centre
to May 2002   Inner City Youth Program
                    Duties: Referrals, I.D. Verifications, Intakes, Councelling, Groups, Reception.

January 2001   Blisston Volunteer Centre
to May 2001   Community Relations, Recognition Projects, Interviewing,
                    Duties: Church Out-Reach Projects, Recruitment Projects, Office Duties.

figure 7.5A WEAK RÉSUMÉ. (Continued)

Work Experience

May 2001 to present Duties:	Ministry of Community and Social Services Valleyview Centre I provide parent relief, caring for an eight year old autistic boy.
September 1994 to 1999	Ministry of Community and Social Services Home Provider Program Duties: I provided day care in my home for five families and took a child care course through the ministry and received a certificate.
April 1993 to July 1993	Sasha Park Community Centre Seniors Outreach Worker Duties: I provided a housekeeping service for seniors.
July 1992 to August 1992	Childrens Aid Society Child Care Worker Duties: I took care of 3 children ages 13, 9, 11, while their mother was undergoing treatment for alcoholism at the Drire Clinic.

Other

May 1998 to present	Board of Directors I have been serving on a founding Board of Directors, working on the development of a housing co-operative. Excellent referrences upon request.

Comments: Figure 7.5A This is a terrible résumé for a brand-new college graduate! First, there is no name on it. Since résumés and letters of application often get separated, your name must be on the document. Also, look closely at the layout. The poor use of white space, with little distinction between main points and subpoints, combined with the lack of bold print, underlining, or indentation, make this résumé very difficult to read. The applicant has provided very little no detail about any of the programs taken, and such a lengthy listing of programs started and abandoned gives the impression of indecision; an employer might feel that this person is a quitter. Note the use of the capital "I" in place of the numeral "1." Even if for some reason you must substitute another figure for the numeral (for instance, if you were using a typewriter that did not have the numeral "1"), you should know it's customary to use a lower-case L — l — in its place. Also, there are numerous misspellings throughout this résumé, and under "Other," this candidate doesn't even tell us which Board of Directors is referred to. Employers like to see evidence of genuine knowledge of the field, something that is lacking here. The original version of this résumé was printed on a dot-matrix printer with a faded ribbon. Needless to say, faced with résumés from highly qualified candidates who have put some real thought and effort into their applications, no employer will bother to puzzle through this messy and ill-conceived résumé. It's headed straight for the round file.

figure 7.5B IMPROVED VERSION. What additions have made this résumé better than Lucy's first one?

*L*uchia *G*aschler
123 Winnetonka Way
Blisston, Ontario K0R 3R5
555-9876

EDUCATION

2000–2001 **SOCIAL SERVICE PROGRAM** — Waskasoo College, Blisston, Ontario
Program covered both theory and practice in counselling, client support, and enabling, including extensive field placement.

1988–1995 **MINI CHILDCARE PROGRAM** — Waskasoo College, Blisston, Ontario
Five-month course covered basic childcare practices and theory and certified me as a Childcare Worker.

FIELD PLACEMENTS

2001–2002 **COUNSELLOR** (Displaced Youth) — Jersey Youth Centre, Inner City Youth Program
Handled referrals, I.D. verifications, intakes, and group counselling.

January–May 2001 **COORDINATOR** — Blisston Volunteer Centre
Handled community relations and interviewing; ran various projects including Recognition, Church Outreach, and Recruitment. I was also responsible for office duties.

EMPLOYMENT

2001–Present **CHILDCARE WORKER** (Valleyview Centre) — Ministry of Community and Social Services
Provide extensive care for an eight year old autistic boy.

1994–1999 **CHILDCARE WORKER** (Home Provider Program) — Ministry of Community and Social Services
Provided ministry-certified home day care for five families.

figure 7.5B IMPROVED VERSION. (Continued)

Lucy Gaschler /2

1993 **SENIORS OUTREACH** Sasha Park Community Centre
Provided housekeeping service for seniors.

1992 **CHILDCARE WORKER** Children's Aid Society
I took over the care of three children, aged 9, 11, and 13, while their mother underwent treatment for alcoholism at the Drire Clinic.

COMMUNITY SERVICE

1998– **BOARD OF DIRECTORS** Allendon Community Association
Present **(Founding Member)** Blisston, Ontario
Participated in numerous projects, including the development of a housing co-operative.

AREAS OF SKILL

Specialized   I am experienced in therapeutic counselling, client support, group dynamics, and enabling. As well, I am familiar with the procedures and requirements of both the Ministry of Community and Social Services and the Children's Aid Society.

Personal   I learn quickly, am enthusiastic and dedicated. I am also organized and disciplined, and work effectively to deadlines.

Interpersonal   I have skill in active listening, supportiveness and questioning techniques. I can interact effectively with clients of diverse backgrounds and with other professionals.

Comments: Figure 7.5B This is a much better résumé. Lucy has given herself a better chance to be considered by her prospective employers, not only because she has corrected her errors and improved the organization of her résumé, but because she has incorporated some of the language of her profession into her presentation. This is something you should try to do whenever you can; employers of new graduates like to see the applicants correctly using the terms associated with the profession because such usage suggests both knowledge and confidence. Note that Lucy's listing of duties and activities has also been improved, and that she has deleted the long list of programs that made her sound like a quitter.

Comments: Figure 7.6A Our last résumé pair belongs to Michael Fedaj. Two acceptable versions are shown here: the first is an example of the functional format; the second, like the previous "improved" résumés, is an analytical version. In the functional approach, the skills are listed first on the résumé, whereas the analytical format places the skills following information about the candidate's education and experience. Which do you feel is the better format? Explain your assessment.

figure 7.6A FUNCTIONAL RÉSUMÉ. How effectively does Mike Fedaj's functional résumé communicate his experience to an employer?

MICHAEL MURRAY FEDAJ
PO Box 1234, Forestville, Ontario K0B 4L0
(519) 632 2791

CAREER GOAL   Developmental Services Worker in a residential facility, with the opportunity to use my training in Wellness and Lifestyle Management

RELEVANT SKILLS

Professional
- assessment
- program planning
- group dynamics
- counselling
- residential care/administration
- interpersonal communication
- effective report writing
- behaviour modification
- promotion and presentation
- learning augmentation

Personal
- honesty
- initiative
- committed
- reliability
- able to meet deadlines
- self-supporting during college

Interpersonal
- leadership
- cheerful
- cooperation
- flexible

EDUCATION

Sep. 2001– Dec. 2001	**Wellness and Lifestyle Certificate** Sir John A Macdonald College; Forestville, Ontario
Feb. 2000– Apr. 2001	**Developmental Services Worker** Sir John A Macdonald College; Forestville, Ontario

figure 7.6A FUNCTIONAL RESUME. (Continued)

Mike Fedaj /2

PLACEMENT EXPERIENCE

Feb. 2001– **Rehabilitation Assistant I**
Apr. 2001 Vanier Centre; Cedarton, Ontario

OTHER EMPLOYMENT

Apr. 1996– **Clerk/Stock Person**
Aug. 2000 IGA Groceteria; Forestville, Ontario

Jun. 1996– **General Labourer**
Sept. 1996 County of Pine Hill, Ontario

REFERENCES A list of referees is attached.

Comments: Figure 7.6B The final example is Mike's analytical résumé (Figure 7.6B). Notice how he has handled his skills segment in this version: it is written in paragraphs, but individual skills are boldfaced to make them stand out. He has used boldfacing throughout the document to make it even more scannable and easier to follow. Once again, notice the layout of Mike's background; he has not included a career objective because his training has prepared him specifically for one kind of position. Note that on this document, the education, as Mike's most recent experience, comes first.

Mike doesn't have a lot of experience, but he has just graduated from a specific career program, and he will impress an employer with his well-developed and professional résumé. It is in such a case that this résumé format really comes in handy: Mike's background might appear sketchy if he had merely listed it in a strictly chronological format.

figure 7.6B ANALYTICAL RÉSUMÉ. Evaluate Mike's analytical résumé to show how it displays the qualities of an effective résumé: visual appeal and attention to the reader's needs. In what way is it more effective than the functional format?

MICHAEL MURRAY FEDAJ
PO Box 1234, Forestville, Ontario K0B 4L0
(519) 632 2791

••••••••••••••••••••••••••

EDUCATION

| Sep. 2001–
Dec. 2001 | **Wellness and
Lifestyle Certificate** | Sir John A Macdonald College
Forestville, Ontario |

This one-semester program included Program Design and Management; Promotion and Presentation; and Physical Wellness.

| Feb. 2000–
Apr. 2001 | **Developmental
Services Worker** | Sir John A Macdonald College
Forestville, Ontario |

Program covered all aspects of Developmental Services, including Labels and Disabilities; Advocacy; Behaviour Modification (both theory and practicum); and Supervision and Administration. The program also an extensive placement component.

PLACEMENT EXPERIENCE

| Feb. 2001–
Apr. 2001 | **Rehabilitation
Assistant I** | Vanier Centre
Cedarton, Ontario |

Duties included assisting with the care of twenty-seven developmentally handicapped adults in a residential setting. My three-month employment was work experience for the Developmental Services. program at Sir John A. Macdonald College.

OTHER EMPLOYMENT

| Apr. 1996–
Aug. 2000 | **Clerk/
Stock Person** | IGA Groceteria
Forestville, Ontario |

figure 7.6B ANALYTICAL RESUME. (Continued)

Mike Fedaj /2

Jun. 1996– **General Labourer** County of Pine Hill
Sept. 1996 Ontario

AREAS OF SKILL

Technical   As a trained Developmental Services Worker, I have developed effective **assessment** and **program planning** skills. My Wellness and Lifestyle Certificate program also added practical skills in **promotion and presentation** as well as an understanding of physical, psychological, and emotional health. I have also developed some experience in residential care administration.

Personal   In both my education and my previous work experience, I have always shown myself to be an **honest, reliable** worker who takes **pride in a job well done**. I am able to take **initiative** and work effectively to deadlines. I was **fully self-supporting** during my college programs, while maintaining an honours standing in my courses.

Interpersonal   I am able to function effectively in a **leadership** role or in **cooperation** with others. I maintain a cheerful outlook and am **flexible** in dealing with other people.

REFERENCES: A list of referees is attached.

The Letter of Application

A résumé is always accompanied by a letter of application, also called a cover letter. Like all professional correspondence, a job application letter must follow the Six C's: it must be complete, concise, clear, coherent, correct, and courteous. It also follows the format of a standard letter — preferably the full block style.

Two Types of Application Letter

There are two types of application letters; both, in a sense, are proposals. As in the résumé, you are promoting your suitability for the job you want. Both types put the reader's concerns foremost.

The *solicited* letter is written in answer to an advertisement for an available position, while the *unsolicited* letter is written to an organization in the hope that a suitable position is currently, or is about to become, available. The advantage of the second, if your timing is right, is obvious: there will be less competition than for an advertised position.

Both letters perform essentially the same task, however, and may be broken down into steps. How many paragraphs each step takes will depend on the background of the individual and the nature of the job applied for.

Remember that the application letter, like all professional writing, must be carefully directed to your reader's requirements and expectations. What you might want to say is not as important as what the employer needs to hear, and what you choose to put into the letter should be conditioned by the information the reader needs to make the decision to interview you. To help determine the reader's expectations, study the job advertisement or position description carefully, and ask yourself what questions an employer will want your application to answer. The following steps can serve as a guideline; you could plan to allow one paragraph for each step, though each step may be shorter or longer than a paragraph.

Step 1 The first thing an employer will want to know upon receiving a letter is, "What is this about?" As in all professional communication, you put your main message first; begin by identifying your reason for writing. If you are answering an advertisement, state the title of the position you are applying for, quoting the competition number if there is one, and the source and date of the advertisement. For an unsolicited letter, state clearly the type of work you desire and enquire whether such a position is currently open or soon to become available. You may wish to use a "re" or subject line for both types of letters, identifying by title or type the position sought.

Step 2 The next thing the employer will want to know is, "What qualifications does this applicant have for the job?" Whether your letter is solicited or unsolicited, you should next provide a very brief outline of the highlights of your background and your reasons for applying for this position. This section need not be elaborate, since your résumé will take care of the details, but it should provide some legitimate reason why you would be a suitable candidate for the position. Remember that the purpose of the letter is to convince an employer to read your résumé, which accompanies the letter. In this paragraph, you may wish explicitly to refer the employer to the résumé.

Step 3 An employer's third concern will be what makes you the best candidate for the job. You will want to be specific about why you are more suitable than the other applicants for the position. You may choose some particularly relevant skills and details from your résumé, qualifying these with brief examples appropriate to the job you seek. This is where you really emphasize your appropriateness for the position; show the employer what you can do for him or her and emphasize your strengths.

Step 4 If you have not yet referred the employer to your résumé, do so at this stage; mention also that you have attached letters of recommendation or other documentation (if you have done so) or invite the employer to contact the references you have listed.

Step 5 Close with a strong statement of confidence in your abilities; thank the employer for considering you and ask for an interview. You might even say that you will call the employer on a specified date to set up an interview. This is a good move if you can carry it off. However, if you really can't imagine yourself making such a call, don't say that you will do so. Instead, request an interview at the employer's convenience. Provide a telephone number where you may be reached or where a message may be left.

Figures 7.7 and 7.8 are effective examples of the solicited and unsolicited application letter.

The Application Form

Completing an application form is relatively straightforward once you have written a résumé. Though it may seem initially like an unnecessary overlap in information, there are good reasons for being able to complete an application form in addition to your résumé. In some agencies, the two are kept on file in different locations: the résumé goes to the appropriate department, while the form is kept in the personnel file. Thus, some will require that you both submit a résumé and complete an application form. Some prefer only a form, because it makes comparison between applicants easier. It's a good idea to know how to complete one in case you are asked to fill one out at the interview.

Forms vary considerably in their thoroughness. The example below is quite detailed. Though a longer form may seem too demanding, it is generally to your advantage because it allows you room to communicate any special skills and

figure 7.7 This solicited letter of application focuses on the employer's needs, making it more likely to be successful.

123 Braemar Way
Blisston, Ontario
K0R 3R5

July 12, 2001

Dr. Nancy Schindelhauer, Director
Addiction Intervention Council
1702 Trutch Street
Toronto, Ontario
M6K 7Y9

Dear Dr. Schindelhauer:

RE: Addiction Intervention Counsellor I
      Competition #12-D-465

Please accept my application for this position, as advertised in *The Edmonton Journal* January 11, 2001. I am very interested in this position, and believe I have the experience you are seeking for this entry-level position.

As my résumé explains, I recently graduated from the Social Service Worker Program at Waskasoo College in Blisston. This program included numerous courses in social support, assessment, behaviour modification, and counselling. During my fourth semester, I also took an elective in addiction services. My placement experience includes work as a counsellor for displaced youth at Jersey Youth Centre, and as coordinator of programs for the Blisston Community Centre. I have worked with the Ministry of Community Services in Ontario and am familiar with government policies and procedures for the administration of community support programs. I have worked with both children and adults and am skilled in interpersonal communication and group dynamics.

I am very interested in meeting with you to discuss my future with the Addiction Intervention Council, and would be available for an interview at your convenience. I may be reached at (905) 555-9876.

Sincerely,

Lucy Gaschler

Lucy Gaschler

figure 7.8 Notice how Mike emphasizes his relevant experience in his unsolicited letter of application.

PO Box 1234
Forestville, Ont.
K0B 4L0

April 21, 2002

Dr. Iqbal Zafar, District Director
Vanier Centre
34 Centre Street
Cedarton, Ontario
K7Y 2F6

Dear Dr. Zafar:

Re: Developmental Services Caseworker

I am a recent graduate of the Developmental Service Worker Program at Sir John A. Macdonald College in Forestville and am very interested in joining the staff of the Vanier Centre, where I spent my three-month placement. I believe you will find my background of interest if you are currently looking for an enthusiastic and competent caseworker at the entry level.

I completed the Development Services program with first class honours overall, and high marks in all my courses. My interest in the overall well-being of my clients also prompted me to complete the Lifestyle and Wellness Certificate, also at Sir John A. Macdonald College. This combination of education has provided me with skills in assessment, advocacy, and behaviour modification, as well as physical wellness and lifestyle enrichment. As well, my three-month DSW placement at the Vanier Centre has only intensified my interest in working in a facility modeled on the work and goals of Jean Vanier. A letter of recommendation from Shariff Omarish, the Chair of the DSW program at Sir John A. Macdonald, is attached.

Though I am relatively new to the DSW field, I am committed to the health and well-being of the developmentally disadvantaged in our community. I am very interested in a career in a residential setting and in following the philosophy of Jean Vanier. You will find me a conscientious, dedicated, and hard-working employee. I would be pleased to speak with you about a possible position with the Vanier Centre in Cedarton, and will be available mornings at 632 2791. Thank you for your consideration.

Sincerely,

Mike Fedaj

abilities that might be overlooked on a shorter form. It can thus help you to make a stronger impression on the employer. However, it does so only if you take the time to complete all the sections carefully and fully. Use the flexibility of a longer form to showcase your unique abilities and to make yourself stand out from the competition.

Your instructor will likely provide you with a full-sized version of the application form shown in Figure 7.9. In filling out the form, complete all sections as fully as possible, taking special care to fill in areas asking for elaboration on the form's standard questions. On this form, you will find such areas under the headings "Career Goals" and "Areas of Expertise." It is important to take advantage of these sections, not only because they allow you to distinguish yourself from other applicants, but also because one of the most common employer complaints about applicants is failure to fill out forms completely.

The "additional information" questions are especially important; they are areas that you can use to your advantage, elaborating on strengths that may not have shown up clearly in the rest of the application form. Read the form carefully before completing it fully.

The Letter of Recommendation

At times, employers will ask for references from people who have known you professionally, either as employers or instructors. Sometimes you can simply append a list of names and contact information to your résumé, but at other times you may need or want to provide a written record of the person's impressions of you.

For a number of reasons it is a good idea to request a letter of recommendation whenever you leave a job or an educational institution. If you apply for a job in an area far away from your previous location, a prospective employer might not bother to phone long distance to speak to your references and may instead hire someone whose references are easier to check. A letter might be sufficient to allay this concern. As well, people who have been familiar with your work move on, retire, get promoted, or just plain forget you. A letter written when your performance is current and fresh in the person's mind is more desirable than a vague recollection written long afterward, which is unlikely to be as enthusiastic.

You should know what a letter of this type should include because you will probably be asking people to write them for you; eventually you may even be writing them for others.

A letter of recommendation is usually written by someone who knows you in an employment or educational context; these two types of reference are considered most appropriate for a job hunt. Most employers no longer accept personal references. However, if for some reason you wish to include a personal letter of reference, it should be written by someone who can evaluate you objectively

figure 7.9   A typical application form.

APPLICATION FOR EMPLOYMENT

Name: _____
           (last)   (first)   (middle)

Address: _____
_____
_____
_____
_____

EMPLOYMENT HISTORY: List in chronological order, beginning with most recent and working back.

From: _____ To: _____ Position Held: _____ Name of Firm: _____
_____
      Duties: _____
_____
_____
_____

From: _____ To: _____ Position Held: _____ Name of Firm: _____
_____
      Duties: _____
_____
_____
_____

From: _____ To: _____ Position Held: _____ Name of Firm: _____
_____
      Duties: _____
_____
_____
_____

figure 7.9 A typical application form. (Continued)

From:_____ To:_____ Position Held:_____ Name of Firm:_____

    Duties: _____

_____

_____

_____

Do you type? _____ wpm speed _____
Do you drive? _____ Licence class _____
Do you speak French? _____ fluently _____ well _____ some _____
Do you write French? _____ fluently _____ well _____ some _____

Are you computer literate? _____ If yes, explain _____

_____

_____

CAREER GOALS: Briefly describe the nature of the work you are interested in and the origin of this interest: _____

_____

_____

_____

_____

_____

_____

_____

_____

_____

_____

figure 7.9 (Continued)

EDUCATIONAL HISTORY: List in chronological order, beginning with most recent and working back.

From:_____ To:_____ Program:_____ Institution:_____ Diploma:_____

    Details:_____

_____

_____

From:_____ To:_____ Position Held:_____ Name of Firm:_____

    Duties:_____

_____

From:_____ To:_____ Position Held:_____ Name of Firm:_____

    Duties:_____

_____

RELATED ACTIVITIES: Describe any school- or community-related activities in which you have taken part, including offices held:

_____

_____

_____

_____

_____

_____

_____

_____

figure 7.9 (Continued)

AREAS OF EXPERTISE: Elaborate on the above factual material by outlining briefly any skills you have developed from your experiences, any strengths you can bring to your position, or any information not already covered above.

_____
_____
_____
_____
_____
_____
_____
_____
_____
_____
_____
_____
_____
_____
_____
_____
_____
_____
_____
_____

To my knowledge, all of the above information is true and accurate.

Date _____ Signature _____

and who will be viewed by the employer as a credible source (from the employer's point of view, credibility may be at least partly a function of the person's status in the community). A physician, a member of the clergy, or a professional in your chosen field is usually a good choice for a personal recommendation. A relative or friend would be considered biased in your favour, and therefore unreliable as a reference for a job. Remember, prospective employers want information regarding your ability to do a job; they will want this information from as objective a source as possible.

In general, an employment reference comes from a professor who knows you well, or a former employer. No matter who is writing the letter of recommendation, its contents are approximately the same. The writer of a letter of recommendation, just like any other letter writer, should consider the needs of the reader and provide answers to the questions the employer is most concerned about.

1. *How long, and in what context, have you known the person you are writing about?* The writer must indicate his or her relationship (supervisor? employer? instructor? academic advisor?) to the job applicant, and the length of time that he or she was the person's employer, teacher, or advisor.
2. *What is your estimation of this person as an employee or a professional or, if it's an educational reference, as a student?* The writer should provide some specific examples — mention grades, work completed, duties of the position, record of advancement, quality of work, or outstanding achievements.
3. *What is your estimation of the subject's personality?* Employers want to know what kind of person they are considering for a position. Will he or she get along with others? Is he or she flexible? Cooperative? Personable? Outgoing?
4. You should make a strong statement of recommendation for the person and may invite the employer to contact you for further information. If the person writing a letter of reference can't strongly recommend the applicant, he or she should not be writing the letter in the first place.

The format for a recommendation letter is like other professional letters. Naming the person about whom you are writing in a "re" or subject line will help the reader more easily identify who is being described in the letter.

points to remember

If you ask someone for a recommendation, keep these points in mind.

1. Be sure that the person approached will give you a positive recommendation; a lukewarm or unenthusiastic letter is as bad as a negative evaluation.
2. Many people are uncertain about what to include in a letter of recommendation. If the person is unsure of what to say, don't be afraid to make suggestions! Ask the person to comment upon the three major areas above and emphasize any qualities that are important to the job you will be seeking.

3. Provide your writer with the correct name and address of the person to whom the letter is addressed, if it is to be sent directly; if not, ask for a general letter addressed "To Whom It May Concern."

Figures 7.10 and 7.11 demonstrate effective letters of recommendation.

Taking Your Job Search Online

Posting Your Résumé to a Web Site

If you have a Web site of your own, you may wish to display your résumé there. If you do decide to post an electronic version of your résumé, you should make sure that the page is readable and attractive, just as you would do for a print version, using visual devices to help organize the information. One major difference, however, between the print version and the electronic version of the résumé is the potential for violations of your privacy. An employer to whom you have sent a hard copy does not have a legal right to distribute or divulge the information on your résumé to anyone else without your explicit permission. By contrast, a résumé on a Web site is vulnerable to anyone who has access to the Internet. Once you have "published" online, your work history and educational experience, along with every other piece of information contained in your résumé, are no longer private. This can be a good thing if it brings you to the attention of an employer; however, you should realize that very few serious employers will seek prospective candidates in this fashion, especially for entry-level positions. As long as potential candidates outnumber available jobs, there is really little incentive for a busy employer to cruise the Internet seeking qualified entry-level candidates; generally they will wait for the candidates to come to them. In any case, placing private information on public view can have some negative and even potentially disastrous consequences if someone decides to misuse the facts you've provided, so you should exercise some caution about what you place online. In my view, more harm than good may come from such a posting because of the potential risks involved with supplying so much information to possibly unscrupulous readers. If you decide that, despite these concerns, you would like to post your résumé on your Web site, I strongly suggest that you remove your home and work addresses and supply only your e-mail address and perhaps a telephone number (a good idea is to provide a hotlink to your e-mail address). For your own safety and security, you should not provide any information that might make you vulnerable to unwanted harassment.

Searching the Job Market Online

Although posting your résumé to a Web site and waiting for prospective employers to come to you is risky and most likely futile, the same cannot be said for using

figure 7.10 Note that this letter satisfies the questions an employer is likely to have and that it supports its claims with examples.

JYC
Jersey Youth Centre

April 12, 2001

143 Lakeview Road
Blisston, On K70 4T6
(905) 534-1914
www.jerseyyouth.ca

To Whom It May Concern:

Re: **Lucy Gaschler**

As the Associate Director of Counselling Services at the Jersey Youth Centre, I had the pleasure of supervising Ms. Gaschler during her placement from the Social Service Worker program at Waskasoo College.

Throughout her placement with us, Ms. Gaschler showed herself more than competent. She was meticulous in her record-keeping, and insightful in her assessments. Though normally a placement student is included as an observer rather than an active participant in counselling sessions, Lucy's insight was such that we encouraged her to take an active role in our counselling strategy meetings. Ms. Gaschler undertook with care all tasks assigned her, including some of the less glamorous "housekeeping" tasks, and she completed them cheerfully and efficiently.

On a personal level, Lucy Gaschler is a positive addition to any workplace. She is a thoroughly delightful employee who interacts effectively with clients and staff alike. Her conscientious good humour was appreciated by all who worked with her, and she made herself a valued member of the Jersey Centre Team.

Overall, Lucy performed well above the recommended standard for placement students, to the extent that we would be delighted to have her join our staff on a permanent basis should we have an opening available. Unfortunately, government funding being what it is, we are unlikely to have an opening in the near future. As a result, I am delighted to recommend Lucy Gaschler as an outstanding young counsellor who will certainly add much to any agency lucky enough to hire her.

Please contact me if I can be of further assistance to you in assessing Lucy's potential as a counsellor. I may be reached at the above number, or at inder_stend@Jerseyyouth.ca.

Sincerely,

Inderjit Stendhal (MSW)
Associate Director, Counselling Services

figure 7.11 — A specific letter of recommendation is addressed to a particular individual, but it covers the same kinds of material as the general letter shown above.

Sir John A. Macdonald College

Murgatroyd Street, PO Box 1234 * Forstville, ON * M6N 4R7 * (905)-5643
www.sirjamacdonald.cc.ca

Dr. Iqbal Zafar, District Director
Vanier Centre
34 Centre Street
Cedarton, Ontario
K7Y 2F6

April 12, 2002

Dear Dr. Zafar:

Re: **Michael Fedaj**

Mike has asked me to write this letter in support of his application for an entry-level position with Vanier Centre. I am delighted to recommend him very positively; as you likely are aware, Mike completed his placement at your institute and received strong evaluations from his immediate supervisor, Yokara McCarthy-Lenin.

I had the pleasure of teaching Mike in three of the core DSW program courses here at Sir John A. Macdonald. I must say I was from the start impressed with Mike's dedication and commitment to the concerns of the disabled, and with his interest in enhancing their access to community support. I also have a great deal of confidence in his mastery of the theory that underlies our approach to DSW, and in his ability to apply that theory in practical settings. I don't mind telling you that some of the program plans that Mike submitted during his stay here were among the best student work I've encountered in ten years in the program. In fact, it was this rare combination of commitment and skill that led me to assign him a placement at the Vanier Centre, which is one of our "plum" placement opportunities.

If Mike has a flaw, it is in his tendency to take on too much and to work himself too hard. Apart from — or perhaps because of — this quality of "over-achievement," Mike's work is invariably outstanding. I know that, should you have an entry-level opening, you will not find a more committed or reliable professional. Mike will fulfil your every expectation. I recommend him most highly for a position, and would be pleased to speak with you should you require further information about his suitability for a position with the Vanier Centre.

Sincerely,

Shariff Omarish, Chair
Developmental Services Worker Program
s_omarish@sirjamacdonald.cc.ca

the Internet as a tool for your job search. Businesses large and small now operate Web sites, and many of these maintain a listing of position openings, as do both provincial and federal governments. Most newspapers also operate Web sites, and many make their classified advertisements, including job ads, available online. Another possibility for an online job search is professional and trade journals and magazines, many of which regularly feature job ads for career-specific positions. There are also databases to which you can subscribe online, that feature current job listings in a given field (not all of these are completely reliable; you should probably make it a policy not to pay for access to job listings).

One very nice advantage of using the Internet to look for job opportunities is that you can locate openings not just locally but also in other cities or provinces, or even in the U.S. or other foreign countries. Once you've found a position that interests you, you may even be able to submit your application online by sending your résumé and application letter as document attachments to an e-mail message. If you are looking for a position in another province or country, you should probably remember that some employers may still be reluctant to consider applicants who have to travel a long distance to the interview and may for this reason prefer local candidates. Nevertheless, the access to job listings provided by the Internet can be a major convenience for the applicant. While the Internet should probably not be the only resource you use for searching out employment opportunities, it is a useful source of information that can aid you in your job search. Even if you use it only as a research tool for gathering information about potential careers, the Internet can be a valuable addition to your job-seeking strategies.

The Job Interview

If your application has been successful, the employer will be interested in talking with you about the position and will invite you for an interview. The interview is the employer's chance to get to know you in person, to determine if you are the right person for the job. In the interview, you will want to maintain the positive impression you created with your résumé and application.

A Tip on Answering Machine Messages

An employer I recently interviewed had just telephoned a job applicant, only to find herself confronted with a long and inane answering machine message. Like most busy employers, she found this exceedingly annoying and unprofessional, and she resented the waste of her time. In her opinion, and that of many other professionals, a number left for work purposes should not waste the caller's time with "humorous" messages. In this instance, the employer left no message; instead, she offered an interview to the next candidate on her list.

At least while you are job hunting, keep the message on your answering machine simple and professional. Silly messages, especially if they are long, may form a negative impression on an employer who has not yet met you. Don't risk losing an interview by frustrating someone who calls for work reasons.

Remember that the employer's first impression of you strongly influences any decision to hire you. This decision is made in many cases within the first minute of the interview, during the employer's first reaction to you; if this impression is negative, the employer may spend the rest of the interview looking for faults to justify this dislike. It's obviously in your best interest to make the employer's first response to you a positive one. You should do all you can to prepare yourself, and thus give yourself an advantage.

A successful interview, like other effective professional communications, depends partly on your preparation. Before your interview think carefully about the needs and interests of your audience — the person who may be paying your salary. What does that person want in an employee? What will he or she be looking for?

Although you cannot completely predict the interviewer's response to you, there are three aspects of that initial impression that you can control so as to make it a good one: your appearance, your attitude, and your background knowledge.

Interview Appearance and Behaviour

1. *Wear appropriate clothes.* For an interview, you should wear slightly more formal attire than you would wear on the job. For professional or office jobs, wear relatively conservative clothes: a suit is fine for both men and women, though for men a sports jacket and dress pants may serve the purpose, and for some jobs a woman may want to wear a dress and jacket. If you are applying for a labour or other blue-collar job, dress accordingly; in this situation, a suit might be considered overdressed. Your clothes should also be comfortable enough that you don't have to repeatedly adjust or fiddle with them. No matter what you're wearing, be sure you're neat and clean; avoid splashy colours or unusual hairdos, and leave the nose ring at home.

2. *Be punctual.* Arrive at the interview with a few minutes to spare, but not more than fifteen minutes early. Know how long it will take you to arrive by whatever means you're travelling and allow yourself enough time for delays. Be sure to take a watch. Occasionally, there may be a legitimate reason why you have to be late — car trouble, an accident, illness. If this happens to you, telephone the interviewer immediately to explain the situation and politely request a later interview. If you miss your interview, you should not expect automatically to be given a second chance; sometimes the employer will be unable or unwilling to reschedule, and you will just have to give up on that job. You should also be aware that even legitimate lateness may create a negative impression that damages your chances, so plan to be on time. Sleeping in or misjudging how long it takes to get to the interview are not acceptable reasons for being late.

3. *Go alone to the interview.* An interview is a formal meeting, not a social event, and bringing someone with you may cause the interviewer to question your

maturity or your awareness of appropriate professional behaviour. A confident applicant is more likely to get the job, and you won't look confident if you bring someone else along.

4. Whether you are male or female, *use a firm, confident grip when you shake hands*. Don't let your hand hang limply, but be sure not to grip too tightly either. As silly as it sounds, it's a good idea to practise your handshake with a friend before going to your first interview.

5. *Don't chew gum or smoke* during the interview, though the interviewer may do either. If the interviewer smokes, don't do so unless you are invited to. Even then you may wish to refuse. And if you are a smoker, don't smoke just before going in to the interview. Non-smoking interviewers can be put off by the reek of smoke on a candidate.

6. *Make eye contact while you speak.* Though some people avoid eye contact simply because they are nervous, this habit can make a very negative impression on an interviewer. It can suggest uncertainty or even dishonesty, neither of which will further your chances. Don't stare at the floor or ceiling or avoid meeting the interviewer's eyes; instead, make eye contact frequently and comfortably. Look away occasionally to avoid appearing overly aggressive.

7. *Speak clearly and use correct grammar.* Employers do judge applicants' intelligence and education by the way they speak, and poor grammar is one of the indicators of weaknesses in either of these areas. Avoid such pitfalls as "I seen," "I done," "I did good in that course," or "between you and I" and keep away from slang expressions.

8. *Watch your body language.* Sit comfortably without slumping in your chair or hooking your feet around the chair legs. Don't fidget, tap your fingers, or fiddle with your clothes. You should appear controlled and any of these is a clear message that you are overly nervous or inexperienced. Don't block your view of the employer, or the employer's of you, with a large briefcase or other unnecessary props. If you are carrying supporting materials in a briefcase, place the case on the floor beside you rather than in the way on the desk.

Attitude

Many interviewers agree that a good attitude is one of the most important things an applicant can bring to the interview. You should appear confident and positive. Although you will most likely feel, and the employer will expect, a little nervousness, you should try to be as relaxed and comfortable as you can. Be yourself — at your very best.

1. *Avoid bragging or overstating your abilities.* Employers, like everyone else, dislike arrogance. Be alert and attentive to questions, enthusiastic and sincere in your answers. Show a willingness to learn and grow with the organization; no matter how much you feel you already know, there is always something else to learn.

2. *Avoid one-word responses.* At the same time, don't take over the interview with long, impossibly complicated replies. Watch the interviewer for cues that will signal when to stop speaking.
3. *Show some interest in the organization* and don't be vague about what you want from your career. Employers like someone who has thought about the future and can show some direction. Indicate a willingness to work hard and start at a reasonable level. You may display ambition, but don't give the impression that you expect to run the organization.
4. *Don't appear obsessed with money, benefits, or vacations.* Don't stress how you can benefit from the position or how much you need it. Remember that the goal of the interviewer is to find out what you can do for the agency, not to hear what it can do for you.
5. *Be courteous at all times.* Don't do or say anything that could be considered rude or discourteous. Remember this especially when you enter and are met by a receptionist or a secretary: rudeness to these people can cost you the job offer, since they often are part of the screening process. Among other things, the employer wants to know how well you will get along with other people in the organization, and one measure of this is how you treat people you meet on the way in. Always remember that first impressions count!

Knowledge

Employers are interested in discovering just how well you know the duties of the position you've applied for; they will want you to demonstrate the skills that you have claimed on your résumé. You should naturally be prepared to discuss your experience, always remembering to show how it is relevant to the position you are looking for.

But there's much more on the employer's mind. Although primarily interested in what you know about the duties of the job, your prospective employer will be impressed if you can demonstrate knowledge of the mandate of the organization. Try to learn as much as you can about the firm before the interview, for example, how large it is and what products or services it offers. You can find out a little about the agency by looking in your local library or checking on the Internet. Here are some questions you might consider answering for yourself before the interview.

1. What is the exact nature of the agency — who are their clients, and what services do they provide?
2. Is it a local agency or is it a provincial or federal office?
3. How extensive is their client base?
4. How long has the agency been in operation?
5. What is their organizational style?

An annual report will give you this information and more that might be useful. If you know someone who works for the organization, try to talk to that person before your interview. If the organization has a Web site, visit it when you are preparing for the interview. It will provide you with important information about how the agency sees itself. Find out as much as you can. Though you may not be asked such questions in the interview, the more you know when you go in, the more confident you will be and the better impression you will make.

Employers' Questions

Employers also want some indication that you are self-aware, that you know yourself and have thought about your goals, and that you have realistic expectations. They will also be interested to see if you can effectively solve the problems you are likely to face on the job. They will try to determine this information through careful questioning. Though every interview is different, and interviewers have different focuses, there are some questions that occur regularly in one form or another. If you think about these before you go to any interview, and about some potential answers, you will have a better chance of handling the questions effectively. As you answer, you should try to tailor your response to fit the job you're applying for. Don't memorize a prepared answer and don't try to be something you're not. Answer fully and sincerely. Here are some samples of favourite employer questions, with strategies for answering them.

1. *Tell me about yourself.* Employers often like to begin the interview with this one, because it not only provides information about you, but it also shows something of your priorities. What you choose to discuss will tell them what you think is important. Be aware that the employer is interested primarily in information relevant to the position you've applied for. Avoid the temptation to deliver the epic of your life. A brief summary of educational and employment highlights, as they have prepared you for the job in question, will work best in answering this question.
2. *What are your strengths?* Don't be falsely modest. Take some time to identify the things you do really well; go back over the skills section of your résumé and be ready with some examples. A mature person knows what his or her strong points are and can state them briefly without either bragging or understating them.
3. *What are your weaknesses?* We all have weaknesses, and a mature adult is aware of his or her own. However, be careful when you're answering this question. Don't identify weaknesses in such a way that they are likely to make an employer think twice about hiring you: such comments as "I never finish what I start" or "I can't get motivated in the morning" won't endear you to an employer. If you have such weaknesses, of course you should be trying to correct them, but an interview is not the place to highlight them. Identify weaknesses that show you are human, but not ones that will make you sound unemployable. For example, you might (if this is true) tell the employer something like "I sometimes take my work too seriously, and don't leave myself enough time for leisure." Or you may identify a not-so-serious

flaw and immediately balance it with a positive: "I sometimes find it hard to take criticism, but even though I find it difficult I usually benefit from constructive comments." Avoid confessing really serious or negative traits, but don't say "I don't have any weaknesses" or "I don't know," and above all make sure you are sincere in your answers. An experienced interviewer can recognize phony or insincere answers and will reject an applicant she believes is misrepresenting himself.

4. *Why do you want to work for this organization?* or *Why do you want this job?* Your research into the organization will give you some information to use in answering this question; don't, however, identify pay or benefits as a primary reason for choosing this agency. Emphasize the position itself, and don't, as an acquaintance of mine did, answer by saying, "because I'm unemployed." Employers want some evidence that they are getting the best, not merely the most desperate, applicant. This question might also appear as "In what ways do you think you can contribute to our mandate?" accompanied by "What can we do for you?" You can best prepare for these questions by thinking them through beforehand and planning how you will answer. Don't memorize an answer though; it is bound to sound false or insincere.

5. *What made you choose [Corrections, Early Childhood Education, Social Services, Recreation Administration, Nursing, etc.] as a career?* There are many acceptable answers to this question, and you will have to choose your own. However, "My father [or mother] is [a corrections officer, an educator, a social service worker, a recreation manager, a nurse, etc.]" is not one of them. Neither is "I knew I'd earn lots of money." The employer wants to know that you've made a thoughtful choice, not just an expedient one.

6. *What was your favourite subject in college, university, or school?* You may wish to identify one or two subjects, but watch out for the other half of this question, which asks you to identify the subject(s) you disliked. You may indicate that there were some subjects you liked better than others, but you should avoid sounding like a complainer. Instead of identifying courses you couldn't stand, indicate that you learned something from all of them, even the ones you didn't particularly enjoy.

7. *How would your friends describe you?* This is another way for an employer to find out a bit about your self-awareness. You should not be overly modest. Again, try to identify real strengths, but avoid sounding arrogant.

8. *What would you like to be doing in five years? ten?* Employers can find out how much thought you've given to your career with this question. They may also be looking for evidence of a commitment to the organization. If you say that you're not planning to stay in this job, or in this field, an employer may not want to spend the time or money on training you for the position. Answering "I don't know" isn't a good idea either; an employer might consider it a sign of indecision or immaturity and it could cost you the job. Try to show that you have given some thought to the future, but that you are flexible and able to adjust your goals as well.

9. *Do you have plans to further your education? Would you be interested in doing so?* Your answer here could depend on whether the employer is wondering if you're open to more training or afraid you'll quit the job in six months to return to full-time study. You should never close any door on yourself. You could indicate that you are willing to take further training if necessary. Even if you don't think right now that you would ever go back to school, remember that with time you might change your mind. On the other hand, you might also want to reassure the employer that you're not going to quit this job as soon as you're trained in order to return to school.

10. One type of question that is often favoured by employers is the situation question. The most common type is one in which the interviewer gives an example of an incident that might happen to you on the job and asks for your solution. There isn't any way to prepare for this question; it's designed to test your awareness of the job's requirements. You might try going over your experience in your memory. Think of difficult situations you have faced and how you handled them; analyze how you might have handled them better than you did. If you consider in advance how you might answer such a question, you will be better prepared for it. The question may also appear in another form, such as:

    Give me an example of a situation in which you showed leadership.
    Tell me about a situation in which you resolved a difficulty.
    Tell me about a situation in which you initiated change.
    Tell me about a situation in which you handled criticism.
    Describe an achievement you are proud of.

11. These questions might also be phrased evaluatively. Instead of asking for an example, the interviewer might simply ask you to outline your capabilities using such questions as:

    How well do you handle pressure?
    How do you handle criticism?
    Are you able to handle change?

    You should always support your answers with brief, specific examples from your work or educational experience.

12. The employer might also probe your attitude toward others with such questions as: *Are you usually right? Are other people's ideas as important as yours?* Of course, you will want to show some openness to others' views and not indicate that you believe only you are ever correct. Provide some balance in your answer: you're not always right, naturally, but you are not always wrong either. You must show that you are capable of making decisions, but that you can also recognize good ideas that others put forward and can compromise. You might also be asked:

    Do you make mistakes?
    How do you handle those?
    Can you give me an example?

Naturally you will want to show that you are aware that you can make mistakes, but also that you can learn from them. If you say you do not make mistakes, the interviewer will reject you outright, because of course we all make errors from time to time, and the measure of us is in how we handle the errors we make.

13. *How would you describe a good [manager, teacher, counsellor, corrections officer, etc.]? What will make you a good [manager, teacher, counsellor, corrections officer, etc.]?*
An acquaintance of mine, unnerved by the interview situation, once answered the latter question with, "I don't know; I just do it!" By now, of course, you know that's not an appropriate answer; a good answer should be thought out beforehand in a way that's relevant to your program or profession.

In answering any of these questions, keep in mind the probable needs and interests of all employers: they will be looking for someone who is confident and capable, but not arrogant or self-absorbed. Admit to mistakes, but show that you have learned from them and can handle criticism effectively. Be honest and not overly modest; be confident but not arrogant. Show that you have both strengths and weaknesses, but that your weaknesses are not serious and can be overcome. Don't cite weaknesses or flaws in character that are likely to damage your employment chances.

Some Reasons Why People Don't Get Hired

Of course, there are many reasons why people aren't hired, some of which you may not be able to control; however, there are some elements that you can control. The following are some of the reasons employers have given for turning down applicants.

Arrived late to the interview.
Dressed inappropriately.
Was poorly groomed.
Was rude to the receptionist.
Seemed unduly nervous.
Fidgeted; did not appear relaxed or confident.
Didn't answer questions fully; rambled on too long.
Could not provide examples to support claims in the résumé.
Attempted to dominate interview.
Was over-confident, arrogant, or self-important.
Criticized former employers.
Appeared more interested in pay and benefits than in work.
Chewed gum.
Was unable or unwilling to provide references.
Spoke poorly, with poor grammar or diction.
Had a limp handshake.
Knew nothing about the organization or was uninformed about the profession.
Was unfamiliar with current trends in the profession.

Had exaggerated on the application or résumé.
Had ambitions far beyond abilities.
Had no clear goals or professional interests.
Appeared whiny or unmotivated.
Could not admit to weaknesses or mistakes; tended to blame others.
Was defensive when answering questions.
Was unwilling to start at the bottom.
Lacked courtesy; was rude or ill-mannered.
Had a poor school record.
Appeared insincere or glib.
Lied on the application or résumé.

What to Expect

Interviews can vary not only in the type and number of questions that employers ask, but in other ways as well. There is no set pattern for interviews and no "right" way to conduct them with respect to length or number of screenings. Employers tend to decide for themselves what selection process best suits their needs, and the more interviews you go to, the greater variety you will see.

For example, the length of time you spend in an interview may be anywhere from twenty minutes to two or even three hours, depending on the type of position and the number of applicants. (An acquaintance of mine recently attended an interview that lasted seven hours! The last one I went to stretched over two days.) Often the person who telephones you to set up the interview will indicate how long it will take; if she or he doesn't volunteer the information, ask for an estimate of how long the interview will last. If you're not sure, allow yourself at least two hours, just to be safe.

You may be interviewed by one person, by two or three together, or even by a committee of five or more. Again, you may be told this ahead of time. But whether you are told or not, be prepared for the possibility that you may be interviewed by a committee; the more responsible the position, the more likely there will be more than one interviewer. In some organizations or institutions, two or three people interview you separately, then compare impressions. These may take place on the same day (you may spend twenty to forty minutes with three different people successively) or on subsequent days. This is neither a good nor a bad sign; it merely shows the employer's personal preference.

In any of these cases, don't be thrown off by interviewers taking notes while you speak. Remember that they have seen several different people in a short space of time and are merely interested in keeping track of what was said. It's really for your benefit — you wouldn't want an interviewer to forget you or confuse you with someone else.

Sometimes, depending on the employer and on the position, you may be asked to complete some form of testing. Occasionally these tests will be vocationally specific — office clerk applicants may have to take a keyboarding test, drivers may be asked to operate a vehicle, or trainers may have to give a sample lesson. In these cases, the interviewer is interested in knowing that you really do have the level of skill needed for the job.

There are other kinds of tests that you may be asked to take: general aptitude or even psychological tests. These are tests you can't really prepare yourself for; they are thought to reveal your general intelligence, attitude, or aptitude for the position you are interested in. Like all trends, aptitude testing goes in and out of favour, and is used more in some fields than in others. Even when they are popular, such tests are not universally employed by all organizations. However, employers who choose to use aptitude testing generally believe it is useful. Your best bet if you are asked to write one of these is to be as honest and forthright as you can. Most of the tests are designed to double-check your responses by asking several questions aimed at the same information, so keep in mind that it's difficult to try to second-guess the tests. Fudged answers can usually be identified by the cross-questions. Simply try to relax as much as possible and do your best. There is nothing to be frightened of, and you will do better if you can keep from being too upset.

There is much talk these days about poor writing skills among college and university graduates, and many employers have expressed concern over such weaknesses. As a result, occasionally an employer will ask applicants to write a piece of professional correspondence — a letter or a memo — right on the spot, in response to a situation such as the ones given in the chapter on letters and memos. You should be prepared to write if necessary; you might review the chapters on the letter and the memo before you go to the interview. In this case, the employer will be looking not only for proper letter or memo format, but also more importantly, for correct grammar and sentence structure, and the other Six C's of professional writing.

You should also know that not all interviewers will be equally skilled. In some agencies, interviewing is typically conducted by skilled personnel specialists, but this isn't always the case. Frequently, in fact, you may be interviewed by the immediate supervisor or even by the person who is vacating the position you are applying for. Since interviewing people is not their area of specialization, they may be inexperienced at the task, sometimes enough that you will be able to detect their uncertainty. However, if you find yourself in such a situation, maintain your cheerful, positive demeanour and answer each question to the best of your ability. Don't let the interviewer's lack of experience make you overconfident or arrogant. Unskilled interviewers are likely to be more sensitive to such nuances than an experienced interviewer would be, and possibly more easily intimidated. They will not appreciate challenges to their authority, however subtle. Maintain your poise and do your best with the questions you are given.

Problem Questions

Employers are no longer permitted to ask an applicant questions that will solicit information about age, marital status, religious affiliation, ethnic background, or family relationships. It is illegal to do so, but occasionally you will encounter an interviewer who asks you such questions anyway, either because of inexperience or because of deliberate disregard for the law. You are obviously not obliged to answer such questions, but refusing to do so may be awkward and could cost you the position.

The decision to answer such queries or not is a personal one, based on your own comfort level. If you don't mind a question about marital status, you may wish to answer it even though, strictly speaking, it's not appropriate for the employer to ask. Sometimes such questions are unthinking expressions of other employer concerns; when this is the case, you will sometimes be able to determine the employer's train of thought from the context of the remark. An employer may really be thinking about overtime and may ask about your marital status because he or she feels overtime might be more difficult for a person with a family. You may choose to phrase your response to address the employer's concern directly. For example, a prospective employer may ask if you are married. You could answer: "If you're concerned about my willingness to work overtime, I am willing to put in all the time the job requires."

If, on the other hand, the interviewer's questions seem a bit too personal or make you very uncomfortable, you may wish to decline to answer. Doing so is tricky, though. If you simply refuse, saying that you don't see the relevance of the question to the job, you will probably turn the interviewer against you. You may try restating the question as in the example, but you should be prepared to balance your need for the job against your willingness to field inappropriate questions. This is entirely a judgement call, and it's important to know for yourself how much is too much. Most interviewers want to see you at your best and will try very hard to put you at ease. However, if you do run into a difficult situation, know how much of such behaviour is tolerable to you, and don't be afraid to leave if you have to. If the interview is that unpleasant, it's unlikely that you would want to work for this agency anyway.

Interviewing, like everything else in this book, is a skill you can learn and polish. You can do this best by practicing. Go to as many interviews as you can, even if you're not sure you would want the job. You can never get too much experience, and every interview you go to will make the next one easier. You might even find that a job that didn't appear so attractive on paper turns out to be just the position you were seeking.

points to remember

1. The job application, and the interview, are opportunities for you to display your suitability for the job.

2. Be sure to identify your reader's needs, values, and expectations in order to "target" your application effectively.

3. Prepare your résumé and application letter carefully to display your strengths, not reveal your weaknesses.

4. Always proofread, and remember to apply the Six C's of professional writing.

5. Word-process your application materials and use a printer cartridge with sufficient ink or toner to produce a dark, sharp image. If you must use a typewriter, make sure it has a new ribbon.

6. Take the goofy messages off your answering machine.

sharpening your skills

1. Collect as many job advertisements as you can find from newspapers, flyers, Web sites, or the placement office of your college. You can look only at jobs related to your field or scan a broad cross-section in all fields. Study them carefully and circle key words — that is, those that appear most frequently and that seem to be most important. Based on your survey, what are the skills that employers seem to value most? Which ones are in greatest demand in your field? Compare your findings with those of others in your class; what implications can you draw for preparing your own job application?

2. Write your own Job Package, including a complete application letter, a résumé of your experience and education, a completed job application form, and a letter of recommendation.
   Letter of Application: Use the job descriptions provided by your instructor or answer an ad from the newspaper, placement office, or an Internet site. Type the letter in one of the formats you've learned.
   Résumé: You may complete this as though you have finished your current year of study. Review the section on résumé writing in this chapter and remember that your résumé must be correct, legible, and clear.
   Application Form: There is an application form on pages 194–197. Photocopy it, or use the copy that your instructor provides for you, and fill it out completely, either by hand (in ink) or on a typewriter. Be sure to sign it.
   Recommendation Letter: Pretending to be a former employer or instructor, write a letter either for yourself or for someone else in your class. In either case, you will be graded for the letter you have written, not for the one someone else has written for you.

3. You are assistant director of the Regional Community Services Centre in Winnipeg. Your director, Jocelyne Kaminski, has struck a hiring committee, with you as chair, for a position advertised as follows in the paper, on your agency's Web site, and through the Placement Office of the local college:

> **VOLUNTEER COORDINATOR**
> Community Support Centre
>
> The Community Support Centre seeks an energetic professional to coordinate its volunteer activities and programs. The CSC offers a varied program of services to local communities, including the Suicide Distress Line, Support for Single Parents, a Streetproofing Your Kids program, Street Teens Outreach and Drop-In Centre, and the Each One Teach One literacy program (in coordination with the Regional Library). The individual we seek has the following qualifications:
>
> - diploma or degree from a recognized institution; community services background preferred
> - good interpersonal and leadership skills
> - proven program-planning skills
> - organizational ability
> - excellent oral and written communication skills
> - able to handle fluctuating workload demands
>
> Volunteer experience is desirable; experience in training or supervising others will be a definite asset. However, we are willing to train the right person. Submit an application letter and résumé, along with the names of three referees, to:
>
> Jocelyne Kaminski, Director
> Community Services Centre
> 555 Hamilton Road
> Winnipeg, MB R0C 0C0

You are responsible for the initial screening of applications, and so far you have received the three submissions that appear below (Figures 7.12 to 7.17). Your job is to read the applications as they come in, placing them into a "discard" pile and a "consider further" pile. Carefully read through the samples below and decide which of them will be included in the group that will later be considered for an interview. Be sure to keep in mind the requirements of the position, and evaluate the submissions according to the criteria you have learned. Remember that, as in real life, not all of the applicants will exactly match the list of desired qualifications; your job is to pick the best of the ones you have received. As you conduct your initial screening, see if you can identify specific weaknesses of these résumés and letters in content, format, and style. Have they clearly identified purpose and placed the reader's needs first? Make a list of the weaknesses you have found and compare them with those identified by your classmates or instructor. Which of the applicants has best targeted her résumé to the demands of the position you have advertised?

4. After screening the following résumés and making your selection of the person you think is best qualified, turn to the weaker applications. Offer an analysis of their weaknesses, and rewrite them so that they are more effective. Compare your rewritten versions with those of your classmates.

online exercises

1. Before starting your job application, you may find it useful to think about the kind of work environment you prefer. Just for fun, go to **www2.ncsu.edu/unity/lockers/users/l/lkj/** and complete the multiple-choice quiz entitled "The Career Key." Do you think the quiz result accurately reflects your work preferences? Compare your results with those of your classmates and instructor. How useful was the quiz in preparing you for your choice of career?

2. For a workbook approach to preparing your résumé, travel to *Resumania! On-Line!* at **www.umn.edu/ohr/ecep/resume/step1.htm**. The whole site is dedicated to developing a résumé suitable to your background and skills; the personalized workbook page will help you get started. If your instructor directs you to do so, complete the workbook according to the directions on the site, and submit it to your instructor before you complete your résumé assignment.

3. It's important to list relevant job skills on your résumé; sometimes, however, it's hard to identify all the skills you may be able to bring to a new job. Travel to the Purdue University On-line Writing Lab, **owl.english.purdue.edu/Files/59.html**, for a checklist of job-related skills. Use the list as a prompt for your own list of relevant job skills; be sure you can think of an example from your own background that shows how you demonstrated each of the skills you select for your résumé.

4. Many Canadian newspapers now have Web sites on which they post their career and classified ads. Go to the *Canadian Newspaper and Magazine Zone* at **www.storm.ca/~gerald/news.shtml** for hotlinks to the major newspapers in your province or region. Go to their career listings and find an advertisement for a job for which you would like to apply. (You may also wish to check out job listings in other regions.) If you wish, you may use one of these ads as the target for your job application package. If so, be sure to include a copy of the advertisement with the package when you submit it to your instructor.

figure 7.12 The application letter is meant to encourage an employer to read the attached résumé. What impression does Leola Bitango's letter make on you?

15 Cedar Avenue
Greyfowl, BC
V8G 1S4

Dear Sir:

Enclosed please find a copy of my résumé for your perusal. I have experience as a secretary.

I look forward to hearing from you at your earliest convenience.

Sincerely,

Leola Bitango

Leola Bitango

figure 7.13 Compare this résumé to the advertisement for the position. How well has Leola targeted her résumé to the job she wants?

-1-

RESUME — LEOLA BITANGO

ADDRESS: 15 Cedar Avenue   SIN: 987 654 321
           Greyfowl, BC
           V8G J9K

PHONE: 678 9087

PREVIOUS WORK EXPERIENCE:

— Clerk Typist Position at British Columbia Social Services for a temporary 6 months. From September/00 to February/01
  Supervisor: Greta Grey Phone: 234 5678 (8:15- 4:30 p.m.)

— Bartender/Server at "Steer's Neighbourhood Pub". Worked from April/94 to September/00.
  Supervisor: Dave Pickard Phone: hm 123-2234 wk 345-2876

— Various Volunteer positions, including supervising in Swan Valley, BC. between the period of 1995 to 1999. Along with cashier positions also.

— Volunteer at St. John's Hospital in Swan Valley, BC. In the Geriatric ward.

EDUCATION:

— Started a program in recreation Leadrship but had to quit because I ran out of money.

— Attended Northeastern High School in Strickland, BC as an Adult Student for a grade 12 general diploma. (1996)

— Correspondence Course for an Program administrator Diploma through Drucker Career Training Centre situated in Vancouver, BC.

— General courses taken in high school were: Sociology, Typing (3 yrs.), English, Business Education and also Psychology.

figure 7.13 (Continued)

-2-

PERSONAL INFORMATION:

BIRTHDATE: 15/05/76

STATUS: Single Parent

SKILLS & KNOWLEDGE:

— Typing at 50 w.p.m.
— Experience working with volunteers
— Can operate a Word Processor and know sign language — S
— Good communication skills both verbal and nonverbal.
— Know most aspects of leadership and group dynamics
— Handle telephone inquiries and good at dealing with the public

EXTRACURRICULAR ACTIVITIES:

— Presently enjoy all indoor and outdoor sports and activities.

REFERENCES:

— Dave Pickard Phone: 123-2234 (hm)   345-2876 (wk)

— Linda Crumb Phone: 453-9876 (hm)   219-0987 (wk)

— Denise Gorland Phone: 573-0287 (hm)

— Mrs. Roest Phone: 2   938-3847 (wk)

figure 7.14 Evaluate Marya Bumanis's letter using the criteria you have learned for letter format and application letter style.

2001 03 10

Jocelyne Kaminski, Director
Community Services Centre
555 Hamilton Road
Winnipeg, MB R0C 0C0

Dear Ms. Kaminski:

Please be advised that I am interested in the position of Volunteer Coordinator at your organization in Winnipeg.

Enclosed is my résumé documenting my experience and education.

Yours truly,

Marya Bumanis

Marya Bumanis

figure 7.15 Check the job requirements listed in the advertisement. How well has Marya addressed the needs of her potential employer?

Marya Bumanis

5555-44 Street, Westock, New Brunswick E4F 2R5
Res. (987) 345 7946
Bus. (987) 344 1230

History

November 1999 to Present	Administrative Assistant to Director of Programs West New Brunswick Youth Centre, Westock, New Brunswick
July/August 2000	Attended Sproxler H.S., Saint John to obtain Grade 12 English
February 1997	Administrative officer, Tartan River Further Education Council, Box 980, Tartan River, New Brunswick • worked out of own home • planned and directed all phases of Council business • received and processed all correspondence • prepared copy and arranged for printing of twice-yearly, twelve-page advertising brochure • prepared financial reports, payroll for 40 instructors, accounts receivable and payable and bookkeeping • taking and transcribing minutes of general and executive meetings • set up and maintained filing system • worked independently at all times • attended seminars and workshops re position
June 1994 to January 1996	Owner-Manager of Totsy Turvy Day Care, Tartan River, New Brunswick
March 1993 to May 1994	Daycare Certificate, Quinpool College, Tartan River, New Brunswick
July 1987	Secretary to Regional Manager, Agricultural Development

figure 7.15 (Continued)

July 1987 to August 1992	PlayCare Assistant Lotsa Tots Play School, Tartan River, New Brunswick
February 1982 to September 1988	Assistant to Regional Dairy Specialist and Regional Livestock Specialist, New Brunswick Agriculture, Tartan River, New Brunswick
February 1984	Graduated with Early Childhood Development diploma, Eastlock College, Eastlock, N.B.
June 1983	Graduated from High School with general diploma from Tartan High School, Tartan River, New Brunswick
Volunteer Work	Elected to Post Secondary Education committee for Westock — council to investigate development of community college in Westock
Personal Information	Married - three children, two living at home Birth date - February 2, 1965

References available upon request

figure 7.16 Evaluate this letter for content and format. How effective will it be in meeting the employer's needs?

General Delivery
Brookfield, Alberta
T0M 9I9

March 11, 2001

Jocelyne Kaminski, Director
Community Services Centre
555 Hamilton Road
Winnipeg, MB R0C 0C0

Dear Ms. Kaminski:

Re: Volunteer Coordinator Position

I am a recent graduate of the Recreation Services Management program at Modern City College in Modern City, and am very interested in relocating to the Winnipeg area; I would like to be considered for this position, currently posted to your Web site.

I completed the Rec Services Management program with first class honours, achieving top marks in my Facility Management and Group Dynamics in Leadership courses. The program provided experience in a variety of skills related to successful management of a recreation facility, including leadership of volunteers through a placement component in which I was particularly successful. Two intensive courses in communication (Effective Written Communication and Interpersonal Interaction) were also part of the program. I earned grades of 9 (+90%) in all my communication courses, and have been commended for my organized and disciplined approach to my written work.

You will find me personable, conscientious, and committed to the "firm-but-fair" approach to dealing with clients and volunteers. I am very interested in joining the staff of the Community Services Centre of Winnipeg. I will be travelling to Winnipeg within the next month and can adjust my itinerary to accommodate your interview schedule. I look forward to speaking with you about this attractive career opportunity. I will be available at (403) 555 5106 mornings. Thank you for your consideration.

Yours truly,

Sharma Salaam

Sharma Salaam

figure 7.17 Considering the qualities that your organization is looking for, how effectively has Sharma Salaam focused on the job requirements?

.Sharma Salaam.

General Delivery
Brookfield, Alberta
T0M 9I9
(403) 555 5106
e-mail: <sharma@col.com>

CAREER OBJECTIVE:

After several years raising a family, I have prepared myself for a career in facility management in a social or recreation services context. I am primarily interested in employment in a setting where my life skills and volunteer experience, as well as my specialized training, will be of most benefit.

EDUCATION:

Sept.1999–   **Recreation Services**   Modern City College
April 2001   **Management**   Modern City, Alberta

The program covered all aspects of facility and staff management, including group and interpersonal communication, leadership skills, program development, promotions, and dynamics of personnel management. I also completed the college's Communication Proficiency Certificate, awarded to students who complete a sequence of five courses in communication. I took three electives in the area, along with my two required courses. The program also included hands-on experience in a placement situation.

May 1999–   **High School**   Modern City College
Aug. 1999   **Equivalency**   Modern City, Alberta

In order to round out my High School courses and prepare myself for entry to the Rec. Services Program, I completed English, and Sociology, and Political Science.

figure 7.17 (Continued)

Sharma Salaam /2

EXPERIENCE:

Nov. 1998– **Program** Coyote River Golf Resort
Apr. 1999   **Planner** Coyote River, Alberta

As occasional help, I assisted in the running of programs for children and teens who accompanied their parents to the resort. I handled a variety of responsibilities from organizing activities, to booking facilities, to supervising the children and teens. I worked with a group of community volunteers.

Jun. 1991– **Partner/** Morton Food Service
Jun. 1995   **Manager**   Brookfield, Alberta

Under contract with Alberta Natural Gas Ltd., I operated a successful on-site catering service with one other individual. Our business was so successful that we won additional contracts and hired additional staff to meet the demand. I handled all aspects of the catering business, including training new staff.

SKILLS:

Technical

As a trained Facility Manager, I am familiar with program design and organization, staff supervision, and booking procedures. I am familiar with WordPerfect and MicroSoft Word, Netscape Composer, and MicroSoft Publisher. I can type accurately (50 wpm) and have learned the basics of Web design.

Personal

I am an honest and meticulous worker and strive to do my best whatever the task. I am organized and punctual and work hard to meet deadlines. I am also able to assume responsibility when necessary to get the job done.

figure 7.17 (Continued)

Sharma Salaam /3

Interpersonal	I genuinely like people and am able to interact effectively in cooperation with others; I maintain a cheerful outlook and am flexible in my approach to situations. I understand that people are sometimes difficult to handle and am able to show tact and patience in my dealings with them. I particularly appreciate the challenges of dealing with volunteers in an organization and am committed to making their experience positive.	
REFEREES:	**Mrs. D. Malvolio** Owner/Manager **(403) 555 6050**	Coyote River Golf Resort PO Box 1378 Brookfield, Alberta T0C 2H0
	Ms Maureen Vapid Rec. Services Management Instructor **(403) 342 3286**	Modern City College PO Box 5005 Modern City, Alberta T4W 5K5

appendix a

Grammar Review

Writing effectively means choosing your words carefully and putting them into an understandable order so that your reader receives the message clearly and without ambiguity. Part of this process involves using correct grammar. Incorrect grammar can sometimes result in unclear or unintended meanings being communicated, and in a business or career situation this can mean lost revenue. It quite literally pays to give some attention to what you're really saying in your work.

As well, people will judge you as surely by the quality of your writing as by your appearance, and though you may consider this unfair, you must recognize that it's a fact of life. You may, like some people, believe that correct spelling and grammar are things that matter only to an English teacher, but this is far from the truth. Even people who are weak in these areas themselves notice someone else's mistakes, and they may be just as unforgiving — in some cases more so — than the average English teacher.

For example, one of the most common complaints that colleges hear from employers, no matter what the field, is that graduates can't write. Much of the problem they see is with grammar; of all writing problems, it is the most visible.

Though this is not intended to be a grammar book, the subject is important enough that this appendix is included to provide you with a handy guide to avoiding the most common grammar errors. If you feel you need a more thorough review, there are plenty of excellent books available. Ask your communication professor to recommend one.

Though there are many ways to mangle the language, the following six errors in grammatical structure seem to occur with frequency.

subject–verb agreement
sentence fragments

run-on sentences
pronoun, tense, and person agreement
modifier errors
faulty parallelism

Before we deal with these, however, it is important to have a clear understanding of what makes a sentence.

Word Groups

Language is constructed principally of words, which can be grouped according to some pretty basic rules. By following these rules we can make three types of word groups:

clauses
sentences
phrases

A CLAUSE is a group of words that contains a subject — a "do-er" or "be-er" of something (this word will usually be a noun or a noun substitute) — and a verb — what the subject does or is.

Joe teaches.	subject: Joe
	verb: teaches
Birds fly.	subject: birds
	verb: fly
Babies cry.	subject: babies
	verb: cry
The class learns.	subject: class
	verb: learns

If these are the only elements contained in the word group, it is considered to be an INDEPENDENT CLAUSE. This means that it is able to stand by itself, and its meaning is complete. Independent clauses are important, because they are the fundamental units from which sentences are made.

Clauses may also be made DEPENDENT by the addition of a joining word called a *subordinate conjunction*. This word reduces the clause to a lesser (or subordinate) role in a sentence; it is no longer the fundamental unit within the sentence. Some subordinate conjunctions are:

although   because
if   when

whenever	which
before	after
who/m	that
though	since

Let's see what these do to our independent clauses from above:

When Joe teaches...
If birds fly...
Because babies cry...
After the students learn...

Suddenly they are no longer complete; they merely set the stage for the really important information that is to follow. In other words, they must now be joined to something else, in fact another independent clause, to make a complete thought.

When Joe teaches, he uses many examples.
If birds fly, people should too.
Because babies cry, they can get attention.
After the students learn, they may be tested.

When you begin to join clauses in this way, you are really building sentences. The rule for a SENTENCE is simple: each sentence *must* contain at least one independent clause; though it may contain other things, the independent clause is an absolute necessity. A SIMPLE SENTENCE contains only an independent clause. You can see that our first grouping of clauses, though made up of only two words each, is also a grouping of sentences. A COMPOUND SENTENCE contains two or more independent clauses joined by *coordinate conjunctions* (and, but, or, nor, yet, and so). A COMPLEX SENTENCE contains a combination of at least one independent clause with one or more dependent clauses. The examples above are complex sentences.

REMEMBER: if there is no independent clause, you do not have a sentence.

The third classification of word groups is easy: anything that is not a clause or a sentence is a PHRASE. To put this another way, anything that does not contain a subject or a verb is a phrase. This is true no matter how long the group of words may be.

climbing up the hill
across the street
beside the store with the big sign out front
over between the drive and the garage
with my dad

Because these groups of words contain neither a subject nor a verb, they are phrases, even though some may be quite long.

Joining Clauses

Independent clauses may be combined into longer sentences in any of several ways. The following are two related independent clauses.

> Dave frequently dribbles. He plays basketball.

These may be joined by:

- using a coordinate conjunction *(and, but, or, nor, yet,* and *so):*

    Dave frequently dribbles, so he plays basketball. (compound sentence)

- using a subordinate conjunction (such as those listed above):

    Because Dave frequently dribbles, he plays basketball. (complex sentence)

- using a semicolon (;):

    Dave frequently dribbles; he plays basketball.

The following are common *incorrect* ways of joining two independent clauses.

- no joining method, simply running two clauses together:

    X Dave frequently dribbles he plays basketball.

- using a comma:

    X Dave frequently dribbles, he plays basketball.

Be sure to use only one of the correct methods at a time. It is, for example, also incorrect to use the semicolon *and* a conjunction to join two clauses:

> X Because Dave frequently dribbles; he plays basketball.
> X Dave frequently dribbles; and he plays basketball.

Six Common Sentence Errors

1. Subject-Verb Agreement

Subjects ("do-ers" of an action or "be-ers" of a state) agree with their verbs in person and number. Singular subjects always take singular verbs, and plural subjects take plural verbs. Singularity of the verb is determined by its subject.

he walks	but	*they* walk
sings		sing
does		do
is		are

Regular verbs are made singular by the addition of "s" to the end. Irregular verbs change form depending on the person (first, second, third — that is, "I/we," "you," or "he/she/it/they") of the pronoun.

I am   you are   he/she is

Luckily, there aren't many irregular verbs in English, and you will be familiar with them from your speech. Just make sure you match them up in your writing. This is easy enough to do when subject and verb come together, but if they are separated by phrases or other words it is more difficult. Here are some quick rules to remember.

a. Subjects compounded with "and" take plural verbs.

   Bob and Devon <u>were</u> with me when it happened.

b. Subjects compounded with "either…or," "neither…nor," and "or" take verbs that agree with the subject *closest* to the verb.

   Neither the Kennedys nor Sheila <u>is</u> happy with the result.
   Neither Sheila nor the Kennedys <u>are</u> happy with the result.

c. Words ending in "-one," "-thing," and "-body" are always singular.

   Everybody <u>was</u> present at last night's meeting.
   Everything <u>is</u> all right.

d. Phrases such as "together with," "in addition to," "along with," "apart from," and "as well as" are not part of the subject and do not influence the choice of verb.

   Joyce, along with her friends, <u>is</u> going to the movie.

e. Collective nouns may take singular or plural verbs, depending on their context. If the group, family, committee, or class acts in unison, it is singular.

   The committee <u>has made</u> a decision.

   If they act individually, the verb is plural.

   The committee <u>have argued</u> about this issue for months.

f. The word "each" is always singular; "both" is always plural.

   Each of these <u>is</u> perfect for my sister.
   Both of them <u>have</u> advantages.

2. Sentence Fragments

Complete sentences always contain at least one independent clause. Do not punctuate phrases or dependent clauses as sentences. A fragment is a part of a sentence that has been treated as a complete sentence.

X Running down the street and around the corner.
X The thing being that I don't like him.
X After I had finished the laundry and the cleaning.
X For example, scrubbing, polishing, and waxing.

To fix these, either:

- join them to an independent clause; or
- add whatever is missing.

In the case of the second example, the word "being" is not a complete verb; therefore this cannot be a sentence. Change the present participle ("being") to the simple present "is."

John was running down the street and around the corner.
The thing is that I don't like him.
After I had finished the laundry and the cleaning, I took a nap.
I hate household chores, for example, scrubbing, polishing, and waxing.

3. Run-on Sentences

This mistake is created by trying to cram too much information into a single sentence; to correct it, break the elements up in some way. The most common run-on sentences are created by putting two independent clauses together with only a comma.

X I slept in, I missed the bus.

This is incorrect. As is explained above, the only permissible ways to join clauses are with a coordinate conjunction, as in the first example sentence, below; with a subordinate conjunction, as in the second example; and with a semicolon, as in the third example.

I slept in, so I missed the bus.
Because I slept in, I missed the bus.
I slept in; I missed the bus.

4. Pronoun, Tense, and Person Agreement

Always strive for consistency in pronouns, person, and tense. Jumping from one to another person or tense is confusing; using ambiguous or inaccurate pronouns is likewise.

X Ted asked the neighbour to move his car. (Whose car? Ted's or the neighbour's?)
X A person should mind their own business. ("A person" is only one; "their" is plural. Pronouns should always agree with their antecedents in number [singular-plural] and gender [he-she-it].)
X His piece of cake was bigger than hers, which made her angry. ("Which" must refer to a single noun antecedent; a pronoun should not be used to refer to a whole idea.)

Maintain consistent tense. Generally, there are three kinds of time you may refer to in writing: past, present, and future. We tend to write about events in the past or present, and the rule is the same for both. If you're writing in the past, stay in the past unless the meaning changes. The same applies to writing in present tense, and future tense, too, if you happen to be using it.

X So he came up to me and says, "Who do you think you are?" (This is incorrect due to the switch from past "came" to present "says.")

Keep person (I, you, he/she, we, you, they) consistent. The most common problem with person agreement is to move from the first person "I" to the second person "you"; if you stop to think about the sentence, it really doesn't make sense.

X My apartment faces a busy highway, so when I'm trying to sleep in, the noise of the traffic keeps you awake. (Why would the traffic keep you awake if I'm the one sleeping?)

The second common error in person agreement is switching from the use of third person "one" or "a person" to second person "you."

X One should always keep your eyes open. (Use "you" or "one," but don't mix them in the same sentence.)

5. Modifier Problems

Modifiers are words or groups of words that describe, explain, intensify, or negate other words or groups of words. The two kinds are *adjectives,* which modify nouns or noun substitutes, and *adverbs,* which modify verbs, adjectives, or other adverbs. Modifier errors occur when the modifier is either misplaced or "dangling." The best rule for correcting both of these problems is to place the modifier as close as possible to the thing it modifies; if that item is not in the sentence, rewrite the sentence so the meaning is clear.

Misplaced Modifiers
In the case of this error, the modifier is in the wrong position in the sentence. Put the modifier as close as possible to the thing modified.

X I only ate half my dinner. (I only ate it; I didn't dance with it or take it to a movie! Probably I intend the "only" to modify the "half.")
I ate only half my dinner.

Dangling Modifiers
The modified element, though implied, does not exist in the sentence. Rewrite the sentence so that the modified element is clear.

X Running alongside the river, a treasure chest lay in the bushes. (Since the treasure chest can't run, this sentence doesn't make sense. Who saw the treasure chest? Who was running?)
Running alongside the river, Mark spotted a treasure chest lying in the bushes.

6. Faulty Parallelism

This error occurs when you are using lists or series of items. Whenever you are speaking of more than one item, place them all in the same grammatical form. Use nouns with nouns, adjectives with adjectives, "-ing" words with "-ing" words, clauses with clauses.

X Professionals include doctors and people who practise law.
X I like running, jumping, and to sing.
X She's pretty, but has ambition too.

Replace such faulty parallelism with corrected forms:

Professionals include doctors and lawyers.
OR
Professionals include people who practise medicine and people who practise law.

I like running, jumping, and singing.
OR
I like to run, jump, and sing.

She's pretty, but ambitious too.
OR
She has beauty and ambition too.

This coverage of grammar is necessarily a brief overview. There are many more subtleties to good grammar than there is room to cover in this book. A good grammar handbook will give you more information, should you require it.

sharpening your skills

The following sentences contain errors of the types explained above. See if you can correct them. The answer key follows.

1. I only lived in Ottawa for four months.

2. Doing his homework, the TV was distracting.

3. The thing being that I really enjoy their company.

4. Take me with you, I'll miss you too much if I stay here alone. In this scary place with no phone.

5. Give me a bite of your sandwich, I haven't had lunch.

6. Darlene's answer almost was right.

7. Genevieve, but not the others, are going camping.

8. I nearly told you a hundred times! Don't call me!

9. A person should mind their own business.
10. One should always keep your eyes open.
11. Doing a test is better than explanations, you can see the rules in action.
12. I didn't want his sympathy, I sent him away forever.
13. If a mosquito bites your face, it should be squashed.
14. On the table was his hat and gloves, so I knew he was home.
15. I only mailed half the letters after lunch.
16. In college I took English, History, and a course in people and society.
17. If I want to do a good job, you should never overlook details.
18. There was three people on the bus: a student, a mail carrier, and a man who worked on cars.
19. I love lasagna. Even though it's fattening.
20. I don't want to go to the party with him. The reason being that I had a lousy time when I dated him before.
21. Jeff looks familiar to me; because I have a friend who looks just like him.
22. There are lots of things you can do in winter. Skiing, skating, and hikes are only three of them.
23. Running up the stairs, someone tripped Erika and she fell on her arm, breaking it in two places.
24. Where is Rebecca's dictionary, she'll be lost without it.
25. Neither Bryce nor his friends is willing to help.
26. If the dog sleeps in your bed, it should be disinfected.
27. Being too large a sandwich, she declined to eat it.
28. It really made me laugh. The day she told us about Ted.
29. He is a kind person who has generosity too.
30. If a person is nervous, they should try to relax more.
31. Suzanne likes to wear soft sweaters, eat exotic food, and taking bubble baths.
32. My sister's boyfriend is stingy, sloppy, and doesn't have much ambition.
33. I noticed a crack in the window walking into the house.
34. Eating a hot dog, mustard dropped onto my shirt.
35. What do you think of this, Red Deer is the fourth largest city in Alberta.

36. When you're stuck. You can use your dictionary for help.
37. Hallowe'en is my least favourite holiday, I'm afraid of ghosts.
38. Although I like Christmas, since I love all the sparkle and magic.
39. I nearly earned a hundred dollars last week.
40. Jerry invited only Buffy and me, I guess you can't come.

answer key

1. I lived in Ottawa for <u>only</u> four months.
2. <u>As he did</u> his homework, the TV was distracting.
   OR Doing his homework, <u>Marshall found</u> the TV distracting.
3. The thing <u>is</u> that I really enjoy their company.
   OR I really enjoy their company.
4. Take me with you; I'll miss you too much if I stay here alone in this scary place with no phone.
5. Give me a bite of your sandwich. I haven't had lunch.
6. Darlene's answer was <u>almost</u> right.
7. Genevieve, but not the others, <u>is</u> going camping.
8. I told you <u>nearly</u> a hundred times! Don't call me!
9. A person should mind <u>her or his</u> own business.
   OR <u>People</u> should mind their own business.
10. One should always keep <u>one's</u> eyes open.
    OR <u>You</u> should always keep your eyes open.
11. Doing a test is better than explanations, <u>because</u> you can see the rules in action.
12. I didn't want his sympathy, <u>so</u> I sent him away forever.
13. <u>A</u> mosquito <u>that</u> bites your face should be squashed.
14. On the table <u>were</u> his hat and gloves, so I knew he was home.
15. I mailed <u>only</u> half the letters after lunch.
16. In college I took English, History, and <u>Sociology</u>.
17. If I want to do a good job, <u>I</u> should never overlook details.
    OR If <u>you</u> want to do a good job, you should never overlook details.

18. There <u>were</u> three people on the bus: a student, a mail carrier, and a <u>mechanic.</u>
19. I love lasagna<u>, even</u> though it's fattening.
20. I don't want to go to the party with him. I had a lousy time when I dated him before.
    OR I don't want to go to the party with him<u>, because</u> I had a lousy time when I dated him before.
21. Jeff looks familiar to me because I have a friend who looks just like him.
22. There are lots of things you can do in winter. Skiing, skating, and <u>hiking</u> are only three of them.
23. Running up the stairs, <u>Erika tripped</u> and fell on her arm, breaking it in two places.
24. Where is Rebecca's dictionary<u>? S</u>he'll be lost without it.
25. Neither Bryce nor his friends <u>are</u> willing to help.
26. <u>Your bed</u> should be disinfected if the dog sleeps in <u>it</u>.
27. <u>Because the sandwich was too large,</u> she declined to eat it.
28. It really made me laugh the day she told us about Ted.
29. He is a kind <u>and generous</u> person.
30. If <u>people are</u> nervous, they should try to relax more.
    OR <u>People who are nervous</u> should try to relax more.
31. Suzanne likes to wear soft sweaters, eat exotic food, and <u>take</u> bubble baths.
32. My sister's boyfriend is stingy, sloppy, and <u>unambitious</u>.
33. <u>Walking into the house,</u> I noticed a crack in the window.
34. <u>As I was</u> eating a hot dog, mustard dropped onto my shirt.
35. What do you think of this<u>?</u> Red Deer is the fourth largest city in Alberta.
36. When you're stuck<u>,</u> you can use your dictionary for help.
37. Hallowe'en is my least favourite holiday, <u>because</u> I'm afraid of ghosts.
38. I like Christmas, since I love all the sparkle and magic.
39. I earned <u>nearly</u> a hundred dollars last week.
40. Jerry invited only Buffy and me, <u>so</u> I guess you can't come.

appendix b

Punctuation

This review is designed to remind you of the basic uses of the most common punctuation marks. Students often find punctuation confusing, but it is important. It is a convention designed to help your reader understand the meaning and intention of your written work. Like road signs on a highway, punctuation marks help the reader find her or his way in the journey through your written work. Though style guides differ somewhat, the following general rules should see you through most basic punctuation needs. For more detailed information, consult a style manual. Remember, no matter which style guide you decide to follow, you must follow a consistent style throughout your document.

Reviewing Common Punctuation Marks

There are three common forms of "full stop" punctuation: the period, the question mark, and the exclamation point.

The Period (.)

1. Use a period to mark the end of a sentence.
2. Use a period following an abbreviation: etc., Dr., Alta.
   Some common abbreviations (TV, VCR) don't require periods. Neither do the two-letter provincial abbreviations used by Canada Post: NS, NB, PE, NF, QC, ON, MB, SK, AB, BC, YT, NT.
3. When an abbreviation falls at the end of the sentence, use only one period, omitting the abbreviation period.

   Since Jerry completed dentistry school, he loves to be called Dr.

The Question Mark (?)

1. Use a question mark only after a direct question.

    Where are you taking that box?
    Why did you bring him with you?

2. Never use a question mark for an indirect question.

    I wonder whether Shirley has a copy of this book.
    I asked him where he intended to take that box.

    A question mark is end punctuation and should not be directly followed by any other form of punctuation — period, comma, or semicolon.

The Exclamation Point (!)

1. Use an exclamation point after an exclamatory word (interjection) or phrase:

    Wow!
    Hey!
    How about that!

2. Use an exclamation point for emphasis when a statement or question is meant to be read with force.

    What did you do that for!
    I just won the lottery!

3. In formal writing, and most business writing, you should avoid the exclamation point. Occasionally it is useful in sales letters, for emphasis, but too many exclamation points will create an overly loud or hysterical impression.

    You can win!
    Act now and save!
    No Down Payment! No Interest!

The Semicolon (;)

1. Use a semicolon to separate two independent clauses that are closely related in meaning.

    I am tired of Shawn; I really wish he would go away.
    I built my first model two years ago; now I'm hooked.
    I have a sinus infection; I went swimming without nose plugs.

2. Use a semicolon before conjunctive adverbs such as "however," "therefore," "thus," and "consequently" when they are used to join two related clauses.

    I don't want to deal with those people ever again; however, they are my relatives.

The Agony and the Exigence:
A Rhetorical Analysis of Two Presentations

Innovations in Training:
A Proposal for Improving Our Report Writing Workshops

4. If your title contains the title of another work, you should treat the title of the other work appropriately, depending on whether it is a short or long work.

Method or Madness? An Analysis of Motive in <u>Hamlet</u>
OR
Method or Madness? An Analysis of Motive in *Hamlet*

Miles to Go Before I Sleep:
Hypothermia in Frost's "Stopping by Woods on a Snowy Evening"

This brief refresher is not intended to be a comprehensive guide to punctuation usage, but should provide enough detail for everyday usage. For a more comprehensive guide to punctuation conventions, you may wish to consult a good English handbook or manual of style such as *The Chicago Manual of Style* or Strunk and White's *The Elements of Style*.

Index

Accident report, 77
Accomplishments, in résumé, 158
Achievements, in résumé, 158
Acknowledgement, messages of, 33
Additional courses or training, in résumé, 157
Agreements, grammatical, 232
Analytical report, 79
Analytical résumé, 152
Answer key for grammar exercise, 236
Answering machine messages, during job search, 202
Apostrophe usage, 242
Appearance, at interview, 203
Appendices, 74
  in formal report, 102
Appendix, see appendices
Application form, 190
  sample, 194
Application packages, sample, 216
Application, letter of, 189
  sample, 191
Assessment report, 78
Attitude, in job search interview, 204
Audience, for a briefing, 140
  in oral presentation, 130
Awards, in résumé, 157
Background knowledge, of reader, 2, 5
Be specific, 4
Behaviour, at interview, 203
Bibliography, how to write one, 80
  in formal report, 102
Body, of a letter, 49
  of a report, see Discussion
Brainstorming a topic for oral presentation, 135
Breach of regulation report, 77
Briefing, how to prepare, 139
Career objective, in résumé, 153
Career progress report, sample form, 84
Central issue, failure to identify, 17

Charts, in formal report, 107
Choosing a topic for oral presentation, 132
Choosing a format for your report, 86
Chronological résumé, 152
Clarity, 1, 7
Clauses, joining, 230
Clauses, phrases, and sentences, 228
Clichés, list of, 19
  avoiding use of, 17
Closing, complimentary, in a letter, 49
Cluster related points, failure to, 21
Coherence, 7
Colon usage, 240
Comma usage, 241
Common faults of professional writing, 17
Common sentence errors, 230
Community service, in résumé, 158
Complaint, messages of, 34
Completeness, 6
  in an occurence or incident report, 76
Complimentary closing, of a letter, 49
Conciseness, 6
Conclusion, 2
  in reports, 73
  in formal report, 102
Congratulations, messages of, 33
Connecting words, 7
Consider your audience, in oral presentation, 130
Contents, of formal report, 100
  of informal report, 87
  of semiformal report, 91
Correctness, 7
Courtesy, 8
Cover, of formal report, 100
Crossover résumé, 151
Date, in letters, 45
  in memos, 51
Delivery, in oral presentations, 140

Diagrams, in formal report, 104
Discussion, in report, 73
  in formal report, 101
Education, in résumé, 143
Employers' questions, in interview, 206
Employment history, in résumé, 154
Employment interview, 202
Evaluation report, 78
Exclamation point, 239
Expectations, of reader, 6
Experience, in résumé, 154
Extemporaneous presentation, 132
Extracurricular activities, in résumé, 157
Failure to identify central issue, 17
  to cluster related points, 21
  to identify desired action, 21
File number, in letters, 51
Finding a topic for oral presentation, 135
Focus on your purpose, 3
  in oral presentation, 130
Focusing topic, for oral presentation, 138
Fonts, serif and sanserif, 54
Form, application, 190
Formal reports, 82
  and informal and semiformal, 82
  and proposals, 99
  contents, 100
  parts of, 100
  sample, 112
  using visuals in, 103
Format, of a bibliography, 80
  of letters and memos, 54
  of reports, how to choose, 86
Full development, 2
Full block letter format, 55
Functional résumé, 151
Fundraising letters, 39
Good-news and bad-news messages, 33
Grammar, answer key, 236
  review, 227
Graphs, in formal report, 104
Guidelines for use of visual aids in
  oral presentation, 145
Hard sell, 40
Headings, in a memo, 51
How to make a notecard for speaking, 137
I was, I saw, I did, 76
Identify desired action, failure to, 21
Importance of practice, 146

Impromptu presentation, 131
Incident report, 74
Incomplete information, 21
Informal reports, 82, 86
  and semiformal reports, 70
  contents of, 87
  sample, 89
Initial, in signing a memo, 53
Injury report, 77
Inside address, in letter, 48
Interview, employment, 202
  for a job, 202
  problem questions, 211
  typical questions, 206
  what to expect, 210
Introduction, in report, 72
  in formal report, 101
Investigative report, 79
Job package, 150
  samples, 216
Job interview, 202
Joining clauses, 230
Knowledge, in job search interview, 205
Layout, of résumé, 158
Letter format, full block, 55
  modified semiblock, 55
  reference guide, 56
  semiblock, 55
Letter, parts of, 45
Letter types
  application, 189
    samples, 191
  recommendation, 193
    samples, 200
  transfer, in formal report, 100
  transmittal, in formal report, 100
Letters, memos, and e-mail messages, 30
Line drawings, in formal report, 104
Main point, put first, 4
Main message statement, 2
Making a request, 32
Manuscript presentation, 131
Memo format, 56
  reference guide, 55
Memorized presentation, 131
Message, in a memo, 53
Misconduct report, 77
Modified semiblock letter format, 55
Modifiers, 233

phrases and dependent clauses as, 20
Name and title, in closing a letter, 50
Needs, of reader, 5
Notations, in a letter, 54
    in a memo, 54
Notecard, for oral presentation, 137
    making, 137
Occurrence report, 74
    sample form, 83
Online exercises, 12, 24, 67, 98, 128, 148, 215
Online sources, in bibliography, 81
Online job market, 199
Online job search, 199
Oral reports and presentations, 129
    delivery in, 140
    how to prepare, 132
    types of, 131
Organization name, in closing a letter, 49
Overuse of phrases and dependent clauses as modifiers, 20
Parallelism, 234
Parts, of a letter, 45
    of a memo or e-mail message, 51
    of a report, 72
    of a résumé, 152
Passive voice, avoiding use of, 19
Period usage, 238
Personal information, in résumé, 153
Persuasive messages, 39
Photographs, in formal report, 103
Phrases and dependent clauses, as modifiers, 20
Planner, for professional writing, 18
    for report writing, 75
Points to remember, 12, 22, 57, 91, 111, 147, 160, 212
Posting your résumé to a Web site, 199
Practice, in oral presentation, 146
Preparing for a briefing, 139
    for a presentation, 132
    to write, 17
Presentations, 129
    how to prepare, 132
Print sources, in bibliography, 80
Problem questions, in interview, 211
Professional writing planner, 18
Progress report, 78
Proposals, 79, 107
    contents of, 108
    sample, 112

Public-service announcements, 40
    contents of, 43
Punctuation, 238
Purpose, failure to identify, 17
    for a briefing, 140
    focus on, 3
    focus on (in oral presentation), 130
Put your main point first, 4
Question mark usage, 239
Questions, in interview, 206
Quotation marks, 243
Re line, in memos, 53
    in letters, 49
Reader, remember, 5
Reasonableness, of requests, 32
Reasons why people don't get hired, 206
Recommendation(s), in a report, 73
    letter of, 193
    summary of, formal report, 101
Reference guide for memo and letter format, 56
References, see bibliography
References, in résumé, 156
Refusals, 43
Remember your reader, 5
Repetition, unnecessary, 21
Report, informal and semiformal, 70
    recommendations, 73
    situations for writing, 74
    why write, 71
Report forms, sample, career progress, 84
    sample, occurrence report, 84
Report forms, standardized, 81
    format, how to choose, 86
    parts of, 72
    formal, 99
incident, 74
    injury, 77
    investigative, 79
Report, parts of
    formal, 100
    informal, 87
    semiformal, 91
Report samples, informal, 89
    formal, 112
    semiformal, 92
    proposal, 112
Report types, accident, 77
    analytical, 79
    assessment, 78

    breach of regulation, 77
    evaluation, 78
    misconduct, 77
    occurrence, 74
    progress, 78
    research, 80
Report writing planner, 75
Request messages, 32
Research report, 80
Responding to a request, 32
Résumé, 151
    parts of, 152
    samples, 164
    types, 151
        analytical, 79
        chronological, 152
        functional, 151
Return address, 45
Run-on sentences, 232
Salutation, in letters, 48
Sample application form, 194
    formal report, 112
    informal report, 89
    job packages, 216
    letters of application, 191
    letters of recommendation, 200
    proposal, 112
    résumés, 164
    semiformal report, 92
Secretary's notations, in a letter, 50
    in a memo, 54
Semiblock letter format, 55
Semicolon usage, 239
Semiformal report, 82, 88
    contents of, 91
    sample, 92
Sentence fragments, 231
Sentence errors, common, 230
Sharpening your skills, 234
Sharpening your professional writing style, 16
Sharpening your skills, 12, 22, 57, 95, 111, 146, 213
Signature, in letters, 50
    in memos, 53
Simplify your message, 5
Situations, for reports, 74
Six C's of professional writing, 6
Skills, in résumé, 155

    artistic, 156
    interpersonal, 156
    practical, 156
    specialized, 155
Solicited letter of application, 189
Speaking context, for a briefing, 140
Speaking context, identify, 130
Specific, be, 4
Standardized report forms, 81
Style in professional writing, 1
Subject line, in letters, 49
    in memos, 53
Subject-verb agreement, 230
Summary, in a report, 72
Summary of recommendations, formal report, 101
Table of contents, in formal report, 101
Taking your job search online, 199
Title page, in formal report, 100
Title treatment, 243
Tone, in oral presentation, 143
Topic for oral presentation, selecting, 132
    finding when you're stuck, 135
Topic invention, 132, 135
Typed name and title, in letters, 50
Types, of application letter, 189
    of oral presentations, 131
    of professional letters, memos, and e-mail messages, 32
    of résumé, 151
Unnecessary repetition, 21
Unsolicited letter of application, 189
Use of clichés, 17
Use of passive voice, 19
Visual aids, in oral presentation, 143, 144
    guidelines for use in oral presentation, 145
Visual presence, in oral presentation, 141
Visuals, in formal report, 103
Vocal presence, in oral presentation, 143
Voice quality, in oral presentation, 143
Volunteer experience, in résumé, 158
Web site, posting your résumé to, 199
When to use a letter or memo, 31
When you can't think of a topic, try this, 135
Why write reports?, 71
Word groups, 228
Writing a response, 32
Writing planner, 18